Being Human, Becoming Human

Princeton Theological Monograph Series

K. C. Hanson, Charles M. Collier, and D. Christopher Spinks,
Series Editors

Recent volumes in the series:

Lisa E. Dahill
*Reading from the Underside of Selfhood: Bonhoeffer
and Spiritual Formation*

Joel Burnell
*Poetry, Prophecy, and Patriotism: Polish Messianism
in Dialogue with Dietrich Bonhoeffer*

Paul Ingram, editor
Constructing a Relational Cosmology

Chris Budden
Following Jesus in Invaded Space

Philip Ruge-Jones
Cross in Tensions

Christian T. Collins Winn
*"Jesus Is Victor": The Significance of the Blumhardts
for the Theology of Karl Barth*

Charles Bellinger
The Trinitarian Self: The Key to the Puzzle of Violence

Mary Clark Moschella
*Living Devotions: Reflections on Immigration, Identity,
and Religious Imagination*

Being Human, Becoming Human

Dietrich Bonhoeffer and Social Thought

Edited by
JENS ZIMMERMANN *and* BRIAN GREGOR

PICKWICK *Publications* · Eugene, Oregon

BEING HUMAN, BECOMING HUMAN
Dietrich Bonhoeffer and Social Thought

Princeton Theological Monograph Series 146

Copyright © 2010 Wipf and Stock Publishers. All rights reserved. Except for brief quotations in critical publications or reviews, no part of this book may be reproduced in any manner without prior written permission from the publisher. Write: Permissions, Wipf and Stock Publishers, 199 W. 8th Ave., Suite 3, Eugene, OR 97401.

New Revised Standard Version Bible, copyright © 1989, Division of Christian Education of the National Council of the Churches of Christ in the United States of America. Used by permission. All rights reserved.

Pickwick Publications
An Imprint of Wipf and Stock Publishers
199 W. 8th Ave., Suite 3
Eugene, OR 97401

www.wipfandstock.com

ISBN 13: 978-1-60899-420-5

Cataloging-in-Publication data

Being human, becoming human : Dietrich Bonhoeffer and social thought / edited by Jens Zimmermann and Brian Gregor.

Princeton Theological Monograph Series 146

xxii + 236 p. ; 23 cm. —Includes bibliographical references and index.

ISBN 13: 978-1-60899-420-5

1. Bonhoeffer, Dietrich, 1906–1945. 2. Kierkegaard, Søren, 1813–1855. 3. Theological anthropology—Christianity. I. Zimmermann, Jens, 1965–. II. Gregor, Brian. III. Title. IV. Series.

BX4827 .B57 B35 2010

Manufactured in the U.S.A.

Contents

List of Contributors / vii

List of Abbreviations / ix

Introduction / xi

Part 1: Bonhoeffer's Humanism

1. Dietrich Bonhoeffer as Christian Humanist
—*John W. de Gruchy* / 3

2. Being Human, Becoming Human: Dietrich Bonhoeffer's Christological Humanism—*Jens Zimmermann* / 25

3. Bonhoeffer's Theology and Economic Humanism: An Exploration in Interdisciplinary Sociality—*Peter Frick* / 49

Part 2: Bonhoeffer on Sociality and the Church

4. Sociality, Discipleship, and Worldly Theology in Bonhoeffer's Christian Humanism—*Clifford J. Green* / 71

5. Community Turned Inside Out: Dietrich Bonhoeffer's Concept of the Church and of Humanity Reconsidered—*Kirsten Busch Nielsen* / 91

6. The Narrow Path: Sociality, Ecclesiology, and the Polyphony of Life in the Thought of Dietrich Bonhoeffer—*Barry Harvey* / 102

Part 3: Discipleship, Conformation, and Responsibility

7. The Christological Presuppositions of Discipleship
—*John H. Yoder* / 127

8. Following-After and Becoming Human: A Study of Bonhoeffer and Kierkegaard—*Brian Gregor* / 152

9   Con-Formation with Jesus Christ: Bonhoeffer, Social Location, and Embodiment—*Lisa E. Dahill* / 176

10 Responding to Human Reality: Responsibility and Responsiveness in Bonhoeffer's Ethics
    —*Ulrik Becker Nissen* / 191

Bibliography / 215

Index / 227

Contributors

LISA E. DAHILL is Associate Professor of Worship and Christian Spirituality at Trinity Lutheran Seminary, Columbus, Ohio, USA; past chair of the Bonhoeffer: Theology and Social Analysis Group of the American Academy of Religion; and a scholar, translator, and lecturer on Bonhoeffer.

PETER FRICK is Associate Professor in Religious Studies at St. Paul's University College, University of Waterloo, Ontario, Canada. He is a member of the International Bonhoeffer Society. His recent books are *Bonhoeffer's Intellectual Formation* (2008), *A Dialogue with Dietrich Bonhoeffer: Collected Essays* (2009), and *Dietrich Bonhoeffer: Meditation and Prayer* (2010).

CLIFFORD J. GREEN is Professor Emeritus of Theology at Hartford Seminary in Connecticut, USA. He is the author of *Bonhoeffer: A Theology of Sociality* (1999) and numerous articles on Bonhoeffer, and serves as the Executive Director of the *Dietrich Bonhoeffer Works English Edition*.

BRIAN GREGOR holds a PhD in philosophy from Boston College, USA. He is co-editor (with Jens Zimmermann) of *Bonhoeffer and Continental Thought: Cruciform Philosophy* and has published several essays on philosophy of religion, ethics, and aesthetics.

JOHN W. DE GRUCHY is Professor Emeritus of Christian Studies at the University of Cape Town and Extraordinary Professor at the University of Stellenbosch, South Africa. He has written widely on the legacy of Dietrich Bonhoeffer. Among his most recent publications is *Confessions of a Christian Humanist*.

BARRY HARVEY (PhD, Duke University) is a native of Denver, Colorado, and Professor of Theology in the Honors College at Baylor University, Texas, USA. An ordained minister and father of two, Harvey is the author of *Another City* and *Can These Bones Live?*

KIRSTEN BUSCH NIELSEN is Professor of Systematic Theology at the University of Copenhagen, Denmark. She has made several contributions to Bonhoeffer scholarship, including her 2008 book *Syndens brudte magt: En undersøgelse af Dietrich Bonhoeffers syndsforståelse* [The Broken Power of Sin: Dietrich Bonhoeffer's Understanding of Sin], forthcoming in German.

ULRIK BECKER NISSEN, PhD, is Associate Professor in the Faculty of Theology, Aarhus University, Denmark, where his research and teaching focuses on Christian ethics pertaining to foundational issues and applied ethics. Currently he is working on the question about the foundation of Christian social ethics in liberal democracies.

JOHN H. YODER was Professor of Christian Ethics in the Department of Theology at the University of Notre Dame in Notre Dame, Indiana, USA. His many publications include *Discipleship as Political Responsibility* (1964), *The Politics of Jesus* (1972), *The Priestly Kingdom* (1984), and *For the Nations* (1997).

JENS ZIMMERMANN holds a Canada Research Chair in Interpretation, Religion, and Culture at Trinity Western University, B.C., Canada. His publications include *Recovering Theological Hermeneutics* (Baker, 2004), *The Passionate Intellect* (coauthored with Norman Klassen; Baker, 2006), and numerous articles in philosophy and theology.

Abbreviations

Dietrich Bonhoeffer Werke

DBW 1	Sanctorum Communio
DBW 2	Akt und Sein
DBW 3	Schöpfung und Fall
DBW 4	Nachfolge
DBW 5	Gemeinsames Leben; Gebetbuch der Bibel
DBW 6	Ethik
DBW 7	Fragmente aus Tegel
DBW 8	Widerstand und Ergebung
DBW 9	Jugend und Studium 1918–1928
DBW 10	Vikariat und Habilitation 1928–1931
DBW 11	Ökumene, Universität, Pfarramt 1931–1932
DBW 12	Berlin 1933
DBW 13	London 1933–1935
DBW 14	Zingst und Finkenwalde 1935–1937
DBW 15	Sammelvikariat 1937–1939
DBW 16	Konspiration und Haft 1939–1945
DBW 17	Register und Ergänzungen

Dietrich Bonhoeffer Works (English)

DBWE 1	Sanctorum Communio
DBWE 2	Act and Being
DBWE 3	Creation and Fall
DBWE 4	Discipleship
DBWE 5	Life Together and Prayerbook of the Bible
DBWE 6	Ethics
DBWE 7	Fiction from Tegel Prison
DBWE 8	Letters and Papers from Prison
DBWE 9	The Young Bonhoeffer: 1918–1927

Abbreviations

DBWE 10   *Barcelona, Berlin, New York: 1928–1931*
DBWE 12   *Berlin: 1932–1933*
DBWE 13   *London: 1933–1935*
DBWE 16   *Conspiracy and Imprisonment: 1940–1945*

GS   Dietrich Bonhoeffer, *Gesammelte Schriften*, 6 Bände

Introduction

THE ESSAYS IN THIS VOLUME DEMONSTRATE BONHOEFFER'S SIGNIFIcance for reflecting on the social and political dimensions of our contemporary world, which is grappling with questions of social identity and religion. As the title indicates, these essays on Bonhoeffer's social thought are motivated by an anthropological concern: When we consider the rapid scientific advances of genetics and globally recurring human atrocities, does it not become apparent that human dignity requires a transcendent reference point? Yet as a generation justly suspicious of easy metaphysical assumptions, we also ask how any one concept of human dignity can offer the kind of transcendence and dynamic quality that is necessary in order to accommodate cultural and historical developments.

Of course, these questions are not new. They usually arise in the light of conceptual and social challenges to the idea that human life is sacred. The German theologian Helmut Thielicke, for example, raised the question of human nature in light of the Nazis' inhuman reign. He concluded that rather than criminal desire, anthropological assumptions were to blame for its racist ideology: "On good grounds I do not believe that definitely criminal instincts drove the Nazis to eliminate the mentally ill and persecute the Jews. In many people idealism and readiness for self-denial were motives in this dreadful business, perverted though these might have been. What triggered them and set rolling the apocalyptic drama of mass murder was not the subjective disposition of the murderers but their table of anthropological values. For if humanity is defined by its utilizability, the diagnosis of unfitness to live follows as night follows day."[1] This challenge remains with us today; even our supposedly civilized Western society experiences once again a deep uncertainty about what it means to be human. For example, in his book *On the Human Condition*, the French philosopher Dominique Janicaud

---

1. Thielicke, *Being Human—Becoming Human*, 8.

argues that in the absence of traditional religious definitions of humanity, and with increasing biotechnical advances in human engineering, Western culture is currently marked by an "unprecedented uncertainty about human identity."[2]

In addition to their role in guarding human dignity, our anthropological presuppositions also shape our view of the individual in relation to society. Too often the pendulum of our social imaginary has swung between the extremes of individualism and collectivism. What conception of human being can provide a via media between these two problematic options? How can we build into our conception of selfhood a simultaneous sense of solidarity with others? And what substantive ethical content is this solidarity to have? Is it merely a solidarity of survival, a sense that we are all in the same earthly boat with equal needs of food, shelter, and love, floating on the ocean of existence without any direction? Or is there a greater map that lends human existence a purpose beyond subsistence and survival? If we follow the question of selfhood in this direction, we find ourselves in the domain of religion.

Recent years have witnessed a renewed openness to the voices of religious traditions within academic discussions regarding society and culture. This openness derives from an epistemological shift in which a positivistic model of truth is increasingly being replaced by a hermeneutical model. Once we understand that reason does not operate *ex nihilo* but in dependence on tradition, this notion of reasoning as fundamentally *situated* and *involved* requires more openness to religious sources of insight than older objectivist epistemologies. In addition, the cultural derivation of those older epistemological models has been exposed and its anthropological premises challenged. This challenge has been especially well developed by the Canadian philosopher Charles Taylor. Taylor has done much to debunk the secularist "subtraction narrative," which describes human development as a progression toward maturity that necessitates the demise of religion. For such an interpretive framework (which all too often continues to reign in the sociology of religion), *any* religious conviction is *by definition* a cultural regress into the dark, primordial abysses of our humanity.[3] Yet this irrational fear of religion, based on a certain interpretation of human history—

2. Janicaud, *Human Condition*, 1.
3. Taylor, *Secular Age*, 432ff.

one that has not fulfilled its promise of progress—, is held by a comparatively small intellectual elite in Western culture. Stubbornly, indeed dogmatically clinging to this social imaginary, this secularist circle is dumbfounded by the persistence of religion and remains incapable of advancing fruitful concepts for interreligious or intercultural dialogue. This form of secularist fundamentalism, still retained by the likes of Richard Dawkins and Christopher Hitchens, becomes increasingly harder to maintain against mounting sociological and philosophical evidence for the importance of religion to society, ethics, and politics.

All these developments show that the door has been opened wide for theological conceptions of human sociality. Yet there remains a postmodern caution to this renewed space for religious insights. Postmodern aversions to *any* substantive universal concepts also seem to apply to concrete theological claims about human existence that are based on revelation. Convinced by Lyotard's warning against metanarratives, and inoculated against theological assertions by Derrida's own assertion that only empty, formal notions of justice or the messianic can prevent their colonization by one particular party, postmoderns are fine with religion as long as it remains without particular form. This impulse goes back to the demand for radical ethical transcendence by the Jewish philosopher Emmanuel Levinas. Levinas maintains that even Martin Buber, who rejects objectifying rationalism in favor of the relational "I-Thou" engagement with reality, does not sufficiently guard against our tendency to explain human dignity within some system or some reciprocal relation.[4] In Levinas's view, any such move toward reciprocity already opens the door to rationalize and thus relativize the irreducible human dignity each person inherently possesses.

Yet, however well intended, Levinas's demand for radical otherness becomes itself problematic. His "Other" indeed constitutes the ultimate barrier to any self-satisfied concept of human being, spun in the isolation of our consciousness and then projected onto humanity as a whole; but it also becomes a barrier on which our desire for sociality and reciprocity are easily shipwrecked. Hans Urs von Balthasar clearly recognized the problem with this constellation and thought that

---

4. Levinas explains that for Buber, "the [I-Thou] relation is straightaway experienced as reciprocity," while he accentuates the asymmetry of this relation: "the principle thing that separates us is what I call the asymmetry of the I-Thou relation" (Interview with François Poirié in Levinas and Robbins, *Is It Righteous to Be?*, 72).

Christian theology offered a way beyond this impasse: "If one does not want to fall back into Idealism (i.e., collectivistic sociologism), get mired in materialism and hedonism, nor be shattered to smithereens on the barrier of the Thou (the Thou as Hell: Sartre), then Christianity remains the only open path which can assign infinite worth to the human Thou, because God ascribed such value to it in election and death on the cross; this assignation becomes only possible, in turn, if the I-Thou-We relation has itself absolute, divine dignity: in the Trinitarian Being of Love."[5] Balthasar's recommendation of the Christian foundation for human sociality demonstrates the complex, even paradoxical elements any adequate concept of sociality has to accommodate: immanence and transcendence, individuality and collectivity, solidarity and ethical discernment.

We have assembled the essays in this book out of the conviction that Bonhoeffer's social thought successfully addresses these demands. Clearly, sociality forms a dominant theme in Bonhoeffer's work. From the introduction of his dissertation, *Sanctorum Communio*, where he notes "the social intention of all the basic Christian concepts,"[6] to his final writings in prison, where he describes Christian faith as being for others,[7] the theme of sociality runs throughout Bonhoeffer's authorship. An equally persistent accent is the Christological orientation of Bonhoeffer's social thought. The phrase "Christ existing as community," which Bonhoeffer coins in his dissertation, captures the ecclesial, communal nature of his anthropology. It has often been remarked that Bonhoeffer is "a Chalcedonian theologian,"[8] which means that his Trinitarian conception of sociality is distinctly incarnational. Thus not only does Bonhoeffer uphold the paradoxical co-existence of individuality and collectivity within the Christian community, but he also extends this picture of sociality to all of humanity. In line with patristic theology, Bonhoeffer regards the incarnation as the recapitulation of humanity, affirmed in the life of Jesus, judged on the cross, and redeemed in the resurrection.

---

5. Balthasar, *Herrlichkeit*, 413 (our translation).
6. *DBWE* 1:21.
7. Bonhoeffer, *Letters and Papers*, 381–82.
8. Green, "Human Sociality," 122.

The essays in this volume will begin to think through what all this means for the broad spectrum of social thought. We can already see, however, that what has been called Bonhoeffer's Christian humanism[9] manages to uphold the divine and the human, transcendence and immanence, by emphasizing true humanity as the *kerygma* of the Christian gospel. All the usual concepts of social thought—concepts such as freedom, responsibility, and solidarity—are configured Christologically, which is to say, incarnationally. Being human means *becoming* human in the image of Christ. This dynamic and ethically concrete repristination of the ancient *imago Dei* theme offers a post-metaphysical conception of human being with many possible applications, some of which are explored in this essay collection.

We conclude our introductory comments by noting two important ramifications of Bonhoeffer's Christological sociality. The first is the cruciform understanding of human ontology. This applies most readily to the church as the body of Christ, for "the new human being is the church community, the body of Christ, or Christ himself."[10] After the recapitulation of humanity in Christ and its restoration in Him to the true image of God, being truly human *as* community is ontologically structured in two concrete forms: "being-with-each-other" and "being-for-each-other."[11] Yet Bonhoeffer also insists that participation in the new humanity of Christ extends a link to all of humanity, since humanity in its entirety was taken up by Christ. Bonhoeffer argues that calling the church Christ's body means that "in the body of Christ all humanity is accepted, included, and borne, and that the church-community of believers is to make this known to the world by word and life. This means not being separated from the world, but calling the world into the community [*Gemeinschaft*] of the body of Christ to which the world in truth already belongs."[12] The church, as Bonhoeffer puts it elsewhere, "now bears the form that in truth is meant for all people. The image according to which it is being formed is the image of humanity."[13] And this image defines truly human existence as relational "being-for-the-other."

---

9. See John de Gruchy's essay in this volume.
10. *DBWE* 4:219.
11. Green, "Human Sociality," 123.
12. *DBWE* 6:67.
13. Ibid., 97.

Restored to true humanity, and being the true humanity in embryo, the "philanthropy of God is the reason for Christians to love every human being as a brother or sister."[14] Christological sociality thus not only sets the church apart from the world but also sends her back into the world in solidarity with every other human being. Participating in the divinely held true humanity of Christian sociality leads us away from an abstract to a concrete ethic: "We can and should speak not about what the good is, can be, or should be for each and every time, but about *how Christ may take form among us today and here*... The concrete Christian ethic stands beyond casuistry and formalism."[15]

The second consequence concerns the accent on interpretation within Bonhoeffer's Christological sociality. He understands that being human in Christ means *becoming* human through implementing God's reconciliation with the world. Christian ethics, as he famously put it, deals not with the ethical problem of "How can I be good," or "How can I do something good," but concerns the entirely different question, "what is the will of God."[16] In describing what doing God's will looks like, Bonhoeffer offers one of the most unique modern theological conceptions by describing the Christian life as living out of what he calls the "ultimate-penultimate" relation. Christian life, says Bonhoeffer, does not mean the adherence to a set of rules, but "Christian life is participation in Christ's encounter with the world."[17] This means two things. First, God has reconciled the world to himself in Christ, who is the eternal Logos through whom all things were made. Hence all of reality is unified as this Christ-reality of reconciliation. Secondly, however, until the final divine renewal of all things, reality is experienced as the tension between the ultimate justifying and reconciling word of God and the penultimate world "preserved and maintained by God for the coming of Christ."[18] This fallen world is still God's good creation; it has been affirmed by Christ, whose redemptive work has confirmed its worth and its relative autonomy—an autonomy that is relative, penultimate,

---

14. *DBWE* 4:285.
15. *DBWE* 6:99.
16. Ibid., 47.
17. Ibid., 159.
18. Ibid., 164.

because it is directed toward its ultimate fulfillment in Christ.[19] The upshot of all this is that the Christ-reality of reconciliation has to be enacted by the Christian discerningly within the ultimate-penultimate relation. Christian knowledge and discernment, in other words, follows the pattern of the Incarnation in having to find the sacred in the profane, yet without reducing the sacred to the profane. The Christian life is one of interpretively discerning what action and mode of sociality is most human because Christ died to enable true humanity. How can Christ's image of God, his servanthood for the sake of true humanity, become reality in any given situation? That is the basis for Christian social comportment.[20]

This vital theme of human sociality links Bonhoeffer with contemporary concerns in theology, philosophy, cultural studies, and science, regarding human reason, human nature, and their socio-cultural expressions. In particular, Bonhoeffer's emphasis on the fundamental relationality of human existence, which he defines Christologically as being-for-others, and the theme of a common humanity in his theological ethics contain rich resources for a wide range of topics in contemporary academic research. Consequently, the contributors to this volume examine Bonhoeffer's wealth of resources for thinking about human being, sociality, and religiosity within our contemporary context.

◆ ◆ ◆

The essays in this volume fall under three main divisions. Part I examines the humanist orientation of Bonhoeffer's thought. In "Dietrich Bonhoeffer as Christian Humanist," John de Gruchy argues that while Bonhoeffer did not refer to himself specifically as a Christian humanist, his life and work from his early formation through to his prison reflections give us good reason for describing him as such. At the same time, Bonhoeffer's legacy helps us critically retrieve the term in ways that give it greater contemporary value and significance. It is a Christological humanism shaped by a genuine encounter with "the other," fashioned in the struggle for truth and justice against dehumanizing power, deep-

---

19. Ibid., 174.
20. Ibid., 74.

ened through suffering, and always affirming human goodness against perversity, hope against despair, and life against death.

Jens Zimmermann, in "Being Human, Becoming Human: Dietrich Bonhoeffer's Christological Humanism," complements de Gruchy's essay by linking Bonhoeffer's Christian humanism to its patristic roots. According to Zimmermann, humanism, including Renaissance humanism, was originally a Christian affair, deriving from the Christological reflections of the church fathers. Bonhoeffer stands firmly within this tradition, and Zimmermann defends this conception of humanism against philosophical (Luc Ferry) and theological (John Howard Yoder) challenges.

In "Bonhoeffer's Theology and Economic Humanism: An Exploration in Interdisciplinary Sociality," Peter Frick offers an exploratory essay that examines Bonhoeffer's own pronouncement, early in his career, that he is seeking a humanistic theology. On the basis of three of Bonhoeffer's basic theological assumptions (the economic realm is part of the one reality of Christ; the church must address the social issues of society; every life is valuable independent of social utility) Frick argues that theology's task is to critique and comment on economic structures by asking whether they enhance or destroy life. In order to achieve such an objective, theology must itself be critical, similar to the attempts of the Frankfurt School, but go beyond mere criticism and engage in constructive, interdisciplinary dialogue that works toward the emergence of authentic humanistic economies.

The essays in Part II examine Bonhoeffer's ecclesiological concept of sociality. In "Sociality, Discipleship, and Worldly Theology in Bonhoeffer's Christian Humanism," Clifford Green revisits his influential interpretation of Bonhoeffer's theology of sociality, asking to what extent it adequately illuminates the dynamics of his theological development, and whether recent research further clarifies his intellectual pilgrimage through the period of *Discipleship* to the emphasis on "worldliness" in his *Ethics* and prison theology. In the process Green's article sheds light on what "being human" meant for Bonhoeffer as a Christian theologian.

In her essay "Community Turned Inside Out: Dietrich Bonhoeffer's Concept of the Church and of Humanity Reconsidered," Kirsten Busch Nielsen focuses on the interdependence of anthropology and ecclesiology in Bonhoeffer's early writings, especially in *Sanctorum Communio*.

Nielsen agrees with the prevailing view that the center of Bonhoeffer's theology lies in Christology, but also argues that Christology is surrounded by an ellipse formed by anthropology and ecclesiology. Bonhoeffer elegantly and provocatively combines the concepts of individuality and sociality in his anthropological discourse, and then examines how these insights shape his interpretation of the doctrines of creation, sin, and reconciliation/church. It is, however, important to recognize that since the relation between individuality and sociality is perverted by sin, we can only consider the community of sinners (the humanity of Adam) a broken one—a non-community. Bonhoeffer's strong concept of sin shapes his combination of anthropology and ecclesiology, thus preserving the dialectic of the *peccatorum communio* and the *sanctorum communio*; it is therefore challenging and should still be considered promising for Protestant ecclesiology.

The theme of ecclesiology also guides Barry Harvey's essay, "The Narrow Path: Sociality, Ecclesiology, and the Polyphony of Life in the Thought of Dietrich Bonhoeffer." Harvey argues that ecclesiology is at the heart of Dietrich Bonhoeffer's social thought and is not dependent on a prior theory of sociality per se. The contention of some that Bonhoeffer relaxes the connection between Christ and the church in his later prison correspondence in order to embrace completely and unreservedly a world come of age therefore misses the mark. In a world that compliments itself on having brought the human species to maturity, Bonhoeffer is correct to hold to the centrality of the church in the construction of a coherent and credible theological concept of sociality. The picture of the church that emerges in Bonhoeffer's later works gestures toward an alternative mode of sociality that bears striking similarities to the forms that Jewish life took following the Babylonian Exile.

The contributions in Part III examine the interrelated themes of discipleship, conformation, and responsibility, all of which are important in Bonhoeffer's social thought. In a previously unpublished essay from 1987, "The Christological Presuppositions of Discipleship," John Howard Yoder offers a distinctly Anabaptist and decidedly critical engagement with Bonhoeffer's concept of discipleship. Yoder begins with a genealogy of Anabaptist thought on discipleship and then proceeds to examine the parallels with Bonhoeffer's thought, comparing and contrasting their conceptions of discipleship as "an ethic for which the concrete humanity of Jesus, in his social decisions, provides the model."

Yoder's concern is with concreteness. Regarding the call to discipleship, then, how does the Christological focus of Bonhoeffer's account relate to the lifestyle of the historical man Jesus? Yoder also presses the question of the concrete ethical consequences of discipleship: What is the disciple called to do, in concrete terms? Yoder's recurring criticism is that Bonhoeffer's ethics of discipleship is not yet *concrete enough*—whether it concerns the relation between the Christ of faith and the Jesus of history, the nature of suffering and rejection in the life of discipleship, the interpretation of the Beatitudes, the practice of pacifism, the notion of being conformed to Christ, the doctrine of the mandates, or the relation between church and state. In Yoder's view, despite Bonhoeffer's emphasis on following after Christ he "was not driven either to concreteness about the pre-passion Jesus nor to any abiding challenge to the axioms of Constantinian political ethics."

The theme of discipleship returns in Brian Gregor's "Following-After and Becoming Human: A Study of Bonhoeffer and Kierkegaard." Gregor's essay conducts a dialogue between Bonhoeffer and Kierkegaard—a dialogue that is promising since these two thinkers share several commitments and concerns: a rejection of idealist accounts of subjectivity, in order to take seriously finitude and concreteness in describing human existence; the attempt to retrieve the biblical concept of following-after Christ to correct the cheap grace that had distorted Lutheran Christendom; and a dialectical approach to thinking about the relations between faith and obedience as well as passivity and activity. Gregor closes by arguing that Kierkegaard can enrich Bonhoeffer's thought by offering a deeper understanding of the role of imagination in following after Christ.

Next is Lisa Dahill's "Con-Formation with Jesus Christ: Bonhoeffer, Social Location, and Embodiment." Dahill observes that despite its centrality to human existence and the incarnational heart of Christian faith, the human body—our physical participation in both creation and the life of God—has not until recently been a major focus of Christian theological reflection. Her essay offers a sketch of Bonhoeffer's theology of the human body, tracing five key features of his view: the body's essential goodness, its rights to life and joy, its role as "limit" to others, its centrality in Christian community, and its indwelling by God. The particular focus of her essay is how the body, understood in these ways, participates in the "conformation with Christ" that is central to

Bonhoeffer's *Ethics* and its vision of the Christian life. She explores this question through the lens of the observed experience of Precious Jones, the title character in the 2009 film *Precious*, and asks how Bonhoeffer's theology of the body and his understanding of being *con*-formed, i.e., formed-with Christ, illumine the embodied human experience glimpsed in this film. How do both Precious Jones and Dietrich Bonhoeffer participate bodily in the suffering of their times—and in the incarnation, suffering, and resurrection of Jesus? What do we learn from these two very different human beings about the significance of our own embodiment in Jesus Christ?

Finally, Ulrik Becker Nissen's essay, "Responding to Human Reality: Responsibility and Responsiveness in Bonhoeffer's Ethics," examines the close relation between responsibility and responsiveness. According to Bonhoeffer, moral responsibility arises in the immediate encounter with the other—a view that brings him close to a situation ethics or ethics of proximity, which may be read as an endorsement of conditions of moral responsibility that are universal to all human beings. At the same time, the Christological foundation of Bonhoeffer's ethics also implies a specific approach to human reality, namely, that it is in Christ that the human being realizes true humanity. Nissen argues that this affirmation of humanity and endorsement of its foundation in Christ reflects an underlying Chalcedonian Christology and that this Christological foundation of Bonhoeffer's ethics makes it possible for him to maintain the universal and specific dimensions of Christian ethics at the same time, as exemplified in the notion of responsibility.

❖ ❖ ❖

A volume of this nature requires the cooperation of many people, so we would like to thank those who have made it possible: the authors for their excellent contributions; Lise van der Eyk for her careful and tireless editorial assistance; K. C. Hanson, Diane Farley, and the rest of the people at Wipf and Stock who have worked on this project; the generous funding of this project by the Canadian Social Sciences and Humanities Research Council (CRC and SSHRC) and the Ernest Fortin Memorial Foundation; Anne Marie Yoder, Martha Yoder Maust, and the Mennonite Church USA Historical Committee and Archives for their help; and finally, our wives and families.

PART ONE

Bonhoeffer's Humanism

1

Dietrich Bonhoeffer as Christian Humanist

John W. de Gruchy

IN 1966 KENNETH KAUNDA, THEN PRESIDENT OF ZAMBIA, PUBLISHED a book entitled *A Humanist in Africa*. He spoke of a humanist revolution then spreading across Africa that aimed at restoring the dignity and national pride of the peoples of the continent, who, for so long, had been dehumanized by the forces of slavery and colonialism. Kaunda wrote as an African, deeply rooted in its culture and tradition, but he also wrote as a Christian, the product of a missionary education. The humanism of which he spoke was not the secular humanism of the West, which he rejected; it was Christian, but not based on a Christianity that emphasized human depravity and contributed to the misery and enslavement of African people. The Christian humanism he affirmed is one that discovers "all that is worth knowing about God through our fellow men [*sic*] and unconditional service of our fellow men," for this is "the purest form of the service of God."[1]

Kaunda's vision of Christian humanism resonates with that of the fourteenth- and fifteenth-century European Renaissance. Critical of forms of Christianity that enslaved the human body, mind, and spirit, it sought to restore and affirm human dignity through a recovery of classical culture and to do so in harmony with Christian faith. In doing so, it led to the affirmation of national identity and freedom and contributed to the reformation of church and society. For reasons such as these the European Renaissance continues to capture the imagination of many today—as in former President Thabo Mbeki's vision of an African

1. Kaunda, *Humanist in Africa*, 39.

Renaissance—who seek the renewal, freedom, and moral regeneration of their own societies.

But such a vision probably attracts us all, irrespective of where we come from, where we live and work, especially faced with the dehumanizing powers and forces at work in our global society. Indeed, many of us are deeply bothered by the dominant alternatives facing us today irrespective of our particular context. On the one hand, there has been a powerful upsurge of religious fundamentalism, which in its Christian form is invariably aligned with right-wing political agendas. We stand together with secular humanists in decrying and opposing such forces that so often result in policies that dehumanize people and degrade the environment in which human life is able to flourish. On the other hand, secular humanism, which pervades much of the academy, despite its pedigree of concern for human rights and its affirmation of human freedom, does not have the spiritual resources to address the deepest human needs. Too often it degenerates into a secularism such as pervades modernity with its pursuit of material self-interests. Christian humanism provides an alternative vision, one that retains a strong core of Christian faith and commitment and, at the same time and precisely because of that, embraces all those who seek to affirm the human in an increasingly dehumanizing global context.

All of this has led me to consider again the legacy of Bonhoeffer, prompted by a comment made by Gerhard Leibholz, the husband of Bonhoeffer's twin sister Sabine. In his foreword to the first British edition of *The Cost of Discipleship,* published in 1948, Leibholz remarked that "Bonhoeffer stood for what is called Christian Humanism today."[2] It is an intriguing comment, but one that also begs many questions. For what, or who, did Leibholz have in mind? Was it the Christian humanism of the French Catholic philosophers? Or was Leibholz speaking about people in his adopted country who demonstrated the connection between Christian faith and humanist values, such as Bishop George Bell of Chichester, whom Leibholz described as "the living Christian conscience of this country?"[3] An intriguing thought when we recall

---

2. See the Foreword to Bonhoeffer, *Cost of Discipleship*, 18.

3. Jasper, *George Bell*, 284. Associated with Bell would have been T. S. Eliot, poet and an editor of the *New English Weekly*, who had courageously supported Leibholz in publishing his appeal on behalf of the German Resistance; the ecumenist J. H. Oldham and those associated with his Christian News-Letter; and the journal *Frontier*, edited by Alec Vidler and then John Lawrence.

Eberhard Bethge's comment that "Karl Barth and George Bell were the only men whose authority" Bonhoeffer "ever truly accepted."[4] Indeed, not only is this an intriguing thought, but the juxtaposition of Barth and Bell goes a long way to helping us understand our subject.

But would Bonhoeffer have recognized himself as a Christian humanist? After all, we recall his reservations about Jacques Maritain's attempt to develop Christian humanism on the basis of Thomist philosophy.[5] So should we not rather simply call him a Christian and forget about all suffixes, whether humanist or any other? Indeed, what purpose does it serve to think of him in these terms? Given the history of humanism in general, is it not too confusing, misleading, and generally unhelpful even with the Christian prefix? So should there be a question mark at the end of the title of my paper that at least hints at some doubt, some hesitation, and some ambiguity? Such questions will stay with us as we proceed. But there are sufficient indicators in Bonhoeffer's legacy and in secondary sources[6] to suggest that the subject is worth pursuing in seeking an alternative Christian vision to the dominant forces of fundamentalism and secularism.

The Early Formation of a Christian Humanist

Bonhoeffer's grandparents, Eberhard Bethge tells us, "saw no discrepancy between" patriotic German nationalism "and the lofty humanist standards that they demanded of themselves and their children."[7] Cemented together by Protestant faith and conviction, the roots of this combination of nationalism and humanism in Germany may be traced back to the Renaissance. After all, it was the Renaissance that, through its recovery of the classical tradition and an authentic biblical text, helped awaken a sense of German identity and pride and set people free to rediscover the liberating message of the Christian gospel.

---

4. Bethge, *Bonhoeffer: A Biography*, 72.

5. Maritain, *True Humanism*; see Bonhoeffer's reference to Maritain's book on humanism in his American Diary, 1939 (*DBW* 15:234). Bonhoeffer was also familiar with Maritain's book *Die Zukunft der Christenheit*; see, for example, footnote references in *DBW* 6:75, 134–35.

6. See, for example, Woelfel, *Bonhoeffer's Theology*, 67; Lange, "Particular Europe," 81–96.

7. Bethge, *Bonhoeffer: A Biography*, 9.

The Bonhoeffer family, including the young Dietrich, was nurtured and educated within this classical humanist tradition, as the many references and allusions to it in Bonhoeffer's writings bear testimony.[8] Its aim was the formation or *Bildung* of character,[9] which in turn was the foundation of civil society or *Burgertum*. But the First World War, and especially the defeat of Germany, created a profound crisis for those who took this patriotic, humanist, and Christian ethos for granted. Radical anti-liberal nationalist and ethnic movements erupted, rejecting all their cherished values and forcing the Bonhoeffer family to make a painful choice between nationalism and humanism. Again in Bethge's words: "In the fate of her sons, Dietrich's mother would be the first to experience the painful break between nationalism and humanism."[10]

The young Bonhoeffer soon became personally aware of the problematic relationship between nationalism and humanism. After briefly flirting with nationalism in Tübingen, he sought to find a more adequate Christian basis for the humanist tradition in which he had been nurtured at home and educated at school. After reading Dostoevsky while a student in Berlin in 1925, the place he encountered liberal humanism at its best, he wrote to his parents expressing his attraction to the Russian ideal of a "supranational panhumanism ... necessarily and emphatically linked to Christianity." This, Bonhoeffer suggested, re-established "the genuine 'Catholicism' of original Christianity."[11] By this stage, a full year had passed since his visit to Rome, where he had experienced the inclusive universality of the church in St. Peter's Basilica in a way that made a lasting impression on him.[12] This, for him, was "genuine 'Catholicism,'" the Catholicism of original Christianity that transcended exclusive ethnic and national boundaries. A Christian humanism, expressed in this way, was an attractive alternative to the pseudo-Christian nationalism that was becoming rampant throughout Germany.

---

8. See, for example, his essay "After Ten Years," which was written for his secular humanist co-conspirators (Bonhoeffer, *Letters and Papers*, 3–17).

9. The German *Bildung* and the English "formation" do not mean precisely the same thing. "Formation" does not convey the ambiguity of *Bildung*, which can mean both copy (*Nachbild*) and model (*Vorbild*); see Gadamer, *Truth and Method*, 12.

10. Bethge, *Bonhoeffer: A Biography*, 9.

11. Ibid., 69.

12. *DBWE* 9:88.

That the relationship between humanism, nationalism, and Christianity continued to interest Bonhoeffer over the next few years is evident from another letter to his parents, this time in 1928 during his vicariate in Barcelona. In it he wrote, "For Italy humanism and the classical period represented the solution to all problems, whereas in Spain there is an element of resistance, which I think is also evident, to a certain degree, time and again among the Germans. Spaniards and Germans, I think, are similar in that neither culture ever completely opened itself up to humanism; instead, a remnant of something else always persisted."[13] What did Bonhoeffer have in mind? What was it that the Italians embraced but the Spaniards and Germans did not? There are several possibilities. But one is surely the fact that classical and contemporary Rome embraced Europe and the world beyond; it was universal in its scope, drawing people of all cultures and tribes into its orbit, whereas Germany and Spain fenced their boundaries and defended their emerging sense of national identity as contiguous with their Christianity. This had had a decided impact on the character of Spanish Catholicism and was expressed in the nationalist and monocultural character of German Protestantism. In both, humanism, internationalism, and, later, ecumenism were swear words in much the same way as they were in apartheid South Africa, where they were also identified with what was called the "Roman danger" (*die Roomse-gevaar*).

Given his background and the broadening cultural experience that was already accumulating from his travels, it is unsurprising that early in his stay in Barcelona, Bonhoeffer made a note in his diary that his theology was becoming humanistic.[14] However, being an enthusiastic disciple of Karl Barth, this turn of events appeared to take him by surprise and caused him to ponder what it might mean. It is clear from his lecture on "Jesus Christ and the Essence of Christianity" later that year in Barcelona what it did not mean. For in that lecture he emphatically rejected humanism along with mysticism and cultural Protestantism for their euphoria about human achievements and their confidence in the ability of men and women to reach God in their own strength.[15] So what, then, did he mean?

13. Bethge, *Bonhoeffer: A Biography*, 102; *DBWE* 10:95.
14. *DBWE* 10:64.
15. Ibid., 356–57.

Clues are provided in his Barcelona lecture and his diary notes from that time. The first has to do with Bonhoeffer's conviction that rather than robbing "humanity of its highest possession" in its opposition to secular humanism, Christian faith restores human values and renews culture, though it does so only "in its perfectly limited, relative" right and not as an absolute.[16] This clearly distinguishes Bonhoeffer's incipient Christian humanism from its secular version. It also distinguishes it from the more liberal forms of Christian humanism with which he was so well acquainted in Berlin. For Bonhoeffer, the good and essential human values affirmed by secularists and liberal Christians, as within his family circle, could only be sustained on theological grounds that prevented them from becoming absolutes that eventually dehumanize, not least through uncritical alignment with nationalism. Was this not one of the chief reasons why he had shifted his allegiance from Harnack to Barth, and why Barth in the first place had attacked the failure of liberal Protestantism to oppose Kaiser Wilhelm in going to war?

If the first clue is an affirmation of Christian faith discerned through the eyes of Barth as the basis for true humanism against secular and liberal Christian humanism, the second clue in the lecture suggests an emerging critique of Barth's theology, not on dogmatic grounds, but on the basis of cultural experience. This is the significance of his query whether Barth had ever traveled beyond the sphere of German culture.[17] For, so unlike Barth, by this stage Bonhoeffer had already traveled through Italy, visited North Africa, and lived in Spain, and this was having an impact on his theological vision, making it more open to influences other than German and contributing to what he would later describe as a turning "from phraseology to reality."[18] In other words, for Bonhoeffer to say that his theology was becoming humanist did not imply a break with Barth's theological critique of liberalism so much as a breaking free of its German confinement. Indeed, in prison, he would ask the question whether "a knowledge of other countries and an intimate contact with them" are "more important for education today than a knowledge of the classics?"[19] This, he said, would "be tapping a

16. Ibid, 356.
17. Ibid., 64.
18. Letter to Eberhard Bethge, 22 April 1944 (Bonhoeffer, *Letters and Papers*, 275).
19. Ibid., 230.

hitherto unused source for the fertilizing of our education, and at the same time carrying on an old European tradition."[20]

The contrast between Christianity and secular or liberal Christian humanism was most strongly expressed by Bonhoeffer during his year at Union Theological Seminary, 1930–1931, when he was also at his most outspoken in defense of Barth's theology. Union's critique of Christian fundamentalism and the radical humanism of Chicago was healthy and necessary, he wrote, but its theological basis was flawed and inadequate. The problem, Bonhoeffer perceived, was that a "radically immanent ethical humanism" influenced by William James's pragmatism and John Dewey's instrumentalism pervaded American theology.[21] Symptomatic of this was, to his consternation, when some American students laughed at the mention of Luther's teaching on the "bondage of the will," finding it comic.[22] Within this context, it was highly unlikely that Bonhoeffer would have confessed that his theology was humanistic in any sense, as he had in Barcelona. At the very least he would have been misunderstood in much the same way as many of us from outside North America today are misunderstood when we resist being labeled liberals. And yet there were several influences at work during that year in North America and at Union that were pushing his theology along that path. We need not rehearse them all, but noteworthy among them was his friendship with Jean Lasserre, whose international spirit and pacifism, marks of Christian humanism from Erasmus onwards, had such a profound influence on him.

Bonhoeffer's travels as a young student, vicar, and church world fellow all contributed to the development of the humanistic dimension of his theology, building on his family nurturing, classical education, and respect for, if not agreement with, his Berlin teachers. But now he had to return to Germany and face the darkening cloud of Nazi terror. The emerging scenario within state and church certainly did not augur well for any ongoing development of his nascent Christian humanism, whether theologically or culturally. It was rather a time to batten down the dogmatic hatches and follow Barth into combat for truth against heresy. Yet it was within this inauspicious context that a most surpris-

20. Ibid., 230–31.
21. *DBW* 10:311.
22. Ibid., 309–10. See also his letter to his Superintendent in Berlin, Max Diestel, written from Havana (ibid., 265–66).

ing turn of events took place that caused Bonhoeffer to make common cause with secular humanists on the basis of his confession of Christ.

Common Cause with Secular Humanists

The aim of Renaissance humanism was the transformation of an increasingly moribund medieval scholastic culture through the retrieval of ancient textual resources and of classical culture.[23] The details of this diverse movement varied according to context,[24] evolving differently depending on circumstances and personality, yet always affirming the dignity, potential, and freedom of humanity, the importance of moral values and virtue, and the importance of classical culture over against all forces, not least ecclesiastical, that denigrated humanity. Renaissance humanism was also the midwife of the Protestant Reformation. But there is irony in the fact. The mainstream of the Reformation was adamant in its insistence on the sole authority of Scripture, the centrality of Christ alone as God's revelation, and the sinfulness of human nature. Such dogmatic claims did not sit comfortably with the broader vision of most humanist scholars either in their search for truth beyond the Christian canon or in their affirmation of human goodness and potential within it.

The controversy between Luther and Erasmus, the quintessential Christian humanist, on the freedom and bondage of the will epitomizes this tension. Marked, as Roland Bainton suggested, by "misunderstanding on the part of Erasmus and exaggeration on the part of Luther,"[25] it highlighted the problems faced by all who take seriously the paradoxes of the gospel. But it also highlighted another problem, namely, what it means to stand for the truth. "You and your peace-loving theology," Luther declared to Erasmus, "you don't care about the truth." But Erasmus did care about the truth, for "what happens to truth when men are embroiled in a war of religion?"[26] Indeed, if the search for truth irrespective of where it was to be found was one of the virtues of the

---

23. See, for example: Witt, "Humanist Movement," 93–94; Skinner, *Foundations*, xxiii–xxv.

24. A useful account of the development of humanism during this period is in Witt, "Humanist Movement," and Hecker, "Humanism," 665–70.

25. Bainton, *Erasmus*, 228.

26. Quoted in ibid., 235.

Renaissance, another was tolerance for the opinion of others as part of that search. But, despite the efforts of many on both sides, Erasmus chief among them, tolerance soon became a casualty in the cause of the Reformation, as did Erasmus himself. And the outcome of Erasmus's controversy with Luther symbolized the waning power of humanism as a reforming project. Those who espoused the humanist project were confined within the boundaries of whatever confessional and institutional framework they found themselves. There was no place for a non-doctrinal, non-confessional Christianity within the new climate of Reformation and post-Reformation struggles.

Tolerance of the opinion of others is seldom a virtue in the thrust and counterthrust of theological controversy when the issues are those of life and death, and where each side claims a monopoly on the truth. We discovered this in the church struggle against apartheid, as did the Confessing Church in Germany. So how did Bonhoeffer's nascent Christian humanism shape up during the *Kirchenkampf* epitomized in the decisions of Barmen and Dahlem and encapsulated in Bonhoeffer's declaration that "there is no salvation outside the Confessing Church"? How, for example, did it relate to the secular humanism of those already engaged in the Resistance?

Peter Gay referred to the four centuries prior to the European Enlightenment as the "era of pagan Christianity," a time "when there was nothing incongruous about the sight of a Christian Humanist, a Christian Stoic, a Christian Platonist, or even a Christian skeptic."[27] But ever since then humanism on the Continent had increasingly lost its Christian character, preparing the way for the secular humanism of the twentieth century with its neo-Marxist and existentialist variants. Atheistic in character, secular humanism emerged as the defender of humanity against religious dogmatism, ecclesiastical triumphalism, and popular superstition. It also became the defender of reason, culture, humanity, tolerance, and freedom, all values cherished by Renaissance humanism but which had become, in Bonhoeffer's words, "battle slogans against the Church, against Christianity, against Jesus Christ himself."[28] Cooperation between secular humanism and the church had become virtually unthinkable. But it became unthinkable not just because of

---

27. Gay, *Rise of Modern Paganism*, 256–57.
28. Bonhoeffer, *Ethics*, 55. Cf. *DBWE* 6:340.

secularization; it was also unthinkable because of a theological failure on the part of the church. Ironically, it took the *Kirchenkampf*, with its strident *"Nein!"* to false gospels, to make rapprochement possible yet again as in the early days of the Reformation.

So it was that in the struggle against Hitler and Nazi tyranny such cooperation began to take place on the part of a handful of confessing Christians and those secular men and women whom Bonhoeffer later described as "the few remaining just, truthful and human men," who put Christians to shame.[29] These secular men and women of the Resistance stood, at best, on the periphery of the church, and their defense of human values was not consciously Christian in orientation. But in defending reason, culture, humanity, freedom, tolerance, and human rights against tyranny, there was, to quote Bonhoeffer, "a kind of alliance and comradeship between the defenders of these endangered values and the Christians."[30] The slogans that had previously been used against Christianity "had now, suddenly and surprisingly, come very near indeed to the Christian standpoint."[31]

The surprising factor in this development was that this rapprochement, as Bonhoeffer stressed, was not at the expense of Christian conviction, for it "took place at a time when everything Christian was more closely hemmed in than ever before and when the cardinal principles of Christian belief were displayed in their hardest and most uncompromising form, in a form which could give greatest offence to all reason, culture, humanity and tolerance."[32] The Christians who began to cooperate with the secular humanists were not liberal Protestants but those most committed to the Confessing Church with its categorical rejection of culture as another source of revelation. The *status confessionis* recognized by Barth and Bonhoeffer paralleled that of Luther's Reformation; it was not Erasmian in temperament, showing tolerance for those Christians who disagreed, but categorical in its rejection of all who were not for "the Christ" of the Barmen Declaration and the "true church" of Dahlem. In fact, as Bonhoeffer noted, the alliance grew in inverse proportion to the degree in which the Confessing Church nar-

29. Ibid., 61.
30. Ibid., 55.
31. Ibid.
32. Ibid.

rowed its field of action.[33] How was this possible? As Bethge reminds us in his essay on Karl-Friedrich Bonhoeffer, members of the Bonhoeffer family who began to identify themselves with the Confessing Church after years of antipathy toward Christianity certainly had problems with the language of Barmen.[34] So how was it that the Barmen Declaration, centered on the "one Word of God" over against any other source of revelation, could later be spoken of positively in relation to humanism?

Barmen was, as Bethge reminded us at the Seattle Conference in 1984 celebrating the fiftieth anniversary of the Declaration, far more than "a verbal happening[;] it was linked with the cries and actions of and for dehumanised groups of men" in such a way that "dogmatics and humanism were bound together,"[35] involving both confessors and their compatriots in great personal risk and cost in a common struggle to rid Germany of tyranny, to defend its victims, and to restore justice. Yet, for Bonhoeffer, this was not simply a pragmatic relationship forced upon the historically alienated by historical circumstances. On the contrary, there was a profoundly theological basis for making common cause with secular humanists engaged in the Resistance. Confessing Christ and costly discipleship made it both possible and necessary.

Let us recall that Bonhoeffer began working on *Discipleship* during his sojourn in London (1933–1935), where he discussed his thoughts with his close friend Franz Hildebrandt.[36] Hildebrandt was critical of the influence that Barth had on Bonhoeffer, but the two friends were unanimous, against Barth, in affirming Luther's *finitum capax infiniti* ("the finite is capable of embodying the infinite").[37] They also shared pacifist convictions and an appreciation for insights from the radical Reformation, and, I suggest, recognized the need for what Hildebrandt called "true humanism."[38] Committed Lutheran as he was, Hildebrandt respected Erasmus and recognized "the decisive part" which humanism played in Lutheran tradition.[39] He also had respect

33. Cf. ibid.
34. Bethge, "Nonreligious Scientist," 49.
35. Bethge, "Self-Interpretation," 183.
36. See the editors' introduction in *DBWE* 4:25.
37. Hildebrandt, "Gospel and Humanitarianism," 250.
38. Hildebrandt, "Interpretation of Luther," 137.
39. See ibid.

for the humanist convictions of sectarians and enthusiasts on matters of "war and peace, violence and liberty, persecution and tolerance" despite what he called their "thoroughly questionable theology."[40] In his doctoral dissertation, "The Gospel and Humanitarianism," submitted to Cambridge in 1941, Hildebrandt went so far as to say that these Christian sectarians knew the gospel better than the Reformers. To remedy the situation, he set out to develop a human rights ethic on a Lutheran confessional basis. In a way so reminiscent of Bonhoeffer's earlier comments in his essay on "The Jewish Question," Hildebrandt wrote that there is a gospel mandate for "the intervention of the church on behalf of the 'victims'" of state terror and that this represented "the most efficient protest against injustice, violence and terror."[41] All of this pointed to what Hildebrandt meant by "true humanism," a humanism embodied in Bonhoeffer's own life.

Many years later, at the Seattle conference in celebration of Barmen, Hildebrandt returned to this question. "The church," he wrote, "is called to make common cause with the humanists for the sake of peace and of the rights of man."[42] Bonhoeffer would surely have fully agreed about the need for such an alliance in opposing state terror and the idolatry that led to the dehumanizing of "the other." After all, and this is the heart of the matter, their opponents in the *Kirchenkampf* were not secular humanists but Christians—German Christians, orthodox Lutherans, and liberal Protestants. These were the targets of their confession of Christ, the ones to whom they refused to show tolerance in the fight for the truth. And the reason was clear. The confession of Christ and the struggle for the "true church" was not for the sake of theological correctness and ecclesial purity but for the sake of the world for which Christ had died. To surrender the truth of the gospel, to deny Christ, meant denying humanity, denying the victims of Nazism, and denying all that was good and great in German culture. To affirm the truth of the gospel, by contrast, meant affirming humanity, expressing solidarity with the victims of injustice, and affirming the good and great in culture. So if confessing Christ separated Bonhoeffer from the many

---

40. Hildebrandt, "Gospel and Humanitarianism," 4.
41. Ibid., 294.
42. Hildebrandt, "Barmen," 300.

Christians who had succumbed to Nazism, that same confession united him with the few secular humanists who stood against it.

If the gospel of costly grace demanded engagement in the struggle against human oppression, for Bonhoeffer it was the Incarnation that provided the theological basis for doing so in company with secular humanists. Already in his earliest essay in *Ethics*, on "Christ, Reality, and the Good," which marks a transition from the Christology of *Discipleship* to that of the *Ethics*,[43] the Incarnation means that in Christ, God and the world are reconciled. The consequences are far-reaching, for no longer is it possible to think in terms of "two spheres," the sacred and the secular.[44] Moreover, in affirming the Incarnation—of God fully and truly human—we are led inexorably to an affirmation of the humanity of God and the dignity of the human. In this regard, consider for a moment Barth's lecture in 1956 on "The Humanity of God." "The allegation that we were teaching that God is everything and man nothing," Barth declares, "was bad. As a matter of fact, certain hymns of praise to humanism were at that time occasionally raised—the Platonic in particular, in which Calvin was nurtured."[45] God could now only be understood in "God's *togetherness* with man,"[46] and, unlike the God of Schleiermacher, "stands up for man."[47] Not even the fall takes away man's humanity, and we must do nothing to speak ill of that humanity, for it is God's gift. Most remarkable is Barth's applause for Blumhardt's statement, "You men are gods": "And with this explanation the statement that the human spirit is naturally Christian may also be valued as an obstinately joyful proclamation. That is what we have to testify to men in view of the humanism *of* God, irrespective of the more or less godlessness of *their* humanism—everything else must be said only in the framework of this statement and promise."[48] Given the fact that Bonhoeffer, even at his most Barthian, was closer to Luther in terms of Christology, it seems appropriate to assume that he would have had no difficulty in joyfully proclaiming such humanism long before Barth. Recall, for example, that very powerful section on "Ethics as Formation," where Bonhoeffer invites us to "Behold the

---

43. On this transition see Bonhoeffer, *Cost of Discipleship*, 305–6.
44. Bonhoeffer, *Ethics*, 196ff. Cf. *DBWE* 6:56ff.
45. Barth, *Humanity of God*, 44.
46. Ibid., 45.
47. Ibid., 53.
48. Ibid., 60.

God who has become man": "God loves man. God loves the world. It is not an ideal man that he loves, but man as he is; not an ideal world, but the world as it is."[49] The gospel of the Incarnation challenges both those who scorn and those who idolize humanity, for they both dehumanize. The reason why "we can live as real men and can love the real man at our side is to be found solely in the incarnation of God, in the unfathomable love of God for man."[50]

Yet, for Bonhoeffer, the Incarnation can never be affirmed in isolation from the cross of Christ. Christ, he always insists, "is both the Incarnate and the Crucified, and he demands to be recognised as both of these alike."[51] As he put it in his essay on "Inheritance and Decay," "Wherever the incarnation of Christ, his becoming man, is more intensely in the foreground of Christian consciousness, there one will seek for the reconciliation of antiquity with Christianity. And wherever the cross of Christ dominates the Christian message, there the breach between Christ and antiquity will be very greatly emphasized."[52] Just as there is no easy reconciliation between classical antiquity and Christianity, so the crucifixion continually reminds us that from a Christian perspective there can be no easy, Romantic, or Idealistic humanism, a humanism incapable of opposing evil and indifferent to the sinful and tragic dimensions of life.

The Christology that made common cause with secular humanists possible, then, was not the result of metaphysical speculation or an apologetic attempt to bring Christianity into harmony with classical culture, but "the concrete suffering of injustice, of the organized lie, of hostility to humanity and of violence[;] it was the persecution of lawfulness, truth, humanity and freedom."[53] This struggle for humanity, to assert humanist values, "impelled those who held such values dear to seek the protection of Christ and therefore to become subject to his claim." Indeed, Bonhoeffer went on to say, "It is not Christ who must justify himself before the world by the acknowledgement of the values of justice, truth and freedom, but it is these values which have come to need

49. Bonhoeffer, *Ethics*, 71. Cf. *DBWE* 6:84.
50. Ibid., 74. Cf. *DBWE* 6:87.
51. Ibid., 91. Cf. *DBWE* 6:107.
52. Ibid.
53. Ibid., 58. Cf. *DBWE* 6:344-45.

justification, and their justification can only be Jesus Christ."⁵⁴ And then, in his essay on "Inheritance and Decay," he writes with equal conviction, "It is only in relation to Christ that there is a genuine inheritance from classical antiquity to the west."⁵⁵ Frits de Lange draws our attention here to a remarkable parallel between what Bonhoeffer is saying and what Thomas Mann, the German novelist and humanist, wrote in 1939 after fleeing Germany: "Liberty, truth, true reason, human dignity—whence did we create these ideas, ideas that are the mainstay and support of our lives and without which our spiritual existence would disintegrate, if not from Christianity, which made them universal law?"⁵⁶

The triumphalist danger of such statements is obvious: the claim that the church alone has all the truth and is guardian of such struggles for justice. Nothing could be further from Bonhoeffer's mind. Rather, it is his understanding of Christ, the persecuted and suffering Christ, that has grown to the point where all these values, these humanist values, are seen to have their origin and find their full meaning in him. In other words, contrary to those Christians who regard these values as anti-Christian, Bonhoeffer claims them for Christ and in doing so embraces those secular humanists who in affirming these values find themselves outside the church.

Bonhoeffer's humanism, so deeply rooted in Christ, then, is not an easy, superficial romanticism or philosophical idealism but an affirmation of life in its fullness amidst struggle and suffering. It is a Christian humanism fully cognizant of the depths to which humanity can plunge, the extent to which evil can run rampant. Fashioned through encountering evil, through struggle and suffering, it is a humanism of the cross. There is no escaping the reality of the cross in affirming humanity or appreciating classical culture. In this regard we recall the deep impression made upon Bonhoeffer when, in Rome as a student, he visited the Belvedere and contemplated the Laocoön, that "classical man of sorrows."⁵⁷ So it is significant that Leibholz's discussion of Bonhoeffer as an example of Christian humanism is located in the section of his essay entitled "Death," where he reflects on

54. Ibid., 59.
55. Ibid., 91. Cf. *DBWE* 6:107.
56. Mann, "Der Problem der Freiheit" (in *Essays*, vol. 11, 1939), qtd in Lange, "Particular Europe," 89.
57. *DBWE* 9:89; Bonhoeffer, *Letters and Papers*, 194.

Bonhoeffer's suffering and martyrdom. Bonhoeffer, writes Leibholz, "offered his life for a new understanding of the personal life which has its roots in the Christian faith."[58]

But Bonhoeffer's Christian humanism does not remain bound by suffering and death. Consider his comments in his essay on "History and Good" on the tension between the affirmation and negation of life, the "yes" and the "no" that find their unity in Christ: "It is the 'yes' to what is created, to becoming and to growth, to the flower and to the fruit, to health, happiness, ability, achievement, worth, success, greatness and honour; in short, it is the 'yes' to the development of the power of life. And it is the 'no' to the defection from the origin, the essence and the goal of life, which is inherent in all this existence from the outset. This 'no' means dying, suffering, poverty, renunciation, resignation, humility, degradation, self-denial, and in this again it already implies the 'yes' to the new life."[59] It is, Bonhoeffer tells us, "from beyond death that one expects the coming of the new man and of the new world, from the power by which death has been vanquished." So if it is the Incarnation that provides the basis for Christian humanism by overcoming the dualism between the sacred and secular, reconciling God and humanity, and asserting human dignity, and the Cross that roots such humanism in the reality of a suffering world and the struggle for justice, it is through the Resurrection that the power of death is broken and human hope fulfilled. It is, Bonhoeffer writes, the "risen Christ who bears the new humanity in himself, the final glorious 'yes' which God addresses to the new man."[60] And the words that best capture what that meant are, for Leibholz, those from Bonhoeffer's prison letter of July 18, 1944 to Eberhard Bethge: "To be a Christian does not mean to be religious in a particular way, to make something of oneself (a sinner, a penitent, or a saint) on the basis of some method or other, but to be a man (*Menschsein*)—not a type of man, but the man that Christ creates in us."[61] In his prison writings, fragmentary as they are but so full of "rich humanity,"[62] Bonhoeffer provides us with a profile of what this

58. Foreword in Bonhoeffer, *Cost of Discipleship*, 18.
59. Bonhoeffer, *Ethics*, 219. Cf. *DBWE* 6:251–52.
60. Ibid., 79. Cf. *DBWE* 6:92.
61. Bonhoeffer, *Letters and Papers*, 361.
62. Woelfel, *Bonhoeffer's Theology*, 26–27.

"mature worldliness" means, a polyphony of life rooted in Christ incarnate, crucified, and risen.

Christian Humanism as "Mature Worldliness"

Bonhoeffer, so he tells us in his prison letters, was always ambivalent about the Renaissance and classicism; they were so alien that he could not make them his own.[63] By contrast, he was more attracted to the late Middle Ages. Already then, before the Renaissance retrieved classical values, "the fundamental concepts of humanism—humanity, tolerance, gentleness, and moderation" were present and more accessible.[64] That is why Bonhoeffer questioned whether the classics provide *the* only foundation for education.[65] A genuine humanism, that is, "a mature worldliness," requires more than an elitist retrieval of classical antiquity; it requires both a return to the biblical understanding of human wholeness and a much broader perspective of the world that comes through an appreciation and appropriation of its rich cultural diversity.

Unlike the "worldliness" of the Renaissance or of the later European Enlightenment, the "mature worldliness" of the Middle Ages was not "emancipated" but Christian.[66] Again, unlike that of the Renaissance, this "mature worldliness" was biblical because it did not separate human nature into "inner" and "outer" spheres, "mind" or "spirit" and "body," but instead regarded human beings in their wholeness (*anthropos teleios*). This was important for Bonhoeffer because, as he tells us, he wanted to start "from the premise that God shouldn't be smuggled into some last secret place, but that we should frankly recognize that the world, and people, have come of age, that we shouldn't run man down in his worldliness, but confront him with God at his strongest point."[67] Bonhoeffer's understanding of "mature worldliness" resonated with his newfound appreciation of ancient Greece, inspired by his prison reading of W. F. Otto's book *The Gods of Greece*. That ancient world of faith sprang, in Otto's words, "from the wealth and depth of human existence, not from its cares and longings." Understood in this way, these gods of

63. Bonhoeffer, *Letters and Papers*, 230.
64. Ibid.
65. Ibid.
66. Ibid., 229–30.
67. Ibid., 346.

Greece, Bonhoeffer comments, are "less offensive than certain brands of Christianity" and could be claimed for Christ.[68] The brands he had in mind were probably those that try anxiously "to reserve some space for God." But Bonhoeffer wanted to speak of God "not on the boundaries but at the centre, not in weakness but in strength; and therefore not in death and guilt but in man's life and goodness."[69]

Bonhoeffer's preference for Greek over Roman antiquity was earlier explored in his essay "Inheritance and Decay," where he argues that while Italy and the Catholic Church sought antiquity in their Roman heritage, Germany and the Reformation church were more inclined to Greek sources. This scandalized western European humanists, the humanists of Holland, France, and England, because while they reconciled antiquity with Christianity, in Germany the return to Greece led away from Christianity and directly to Nietzsche and the "anti-Christ."[70] But it was precisely Nietzsche's radical critique that had to be engaged: "Hatred of 'the world,' condemnations of the passions, fear of beauty and sensuality, a beyond invented the better to slander this life ... a sign of abysmal sickness, weariness, discouragement, exhaustion, and the impoverishment of life."[71] From the early 1930s Bonhoeffer had been engaged in an ongoing debate with Nietzsche's critique of Christianity as weak and hostile to life.[72] He recognized the extent to which Nietzsche's espousal of classical Greek culture was a legitimate reaction to the rejection of the natural in German Lutheranism[73] and shared with him a "lust for life." But such life, he claimed, is in Christ, who gives the world its true secularity. This led Bonhoeffer to his strong affirmation of the body and the earth and his celebration of human freedom, *hilaritas*, and life. These themes, which burst forth so passionately in the *Letters and Papers from Prison*, find their theological formulation in what it means to be a Christian in a "world come of age."

If the "gods of ancient Greece" were one source for Bonhoeffer's reflections on "mature worldliness," a more dominant one derived

68. Ibid., 333.
69. Ibid., 282.
70. Bonhoeffer, *Ethics*, 90–91.
71. Nietzsche, *Birth of Tragedy*, 22–24.
72. Bonhoeffer engages Nietzsche already in his reflections on ethics while a vicar in Barcelona (1928) (*DBWE* 10:363, 366–67).
73. Bonhoeffer, *No Rusty Swords*, 91.

from his reading of the Old Testament. In this regard we may refer to Martin Buber's "Hebrew humanism," which was a later attempt to do much the same from the perspective of the Hebrew Scriptures.[74] The Old Testament literally "earthed" Christianity in this world, enabling us to love this world as God's world. "This world," Bonhoeffer writes, "must not be prematurely written off; in this the Old and New Testaments are at one. Redemption myths arise from human boundary-experiences, but Christ takes hold of a man at the centre of his life."[75] All of this meant being concerned about *this* world, "not in the anthropocentric sense of liberal, mystic pietistic, ethical theology, but in the biblical sense of the creation and of the incarnation, crucifixion, and resurrection of Jesus Christ."[76] So, too, being a Christian was not being religious but being truly human, *Mensch*, in the same way that Jesus was a human being. This did not "mean the shallow and banal this-worldliness of the enlightened, the busy, the comfortable, or lascivious, but the profound this-worldliness, characterized by discipline and the constant knowledge of death and resurrection."[77]

Alongside his new interest in Greek culture and his reading of the Old Testament we must also place Bonhoeffer's renewed interest in the liberal humanist tradition in which he was educated and notably his interest in the writings of Wilhelm Dilthey and his "philosophy of life."[78] Could anything be more humanistic than the notion of a "world come of age" or living *etsi deus non daretur*? And we need to remember that much of this was stimulated by his interest in science and his ongoing attempt to respond to the humanist and ethical challenge of his elder brother Karl-Friedrich's reservations about Christian theology.[79]

Bonhoeffer's understanding of God and "mature worldliness" recurs in a variety of ways that explicate what he meant and give us an insight into his own self-understanding. For example, he writes about the wholeness of "the fully grown man that enables him to face the existing situation squarely." Mastering his longings, he lives "fully in the

---

74. Hodes, *Encounter with Martin Buber*, 82–102.
75. Bonhoeffer, *Letters and Papers*, 337.
76. Ibid., 286.
77. Ibid., 369.
78. See the discussion in Wüstenberg, *Glauben als Leben*, 136–46.
79. See Bethge, "Nonreligious Scientist," 55–56.

present."[80] Indeed, for Bonhoeffer, the "man who allows himself to be torn into fragments by events and questions has not passed the test for the present and the future."[81] Being a Christian is all about being "whole" and doing the "whole thing" in contrast to being double-minded.[82] Yet at the same time "Christianity puts us into many different dimensions of life at the same time; we make room in ourselves, to some extent, for God and the whole world."[83] And, writing to Renate and Eberhard, he says that to "renounce a full life in its real joys in order to avoid pain is neither Christian nor human":[84] "I think we honor God more if we gratefully accept the life that he gives us with all its blessings, loving and drinking it to the full, and also grieving deeply and sincerely when we have impaired or wasted any of the good things of life . . . than if we are insensitive to life's blessings and may therefore also be insensitive to pain."[85]

This is part of what human freedom is truly about, without which someone may be "a good father, citizen, and worker, indeed even a Christian," but, Bonhoeffer writes, "I doubt whether he is a complete man and therefore a Christian in the widest sense of the term."[86] That wider sense of what it means to be a Christian is precisely what Christian humanism is about.

There are many dimensions to this Christian humanism as portrayed in Bonhoeffer's prison writings, a subject that cannot be exhausted here. We think immediately of his question whether it was possible "to regain the idea of the church as providing an understanding of the area of freedom (art, education [*Bildung*], friendship, play), so that Kierkegaard's 'aesthetic existence' would not be banished from the church's sphere, but would be re-established within it?"[87] Such "aesthetic existence" is eminently Christian.[88] We may also refer to Bonhoeffer's humor and optimism, despite the circumstances in which he found

80. Bonhoeffer, *Letters and Papers*, 233.
81. Ibid., 200.
82. Ibid.
83. Ibid., 310.
84. Ibid., 91.
85. Ibid., 191–92.
86. Ibid., 193.
87. Ibid.
88. See the discussion in de Gruchy, *Christianity, Art, and Transformation*, 147–58.

himself. And, of course, being fully human was never something individualistic but always achieved together with other people.[89] This, as we well know, was foundational for Bonhoeffer's theology from the outset, and it is nowhere more apparent than in his prison reflections where he experienced the absence of "the other" so starkly: "But what is the finest book, or picture, or house, or estate, to me, compared with my wife, my parents, or my friend? One can, of course, speak like that only if one has found others in one's life. For many today man is just a part of the world of things, because the experience of the human simply eludes them."[90] Ronald Gregor Smith helps us bring the matter to a head. "Bonhoeffer," he writes, "did not relapse into a sentimental Jesusology. Consequently, he did not restrict his theology till it was indistinguishable from a naïve variation of liberal humanism." He continues: "It is a humanism, certainly, of which he is speaking, but the humanism of a liberated humanity in a world which has its own way to go in self-responsibility. But it is at the same time a humanism which is human only in the relation with others, a relation whose reality is both released and confirmed in the being of God for the world in his suffering in Christ. 'Only a suffering God can help.'"[91] This is Bonhoeffer's "Christian Humanism," what Frits de Lange calls "a critical humanism, a humanism which discloses rather than legitimizes power, a humanism in which one person fails to inherit humanity when another does not, a 'humanism of the other man' (Levinas)."[92] Yes, indeed, Christian humanism is a humanism for "the other," a humanism shaped by Jesus, "the man for others."

We began by referring to the way in which Kenneth Kaunda, the former president of Zambia, described himself as a Christian humanist. He did so to distinguish himself from a secular humanism that lacked transcendence and a religious fundamentalism that denied humanism. What I have sought to do is to suggest that in Bonhoeffer's life and writings we have a profound exposition of what Christian humanism can and should be for us today. It is a humanism deeply rooted in the life, death, and resurrection of Jesus Christ, a humanism that is shaped not just by education but also by a genuine encounter with "the other," a

89. Bonhoeffer, *Letters and Papers*, 200.
90. Ibid., 386.
91. Smith, *Secular Christianity*, 21.
92. Lange, "Particular Europe," 93.

humanism that is fashioned in the struggle for truth and justice against dehumanizing power, a humanism that is deepened through suffering, yet one that is always affirming human goodness against perversity, hope against despair, and life against death. All this is the meaning of Jesus Christ, for us, today, for God himself, Bonhoeffer wrote in "After Ten Years," "did not despise humanity, but became human for the sake of men and women."[93]

---

93. Bonhoeffer, *Letters and Papers*, 10 (translation slightly altered).

2

Being Human, Becoming Human
Dietrich Bonhoeffer's Christological Humanism

Jens Zimmermann

Introduction

JOHN DE GRUCHY'S WORK, BOTH IN HIS ESSAY IN THIS VOLUME AND in previous publications,[1] already suggests that Bonhoeffer's theology is best characterized as a Christian humanism. De Gruchy seeks to recover Christian humanism as an alternative cultural stance to scientific fundamentalism on the one hand and to religious fundamentalism on the other,[2] especially when the latter conflates religion and nationalism.[3] Let me say from the outset that I fundamentally agree with de Gruchy's desire to affirm a humanist identity for Christians and that Bonhoeffer is indeed a rich resource for doing so. As the title of my contribution suggests, *Being Human, Becoming Human* is what both Christian humanism and Bonhoeffer's theology are essentially about. Indeed, I would not hesitate to say, not only with Bonhoeffer but also with the Catholic philosopher Jacques Maritain, Christianity *is* in fact the first religious humanism *par excellence*, because God became human, was crucified, and rose from the dead so that we could become

---

1. See, for example, de Gruchy, *Confessions of a Christian Humanist*. Less prominently, Clifford Green has also identified Bonhoeffer's theology with Christian humanism. See, for example, Green's introduction to Bonhoeffer's *Ethics* (*DBWE* 6:1–44).

2. De Gruchy, "Christian Humanism," 2–3.

3. De Gruchy cites Eberhard Bethge's unpleasant experience in Jerry Falwell's church, which identified Jesus with American nationalism and thus invited the comparison of American Christian nationalism with the nationalistic Christ of the German Christians during the Nazi regime (ibid., 7).

truly human. It is because I basically agree with de Gruchy's project that I want to *radicalize* his proposal. By radicalizing I mean taking Christian humanism back to its conceptual and historical roots in two ways: first, by linking Bonhoeffer's humanism to the Christological roots of patristic humanism, and second, by defending Bonhoeffer's Christological humanism against two possible complaints. The first complaint arises from secular philosophies that argue that Bonhoeffer's humanism is still too God-centered, too much rooted in divine authority. The second complaint emerges from the Anabaptist theology of John Howard Yoder, who judges Bonhoeffer's humanism to be too abstract and not counterculturally enough because his abstract Hellenistic Christology fails to incorporate Jesus's actual life and teaching.

The Theological Roots of Christian Humanism

In one of his essays, de Gruchy joins Karl Barth in pondering the question whether recovering the term "Christian humanism" is useful and concludes that it is, provided such a notion is "defined by the gospel, rooted in the biblical tradition," and affirms "a genuine transcendence."[4] I would affirm even more strongly that recovering Christian humanism is not just useful but *needed*, because the interpretation of Christianity connoted by this term "Christian humanism" reflects the faithful engagement of the early church with culture, an engagement that has decisively shaped Western concepts and values. Any honest genealogy of humanism shows us that the ideals of secular humanism are impossible without their Christian antecedents. When we look not for the actual use of the term humanism but for the basic concepts we associate with this term—a focus on a common humanity marked by human freedom, dignity, and creative ability—when we do this, we find that humanism originates from Judaic and Christian roots.[5] It is true, of course, that Roman philosophy already associated the term *humanitas* with social virtue and an ideal of soul formation.[6] And yet concepts such as the radical contingency of being, the predictability and consistent intelligi-

---

4. Ibid.

5. For quasi-contemporary articulations of Jewish Humanism see for instance Buber's *Reden über das Judentum* (English title: *Judaism*), in which he already sketches a this-worldly religion whose goal is to make social relations more god-like.

6. Buck, *Humanismus*, 24.

bility of the universe (which enabled modern science), the concept of personhood, of human dignity, of human rights, of sociality, and many others we often use without considering their roots, originate in the amalgamation of Jewish, Christian, and Greek thought in early Christian theology. It was above all patristic theology that founded Christian humanism and decisively shaped Western culture.

In designating patristic theology a humanism, I am following the Catholic theologian and patristic scholar Henri de Lubac, who claimed that the church fathers' theology could be summed up as an all-embracing humanism.[7] For Lubac, early church theology is essentially a Christological anthropology, an interpretation of the Incarnation summed up by the representative statement of Athanasius: "God became human so that we might become God."[8] In other words, secular humanists and defenders of Christianity are equally wrong in ascribing talk about human divinization to a movement away from God and religion. On the contrary, the affirmation of human dignity and its elevation to divine status belongs first and foremost to the Christian tradition. *Theosis* or deification as the fulfillment of humanity's divine image is a main theme of Christian theology that remains present, albeit at varying levels of intensity, from patristic theology all the way to

---

7. Lubac, *Catholicisme*, 278. In Lubac's words: "Nous ne pourrons revivre le large humanisme des Pères et retrouver l'esprit de leur exégèse mystique que dans un effort d'assimilation transformatrice"; see also p. 323.

8. So, for example, Clement of Alexandria: "[Y]eah I say, the Word of God became man, that thou mayest learn from man how man may become God" ("Exhortation to the Heathen," 174). Likewise, Irenaeus affirms that "it was for this end that the Word of God was made man, and He who was the Son of God became the Son of man, that man, having been taken into the Word, and receiving the adoption, might become the son of God. For by no other means could we have attained to incorruptibility and immortality, unless we had been united to incorruptibility and immortality" ("Irenaeus Against Heresies," 448); and Athanasius repeats this sentiment: "He, indeed, assumed humanity that we might become God"—and explains that "He manifested Himself by means of a body in order that we might perceive the Mind of the unseen Father. He endured shame from men that we might inherit immortality" (*On the Incarnation*, 93).

Aquinas,[9] Calvin, Luther, and Dietrich Bonhoeffer.[10] Through the influence of Augustine, the idea of being conformed to the *imago Dei* defines education as the training of reason and character in the service of humanity well into the late Middle Ages and resurfaces in Renaissance humanism.

When we interpret the history of humanism in light of its Christian origins, and when we recognize the centrality of the *imago Dei* and its attendant theme of divinization, Renaissance humanism no longer appears simply as the beginning of the modern Promethean self but, as scholarship has shown, becomes the reprise of patristic theology, albeit with a renewed emphasis on Neo-Platonism. While the nature of Renaissance humanism is not our main focus, a brief corrective of its standard misinterpretation as proto-secularism justifies our claim that Bonhoeffer's Christian humanism has greater affinity with the humanist tradition than secular humanism does.

---

9. Aquinas follows Augustine's lead: "the full participation of the Divinity, which is the true bliss of man and end of human life; and this is bestowed upon us by Christ's humanity; for Augustine says in a sermon (xiii de Temp): 'God was made man, that man might be made God'" (*Summa Theologica*, Part III, Q.1, Art. 2, 703–4). Theresia Heither confirms deification in Origen's theology. Centered on the divine Logos, human beings are to feed on the Word of God in order to become a true image of the Logos: "The Logos first takes on the human word and becomes accessible in the word of scripture. Later He becomes one with the entire human nature in Jesus Christ. Divine-human Word of scripture and divine-human person of Jesus Christ are basically one and the same, and are the one path to God for humanity, for humankind the only way to God; this enacts the process of salvation, that is, the deification of human beings." ("Theologische Voraussetzungen," 17–18 [all translations from the German are mine unless otherwise noted]).

10. Currently the most comprehensive study on deification in Luther is Reinhard Flogaus's *Theosis bei Palamas und Luther*. After a thorough analysis of both thinkers, Flogaus rejects the thesis advanced by Finnish Luther research that Luther's concept of participation in Christ depends on a realist epistemology and on a "scholastic-philosophical understanding of substance" (Flogaus, *Theosis*, 381). Palamas's Greek notion of *theosis* assumes the *Identity* and *Unity* of being, while Luther's ontological statements concerning soteriology are characterized by Dialectics (383). As a result, God reveals himself for Luther in the crucified rather than the glorified Christ, and for Palamas, by contrast, in the face of the glorified one, "even if not in a fundamentally new way, but as the surpassing fulfillment of the earlier revelations of the divine energy in mystical visions of pre-Christian patriarchs and prophets" (385). Nonetheless, Flogaus maintains the importance of *theosis* in Luther's theology and that this topic could indeed be an important means for ecumenical dialogue (383). For deification in Calvin see Billings, *Calvin, Participation, and the Gift*.

The primary sources of humanist writings show us that Renaissance humanists understood the growing complexity of European life within the context of divine providence and viewed the growth of human achievements as a manifestation of the creativity rooted in the divine image. They "fully believed in God's providential care for man's well-being in this world and the next, His planned beatification, even divinization of those upon whom His grace shone."[11] What society needed, particularly in view of the seeming inability of the church to deal with the evolving culture, was a clear sense of human nature and the divine, a clear exposition of human identity and purpose as created in His likeness.

It cannot be stressed enough that even if Renaissance humanism is not a coherent philosophical or theological movement, the common goal of the Renaissance humanists was the Christianization of culture. Far from a return to paganism, for many dominant Renaissance humanists, humanism was

> a plea for a renewal of a theology of grace as the acceptance that divine force alone was capable of restructuring the naturally egotistical motivations of mankind towards higher ethical and religious goals. Moreover, the capacity and drive of man to command and shape his world was regarded as an emulation of divinity, since it was in this respect that man was created in the image and likeness of God. Instead of viewing the secular, non-religious, or even anti-religious aspects of the Renaissance period as typical and central to the culture, these are seen as incorporated into a new religious vision of *Homo triumphans* that found its inspiration in the patristic Christian tradition brilliantly combined with the non-rational aspects of the ancient rhetorical tradition and its ethics.[12]

On such a reading we will find greater continuity in Renaissance humanism with ancient Christian themes than with modern notions of autonomous selfhood.

Many of us grew up with an oppositional logic of intellectual history in which human apotheosis is the result of secularization. Man becomes divine, that is, more mature and responsible, the more religion and belief in revelation recede. Most attempts to link the maturity of

---

11. Trinkaus, *In Our Image and Likeness*, 1:xix.
12. Ibid., 1:xx–xxi.

humanity to the emancipation from revelation and religious doctrine are heir to this "subtraction narrative" of secularization.[13] Theological versions of this argument posit that human self-assertion arrives providentially through a God who takes on humanity and suffers to the point of self-cancellation.[14] God kills himself, as it were, to make room for human self-assertion (Hans Blumenberg). Bonhoeffer's idea of religionless Christianity has often been mentioned in this context; yet, as I hope to show, Bonhoeffer's Christian humanism owes more to the older Christian, patristic tradition, which should be evident by his dogged insistence that not just the cross but also incarnation and resurrection define God's relation to the world and the Christian's being in the world.

I have recalled these patristic origins of humanism because Bonhoeffer's own Christian humanism seems to fit better into this tradition than into the subtraction narrative of secularization, which equates human maturity and progress with the emancipation from religion.[15] John de Gruchy has already pointed out that Bonhoeffer's Christian humanism is essentially a *Christological* humanism. The central theme in Bonhoeffer of Christianity as new humanity, together with its strong emphasis on human sociality and solidarity, derives from a Trinitarian, incarnational Christology. We also need to see, however, that for this very reason, Bonhoeffer's Christological humanism is a repristination of patristic humanism. Especially when we read sermons and theological reflections on the Eucharist in early church theology, we find typical Bonhoefferian themes which I can only sketch rather than fully explain in this essay.

The first is that the universal goal of God's historical self-disclosure to and his covenant relation with Israel had always been a renewed humanity, a goal achieved in the God-man Jesus the Messiah. Patristic humanism takes up and develops the apostle Paul's argument

---

13. Charles Taylor has coined this term and defines the view of human development it entails in *A Secular Age*.

14. This is true for death of God theology as well as for many explanations of our passage to modernity. See, for instance, Hans Blumenberg's view on this in Stoellger, *Metaphor und Lebenswelt*, 418.

15. As Barry Harvey points out in his essay included in this volume, Bonhoeffer's prison theology with its emphasis on "a world come of age" has to be interpreted in light of his Christologically and thus ecclesially grounded notion of sociality.

that in the Messiah a new humanity is created wherein ethnic and social divisions have been overcome.[16] In the Incarnation, God recapitulates humanity and recreates it fully in his image. From its beginnings in the church father Irenaeus, this Christological humanism expresses a fundamental ontological unity of all human beings in the divine Logos becoming flesh. For Irenaeus, the Incarnation draws into itself *all* of humanity, offering to the Father true humanity, the true *imago Dei*.[17] Christ is "the perfect human being" consisting "in the co-mingling and the union of the soul receiving the spirit of the Father, and the admixture of that fleshly nature which was moulded after the image of God."[18]

This incarnation is a "recapitulation" of humanity,[19] a second creation which does not abolish but redeems the first.[20] Irenaeus's concept of recapitulation is not a remote or abstract notion. He emphasizes that as the concrete human being Jesus the incarnate Word undergoes every stage of human development, thus summing up lived human life and redeeming it in his perfect humanity.[21] Bonhoeffer affirms the same universal soteriological function of Jesus's concrete historical life. In Jesus humanity has been affirmed, judged, and redeemed. Jesus, he writes, "is not *a* human being, but *the* human being. What happens to him happens to human beings. It happens to all and therefore to us. The

---

16. For this theme, see especially the work of N. T. Wright. For example: *What Saint Paul Really Said*, 136; *Paul*, 92–93; *Justification*, 104 (God's people summed up in Christ) and 108–9 (new humanity). Theologically this tradition is also recognized by Jüngel in *Das Evangelium*: "Because the eternal God identified himself with this human being, because the human being Jesus *is* the son of God, therefore *humanity as a whole* is integrated into this being human. Therefore *all of us* are present in this one being . . . for this reason, the truly human human being (*homo humanus*) Jesus is identical with human nature (*natura humana*)." Jüngel, unlike Yoder, appreciates the strength of patristic theology's substance ontology: "With this concept, the old theology with its language and thinking of substance-ontology has unfolded the *universal* ramifications of the identity of the son of God with the irreducibly unique human being Jesus and dared to think that Jesus Christ is the *sacramentum mundi*, the acknowledged great sacrament per se (cf. 1 Tim 3:16)" (138; italics his).

17. Irenaeus, "Against Heresies," 445, 449.

18. Ibid., 531.

19. In his prison letters, Bonhoeffer recognizes the importance of and finds consolation in Irenaeus's repristination of Paul's notion that all things are recapitulated in Christ. Nothing is lost (*DBW* 8:246–47).

20. Irenaeus, "Against Heresies," 454. Cf. also: "For by summing up in Himself the whole human race from the beginning, to the end, He has also summed up its death" (ibid., 551).

21. Ibid., 391 (2.22.4).

name of Jesus embraces in itself the whole of humanity and the whole of God."[22]

From this Christological definition of humanity follows another common element. Based on the Trinity, patristic humanism, like Bonhoeffer, believes in the essentially social nature of human being. The Trinitarian shape of human sociality allows for a unique balance of individual and collective identity. In Christ every person attains an individual identity grounded in personal transcendence, yet is also linked to humanity as a whole. In the Incarnation, with its unique union of human and divine, of the particular and the transcendent, of the historical and the eternal, of the ethnic and the collective human race, the very idea of a common humanity is born. In patristic Christology "[t]hat image of God, the image of the Word, which the incarnate Word restores and gives back its glory, is 'I myself'; it is also the other, every other. It is that aspect of *me* in which I coincide with every other man; it is the hallmark of our common origin and the summons to our common destiny. It is our very unity in God."[23] And so for the fathers, the deepest mystery of our unity with the Trinity defines our humanity as sociality in communion with God: "we are fully persons only within the Person of the Son, by whom and with whom we share in the circumincession [mutual co-inhabiting] of the Trinity."[24]

It is not hard to hear echoes of this participatory language in Bonhoeffer's Christology. He, too, speaks of Trinitarian indwelling, and from *Sanctorum Communio* all the way to *Ethics*, Bonhoeffer emphasizes the social nature of faith, observing, just like the fathers, the balance between individual and collective. The church is "Christ existing as community," she is "the new human being," a single entity,[25] but this unity is not a mystical melting pot, because each individual is recognized by God.[26] Together with early church theology, he also

---

22. "Ethics as Formation" in *DBWE* 6:85. Bonhoeffer's expression intentionally links the concrete Person of Jesus to the universal humanity. This is not the "transfiguration of noble humanity," but God's "bearing bodily" the nature, essence, guilt, and suffering of human beings (ibid., 84).

23. Lubac, *Catholicism*, 340.

24. Ibid., 342.

25. *DBW* 4:232.

26. "Between us lies the boundary of being created as individual persons. The Christian notion of community with God can be realized only on the basis of this

defines the idea of freedom within this framework of social relations. Freedom, as he once put it, is not an abstract concept but "a relation and nothing else."[27]

We can summarize the basic theological anthropology of Christological humanism advanced by Bonhoeffer and patristic theology as *participatory ontology*. Like the church fathers, Bonhoeffer defines Christian existence as participation in the new humanity inaugurated by Christ. In his words, "Christian life means being human in the power of Christ's becoming human."[28] But if one is most fully human only in Christ, what about those who are not thus in communion with God? The concept of a new humanity inevitably raises the question about the "old humanity." Do Christians have to view others as less human? To put it differently, what is the relation of the church to the world? In answering this question, we find yet another similarity between Bonhoeffer and early Christian humanism, for both make Christ the ontological center of humanity, who thus links the new and old human self and therefore also church and world.

When we turn to actual Eucharistic sermons from the early church, we can see the same connections Bonhoeffer makes between church and world; indeed, we can hear the same language that he uses in describing the new humanity and its relation to humanity as a whole. For example, we find in the Eucharistic Christology of the church fathers the notion that communion with the incarnate God leads the human self out of its egoistic isolation toward solidarity with others, not only within the church but also to all other human beings, especially those who count as the "least of humans."[29] Bonhoeffer's language of "one humanity in Christ" and our responsibility for all fellow human beings clearly echoes Augustine's similar sentiments in his Christology sermons, as,

---

interpretation of community. Otherwise, community with God becomes unification in the sense of transgressing the boundary of the I-You relation—that is, mystical fusion" (*DBWE* 1:84).

27. *DBW* 3:58.

28. *DBWE* 6:159.

29. Tillard, *Flesh of the Church*, 30. Later in the book Tillard describes the Eucharistic self in similar terms as Bonhoeffer: "Because they are saved 'in Christ', baptized in the one Spirit and nourished with the one bread, Christians are in essence *beings-who-are-with*, not individuals but persons-in-communion. For them, indeed, the necessary relationship *with* others no longer depends on a command or a mandate. It is the very definition of being a Christian" (ibid., 94).

for example, in his commentary on Psalm 101: "It is therefore obvious that we belong to Christ and *that being his members and his body, we are, with our head, one human being.*"[30] Like Bonhoeffer, Augustine also emphasizes that this unity is a work of faith, "a concrete unity which is not of the sociological order—since it is due to their being seized by the Spirit of God—but which nevertheless assumes the density and variety of all that is human."[31] While the essential ontological unity of the new humanity maintains the tension between spiritual equality and social differences in rank and wealth, it also calls for social action across race, class, and gender divides. Especially the Eucharistic addresses of Chrysostom sound in this regard much like Bonhoeffer's admonition to recognize our responsibility to every other suffering human being. Chrysostom admonishes participants of the Eucharist to remember the ontological link between the Christian, the self-giving Christ, and the world: "What profit is there if Christ's table is set with golden cups but he dies from hunger? First feed him and relieve his hunger; then abundantly deck out his table also . . . Therefore do not ignore your sisters and brothers in distress while you adorn Christ's house, for they are more a temple than the other."[32] The Christology emerging mostly from Eucharistic theologies of the first four hundred years of the Eastern and Western church conveys in essence the same message as Bonhoeffer does concerning the notion of a new humanity and its relation to the world. In the fathers we find a church that "is essentially the presence of a space in which the fabric of the 'humanity-that-God-wants is restored'" and therefore constitutes the foundation for a truly human image of a self whose being in community frees it toward responsibility. Bonhoeffer's ontological structure of "being-with" and "being-for" the other, which shapes the new humanity in the image of Christ, also dominates the Eucharistic Christology of the church fathers.[33]

Moreover, given his own understanding of Christian ethics as Christ-formation, Bonhoeffer certainly would have resonated with Augustine's image of Christ-formation within the new creation: "And then, here you are, singing in [Christ] and exulting in him because

30. Quoted in ibid., 55.
31. Ibid., 61.
32. Quoted in ibid., 71.
33. Ibid., 94.

he himself toils in you, thirsts in you, is hungry in you and in tribulation in you. He again dies in you and you, in him, are already risen."[34] Augustine's thoughts closely resemble Bonhoeffer's idea of ethics as the formation of Christ in the believer, of one's participation in the Christ event of incarnation, death, and resurrection. The church is, therefore, "not primarily a preacher of ethics, an agent of philanthropic endeavors, or a creator of magnanimous ideologies,"[35] but it is first of all a representation of God's love to the world, an invitation to accept the gift of being truly human offered in Christ. It is not hard to recognize Bonhoeffer's ethical imperative of "doing God's will," by embodying in one's life through interpretive discernment God's reconciliation of the world to himself in Christ's life, death, and resurrection.

These few examples should suffice to show that Bonhoeffer's Christological humanism very much reflects the patristic origins of Christian humanism. The same Christological foundation of humanism issues in a similar refusal to separate the church from humanity as a whole. Bonhoeffer's strong expression of solidarity is completely one with ancient Christian humanism. We recall his famous passage from *The Cost of Discipleship*:

> In Christ's incarnation all of humanity regains the dignity of bearing the image of God. Whoever from now on attacks the least of the people attacks Christ, who took on human form and who in himself has restored the image of God for all who bear a human countenance. . . . In as much as we participate in Christ, the incarnate one, we also have a part in all of humanity, which is borne by him. Since we know ourselves to be accepted and borne within the humanity of Jesus, our new humanity now also consists in bearing the troubles and the sins of all others. The incarnate one transforms his disciples into brothers and sisters of all human beings.[36]

---

34. Quoted from Augustine's commentary on Psalm 101 in ibid., 55.

35. Ibid., 137.

36. *DBWE* 4:285. This transformation is patterned according to the entire Christ event: "Christ does not rest with his work in us, until he shaped us into the form of Christ. It is the entire *form* (Gestalt) *of the incarnated, the crucified, and the glorified*, to which we are to conform." And because all of humanity is taken up into and sustained by Christ, therefore the new humanity of the Christian existence "now also consists in bearing the hardship and guilt of others" (ibid.).

It is important to emphasize that this transformation occurs not because of an abstract ideal of transcendence but because of the real presence of God in the believing community through prayer, sacrament, and the preaching of God's word.[37] As heir to a long historical development on the nature of God's presence in the church, Bonhoeffer struggles more than his patristic predecessors with the mediation of this real presence, but he holds with them that being Christian means having one's being reshaped in the image of Jesus as a being-for-others. Being human, one might say, means becoming human according to the divine image of love for humanity.

For Bonhoeffer, as for early Christian humanism, human maturity, our full humanity, comes about in communion with God, within which true freedom and responsibility become possible. Bonhoeffer, of course, wrestles with problems the church fathers did not have to face, problems stemming mostly from our modern dualism of reason and belief unknown to the ancient world. Yet even in dealing with modern issues concerning revelation and reality, Bonhoeffer follows ancient Christology in affirming the Christological orientation of creation with his concept of one Christ-reality.[38] It is also clear that Bonhoeffer, already influenced by so-called postmodern views of reason, has greater hermeneutical sensitivity than the fathers. Realizing the "one Christ-reality" is neither conformity to the world nor shunning or violently transforming it into whatever we deem heaven to look like. Christian ethics is participating in the will of God, which is "nothing but the becoming real of the Christ-reality in us and in our world." The will of God is neither identical with what is, nor an abstract ideal we have to bring to life. Rather, having already become true in Christ, we strive to participate in this reality by living it out using every ounce of intelligence, discernment, and sensitivity to our social responsibilities. No ideological template counts; no interpretation is absolute. What counts is being human and becoming human in Christ; becoming human as conformation to the image of Christ participates in the God-man's own work of restoring our full humanity.

---

37. "Christology Lectures," *DBWE* 12:321–23.
38. *DBWE* 6:74.

Thus the Christian vocation consists of witnessing to this restored humanity and of furthering the humanity of others.[39] Both of these activities require discerning interpretation of one's sociopolitical environment. Bonhoeffer's strong emphasis on interpretation clearly arises from his modern context, but his evident conviction that all human knowledge is based on some interpretive framework akin to belief is also already present in patristic theology. Clement of Alexandria, for example, already argues that all knowledge requires tacit interpretive frameworks. Without minimizing the differences between premodern and postmodern cultures, one can nevertheless justly claim that an interpretive view of knowledge has always existed within the core of Christian belief.[40]

Secular Objections to Bonhoeffer's Christological Humanism

When surveying the philosophical and theological landscape of modern thought, we can observe two objections to Bonhoeffer's Christian humanism. On the one hand, secular philosophy will object that it is altogether still too particular, too Christ-centered. On the other hand, certain theologies concerned particularly with social justice will deem his Christology too abstract, and thus not human enough. My final section will briefly respond to those two objections.

Secular philosophers, especially those concerned with public affairs, recognize the bankruptcy of radically secular reasoning and seek to harness the power of the religious imagination for a nonreligious humanism. For example, the French philosopher Luc Ferry, former minister of education in France, advocates a "transcendental humanism." Against reductive views of human beings as mere machines or instinctual organisms, he insists on the mystery of the sacred in humans

---

39. See, for example, ibid., 83.

40. Clement asserts what philosophical hermeneutics, beginning with Heidegger, have carried forward from Greek thinking into our time: faith is "a preconception of the mind," and "without preconception, no one can either inquire, or doubt, or judge, or even argue. How can one without a preconceived idea of what he is aiming after, learn about that which is the subject of his investigation?" (Clement, "Stromata," 351 [2.5]; in contrast to Irenaeus's text, which features section numbers, the numbers here in square brackets refer to book and chapter.)

that transcends their animal nature.[41] As the title of his book *Man Made God* suggests, transcendent values such as human worth and human rights are now relocated from divine transcendence into the human consciousness. This relocation is necessary because emancipated modern man can no longer accept arguments from external authority. For this reason, Ferry cannot go along with the Christian humanism of John Paul II, whom he otherwise much admires, because the Pope will not concede that universal, transcendent values reside in us rather than in God. Ferry insists, however, that true humanism locates transcendence solely in each individual to safeguard human freedom and autonomy.[42]

In light of Bonhoeffer's Christian humanism, we could respond that Ferry's proposal should be praised for its attempt to unite religious values with a secular view of freedom, but that his suggestion suffers from two problems. The first is philosophical. Ferry proceeds from an individualistic and idealistic view of the human self, for otherwise he would not oppose authority and freedom. In fact, however, human experience teaches us that practical reasoning is communicative. Many, if not most, of the things we know and that influence our decisions come to us through others, and many advances or insights have been prepared for us by others. Authority naturally exists because of who we are and how we navigate life. The difference with Bonhoeffer's Christian humanism is obvious: Ferry starts with an individualistic self and has to construct community afterwards. Bonhoeffer, by contrast, begins with a social self that assumes community. Therefore, he does not have to oppose freedom and authority but can view them as correlates. The other has a claim on me and I respond in freedom. Freedom, we recall Bonhoeffer's words, is a relation and nothing else.

Ferry's second problem follows from the first: his opposition of authority and individual freedom blinds him to the resources the Incarnation offers for holding together transcendence and immanence. Christian humanism, as we have seen, is both theocentric *and* anthro-

---

41. "This is why transcendent humanism is a humanism of man made god. If human beings were not in some way gods, they would no longer be human beings. We have to presuppose in them something of the sacred or accept their reduction to mere animality" (Ferry, *Man Made God*, 139).

42. Ferry asks, "Is Christianity a humanism?" and answers, it depends. If Christianity "instead of anthropocentrism enjoins us to return to theocentrism," it imposes an external authority for our decision making that modern man cannot accept (ibid., 131).

pocentric because of the God-man Jesus. We can also say that, given the patristic interpretation of the Incarnation, Ferry does not have to make man God; Christian theology already did that for him. Yet in the Christian view becoming like God is possible only in relation *with* God, not against Him. Deification means becoming divine according to the divine kenosis in the Incarnation. Becoming like God meant becoming more Christ-like and thus becoming more truly concerned about others. True humanity means becoming like God in his downward movement toward man. As Eberhard Jüngel explains, "this movement of God down toward man refuses man the ascent to divinity. Just as God revealed his Lordship in humility, so the likeness of God is defined only through participation in this humility toward 'the glory of the children of God' (Rom. 8:21)."[43] Becoming like God meant becoming like God in his *kenosis* for the sake of humanity.

Deriving its energy and hope from this relation, Christian humanism much more truly offers a "transcendence inscribed in the immanence of human subjectivity" than Ferry's secular humanism, and it does so through participation in the new humanity of the God-man. The Christian's relation to God is "a new life as 'being-for-others,' through participating in the being of Jesus. Not the infinite distant tasks, but the concrete reachable neighbour is the transcendent."[44] This participation, as Bonhoeffer saw, illumines what the Old Testament idea of *imago Dei* really meant and opens up a social and political realism for action grounded in actual hope, calling us not to turn the world into the kingdom of God but to take "the next necessary step that corresponds to God's becoming human in Christ."[45]

Theological Objections to Bonhoeffer's Christological Humanism

For some theological critics, however, Bonhoeffer's *imago Dei* Christology is still not concrete enough. This, at least, is the verdict of John Howard Yoder, who is otherwise very sympathetic to Bonhoeffer. For him, what Frits de Lange once called Bonhoeffer's "ethical humanism"[46] is prob-

43. Jüngel, *Entsprechungen*, 316.
44. *DBW* 8:558.
45. *DBW* 6:225.
46. De Lange, "Particular Europe," 92. De Lange points out that for Bonhoeffer "the only future for the Christian faith and European culture is a common future, in mu-

lematic because its Christology does not sufficiently incorporate the actual life and teachings of the Jesus who walked on Palestinian soil. Yoder does *not* imply a gap between the historical Jesus and the Jesus of faith; he follows Bonhoeffer's rejection of this artificial paradigm.[47] On the contrary, Yoder is concerned with taking up Jesus's whole earthly career into Christology, in faithfulness to the Chalcedonian creed, which declared Christ not only truly God but also truly human.[48] For Yoder, the history of Christology may be divided into two different ways of interpreting the Incarnation.

The first he calls "logological" because it is preoccupied with the astonishing fact that the eternal Logos became a human being. According to Yoder, this approach has two faults: its metaphysical attitude abstracts too much from Jesus's life and teachings, and it views the Christ event as the fulfillment of natural reason. Thus, the emphasis is too much on the affirmation of creation. In Yoder's words, "For eastern Orthodoxy and Anglicanism, in different ways, and likewise for some recent mainstream styles of social ethics in western Protestantism, the word 'incarnation' serves as the label for a commitment to the sweeping acceptance of things as they are. We know things by observing their obvious 'nature'... The problem of Christology is how the transcendent logos could thus take on humanity; what humanity is or should be is not the problem, since we know thereby the self-evidence of 'nature.'"[49]

In contrast to this approach, Yoder suggests an alternative way of interpreting the Incarnation by demanding that Jesus's particular life form the categories of what being human means.[50] This "Jesulogical

---

tual recognition and influence. Separately, neither has a future at all" (ibid., 91). Both Christianity and European culture depend for their future on recalling the importance of the Incarnation. De Lange, while not sharing Bonhoeffer's political conservatism and also having qualms about his preoccupation with cultural unity, nonetheless agrees with Bonhoeffer's attempt to formulate a Christian, ethical, and incarnational humanism marked by responsibility for the other" (ibid., 93).

47. Yoder, "Christological Presuppositions," 158 (included in this volume).

48. The creed's terms are *theos aleithos kai anthropos aleithos*. Yoder wants to take up the "whole Jesus," his "whole career," to do justice to "the true purpose of the Chalcedonian affirmation that he who is confessed as *vere Deus* had to be first seen as *vere homo*" (ibid., 163).

49. Ibid., 157.

50. "Then the epistemological approach will be the just the reverse. 'Jesus as the Christ' means that the words and work of that man are not only our way to know God but also the only true way to know Man. The definition of 'man' we find in the streets or

path," discovered by the Anabaptists, has a different focus. To cite Yoder: "Not 'becoming man' but 'becoming *that* man' is then the wonder and the scandal of the incarnation."[51] When Jesus's teachings and actions are allowed to shape our categories of what it means to be human and of an ideal society, neither natural theology nor involvement in governments, which usually have to use violence as a matter of course, are legitimate for Christians. For Yoder, applying the gospel categories to politics clearly shows that Christians should be more suspicious of government and allow themselves, following their master, to be pushed to the political margin.

Yoder's misgivings with Bonhoeffer's theology are that whenever Bonhoeffer falls into typically Lutheran ways of thinking, he succumbs to the "logological" path. Thus Bonhoeffer's Christology lectures, his concern about the inner (existential) state of the soul, and his notion of the mandates by which secular government serves to uphold God's purposes—all these elements betray Bonhoeffer's "logological" proclivities, and his interpreters have generally read him this way. Yoder argues, however, that Bonhoeffer's work also contains elements of a different, less "logological" Christology. Yoder perceives among the "logological" obstructions another, more "Jesulogical," Bonhoeffer in *Discipleship*, who increasingly comes through, especially in the prison writings. The Bonhoeffer who wanted a this-worldly and religionless Christianity, had he only known it, would have embraced the Anabaptist tradition of viewing the church as a counterculture, for which the concrete humanity of Jesus, in his social decisions, provides the discipleship model.[52]

Despite the tantalizing vision of Bonhoeffer's conversion to Anabaptism, we should resist Yoder's "Jesulogical" hermeneutic for a number of reasons, but I will only mention two: First, Yoder's own ex-

---

in sociology or in Heidegger or Husserl is not that manhood which God willed, created, restored, assumed. The problem of Christology is not whether or how God could or did become man, but what kind of man He chose to be" (ibid., 157).

51. Ibid.

52. Ibid., 146. This assumption is also challenged by the fact that Bonhoeffer admired the "worldliness" of medieval Christianity, which also presupposes the kind of "logological" Christology Yoder objects to. See Bonhoeffer, *Letters and Papers*, 229–30: "The fundamental concepts of humanism–humanity, tolerance, gentleness, and moderation are already present in their finest form in Wolfram von Eschenbach," etc. Moreover, Bonhoeffer is against "leaving the world to its own devices," as if God had withdrawn from it. See *DBW* 8:416.

amples of concreteness are themselves already abstractions. For where do we draw the line on importing the particular "thatness" of Jesus, for example, as a first-century Jewish male, into Christian discipleship? What about circumcision or patriarchy? In other words, Yoder's hermeneutic is itself open to the danger of literalism, historicism, and even a certain fundamentalism *because* it wants concreteness. Bonhoeffer's more general hermeneutic of working out God's reconciliation with the world in Christ *within* and not only against existing political and social structures does more justice to the correlation of particularity and universality in the Incarnation.[53] Bonhoeffer's retention of patristic theology is precisely what allows the universal identification of every Christian with *that* Man Jesus.[54] As we will delineate in a few paragraphs, Bonhoeffer's cultural context may make his Christology appear less "Jesulogical" than Yoder would like, but Bonhoeffer clearly intends

---

53. Yoder, it seems, stills works with the problematic distinction between a more Jewish and a more Hellenistic Christology, sometimes termed "functional" and "ontic" or ontological Christology. Functional Christology is associated with early Jewish Christology while ontological Christology is linked to patristic Christology and its application of Greek philosophical categories of divine nature to Christ. Yet, as Richard Bauckham has shown, this is to misunderstand Jewish monotheism itself (possibly reading it through Greek eyes), since Jewish monotheism itself offers a different category of *divine identity*. Christology is not divided between either an approach that "speaks simply of what Jesus does" or one that "speaks of his divine nature. Once the category of divine identity replaces those of function and nature as the primary and comprehensive category for understanding both Jewish monotheism and early Christology, then we can see that the New Testament's lack of concern with the nature of Christ is by no means an indication of a merely functional Christology" (*God Crucified*, 42). The opposition which Yoder draws between "logological" and "Jesulogical" is false because already in the New Testament both concerns are united under the question of identity: "Once we rid ourselves of the prejudice that high Christology must speak of Christ's divine nature, we can see the obvious fact that the Christology of divine identity common to the whole New Testament is the highest Christology of all. It identifies Jesus as intrinsic to who God is" (ibid.). The category of identity, I would suggest, is intrinsic to Bonhoeffer's theology, so that when he asks "Who is Christ for us today," this does not exclude but rather includes Jesus's life and action, thus already pursuing what Yoder wants.

54. See here also Jüngel, *Das Evangelium*, 138. Richard Bauckham also defends the older Christology when he claims that "[i]nitially, however, focusing on the earthly Jesus turns the issue of the divine identity around. For the early Christians, the inclusion of the exalted Jesus in the divine identity meant that the Jesus who lived a truly and fully human life from conception to death, the man who suffered rejection and shameful death, also belonged to the unique divine identity." This way ensures that we view Jesus as the revelation of God (*God Crucified*, 46).

concreteness: "Jesus is not *a* human being but *the* human being. What happens to him happens to human beings. It happens to all and therefore to us."[55]

Second, Yoder's "Jesulogical" position erroneously rejects the correlation of faith and reason that Bonhoeffer demonstrates so ably in his works. The beauty of Bonhoeffer's approach is that his incarnational Christology has benefited from Barth just as much as from Augustine and Luther. Yes, revelation shapes our categories of what it means to be human, but for Bonhoeffer revelation also exists within given ontological structures, because God created them reasonable. Bonhoeffer consistently displays this incarnational view, from working with social categories in *Sanctorum Communio* all the way to his call for rediscovering the category of the natural for Protestant ethics.[56] The correlation of faith and reason on the basis of Christology grounds Bonhoeffer's desire to listen to all sources of truth, including philosophy and natural science. And yet, remaining true to his incarnational motto of finding the sacred in the profane, Bonhoeffer never forgets that God's revelation is the ultimate Word, which does not allow simple deductions from given natural concepts for theology.[57]

Yoder, who no doubt is aiming for a balance and wants to supplement Chalcedonian Christology,[58] does not realize that Bonhoeffer pursues the same balance. A close reading of the Christology lectures demonstrates that Bonhoeffer tries to maintain exactly the kind of link between Jesus and Christ, between the historical figure who walked on Palestinian soil and the *kyrios* envisioned by Yoder. Bonhoeffer follows Luther in not separating Jesus from Christ and realizes that Chalcedon was indeed an answer to the "how" question; yet he also realizes that the historical context required nothing less: "For the early church, what was decisive was that God could not become an individual human person, because then God could not redeem humanity and [the human being] would fall back into sin."[59] Yet Chalcedon also goes beyond the mere "how" question, for this creedal formulation equally intends the "who"

---

55. *DBWE* 6:85.
56. Ibid., 171.
57. *DBWE* 12:319.
58. See note 77 on p. 151 in this volume.
59. Ibid., 334.

question.[60] Bonhoeffer's argument is, once again, essentially ecclesial and thus captures the essential sociality of being human. Jesus is present in his church as Jesus the Christ. But both of these halves, Jesus and the Christ, are joined in his personality, a personality itself marked by its participation in the Trinity. Jesus the Christ only exists as all of these aspects held together. This is why Christology should not get hung up on "interpreting the 'is' but rather ask who is *this* man, of whom it is said 'he is God.'"[61]

Because Bonhoeffer refuses to allow even the thinnest wedge to enter between Jesus and the Christ, he often uses the term Christ when Yoder might prefer to refer to Jesus. Indeed, it may well be that Bonhoeffer favors the term Jesus Christ as a constant reminder that this term transcends *any* theological and ideological interpretations of the gospel. Bonhoeffer is arguing at the same time against a disembodied Jesus of inwardness and also against the reduction of Jesus to a great moral teacher by liberal Protestantism.[62] Once again, Bonhoeffer sees himself in accord with patristic theology in arguing for this unified Christology. For the "ancient church," he claims, Christ was not an idea but an "event" (*Ereignis*).

Yoder may have seen greater continuity in Bonhoeffer's Christology had he taken into account the political context of the Christology lectures. In light of the just emergent Nazi ideology,[63] Bonhoeffer was always sensitive to possible dangers of political theologies and questioned Christian political radicalism as much as Christian idealism. The relevance of Bonhoeffer's Christology is underscored by Oliver O'Donovan's caution against "political Jesulogy." This tendency to focus on the life of Jesus for political activism departed from a high Christology and focused on the life of Jesus for practical political purposes. Yet O'Donovan insists that "a secure political theology must base itself on the 'hidden council of God' which worked also through Caiaphas and Pilate."[64] It may seem at first that high Christology and its consequent understanding of faith is counterproductive to politics:

60. Ibid., 350.
61. Ibid.
62. Ibid., 328–29. As Bonhoeffer knew, these positions are not that far apart.
63. For a description of socio-historical context for the Christology lectures, see Larry L. Rasmussen's excellent introduction to *DBWE* 12, especially pp. 3–5.
64. O'Donovan, *Desire of the Nations*, 121–22.

How can an immortal individual depend upon the community to sustain the conditions of life? How can those who have God's Spirit in their hearts need the knowledge of God that is gained in the public realm? How can a community without local or national limits avoid evaporating into an indeterminate ideal with no concrete social presence? These are the objections which classical republicans, ancient and modern, have made to Christianity, accusing it of replacing political society with a communion of immortal souls with divine thoughts, defying political structures.[65]

O'Donovan thus understands Yoder's concern that abstract Christology leads to a political otherworldliness. Yet O'Donovan, like Bonhoeffer, shows that such a view results from a reductive view of the political as referring only to social structures and social goods; yet why should the transcendent be excluded from the political? Adapting Jesus's actions as a blueprint for political action poses its own danger, namely, that political subversion becomes its own ideology. Instead, O'Donovan warns that political theology, rightly conceived, has a critical and a positive function: "Ideas of what government is must be corrected in the light of that imperious government which the Spirit wields through the conscience of each worshipper." This "liberal" mode of political theology is accompanied by a constructive side "which is to show how the extension of the Gospel of the Kingdom into the Paschal Gospel elevates, rather than destroys, our experience of community. Political theology has an ecclesiastical mode, which takes the church seriously as a society and shows how the rule of God is realized there. The independence, then, of the individual believer is not antisocial." Presumably Yoder would agree with O'Donovan that the key to this balanced, right understanding of criticism and affirmation is Christology.[66]

Yoder claims that in his definition of the Christ event as "cradle, cross, and resurrection" Bonhoeffer jumps too quickly from the cradle to the cross, thus missing the entire concrete dimension of Jesus's life, and hence follows a Lutheran two-kingdom path of acquiescence in government authority. Yoder fails to realize that Bonhoeffer's theology is very much political but it is so *because* it insists on keeping to the high Christology of the early church for whom, too, there was only one

65. Ibid., 122.
66. Ibid., 123.

Christ-reality. One, often overlooked, theological reason for this hesitancy to draw direct political implications from Jesus's life is a particular aspect of Bonhoeffer's incarnational theology: Jesus's life, in taking on sinful humanity, has also entered into the ambiguities of interpretation that attends all human action; therefore, his concrete actions cannot simply be guideposts for political theology.[67] This approach is consistent with Bonhoeffer's hermeneutic I mentioned earlier: rather than finding in Jesus's life and actions a blueprint for a more political Christianity, he was concerned about the will of God for each respective cultural moment, but not in a relativistic sense; rather, it always meant the discerning application of the Christ event to one's culture. In a seminar on New Testament interpretation, Bonhoeffer argued that relevant exegesis grasps where Christ challenges present conditions. The preacher, he explains, has to show that the so-called "concrete situation" of any congregation is "the general situation of every person before God, of every human being in his pride, his unbelief, his neglect of social responsibility, in his questioning." It is important, says Bonhoeffer, that before the textual presence of Christ, he who considered himself in his importance as a man, as a National Socialist, or as a Jew, now sees himself in more general terms as "sinner, called-one, or forgiven one," for "precisely that the congregation's so-called concrete situation is *ultimately not taken seriously*, frees the eye for the true situation of man before God."[68] If this sounds too much like an inward piety, we forget Bonhoeffer's interpretive ethics: the very meaning of responsibility is the discerning enacting of God's redemptive action in Christ. What one is to do remains a decision that requires acknowledgement of one's social responsibilities, and the burden of this freedom cannot be transferred over to finding political principles in the scriptures.

This discerning hermeneutic is complemented by Bonhoeffer's ecclesial, social view of the church as the new humanity. Being human is becoming human through participation in Jesus the Christ as his body the church. Bonhoeffer is concerned with "how" this happens only insofar as he describes this participation as occurring in the sacraments of preaching, baptism, and the Eucharist. He is more concerned with the "person" who becomes present in the church and whose image

---

67. *DBWE* 12:357.
68. *DBW* 14:410.

works itself out within His body, the new humanity, without impeding the personality of each member. This holistic Christology remains in place from the Christology lectures and is further developed in the *Cost of Discipleship* and persists in his later writings. In order to correct Yoder's misperception of a "logological" Bonhoeffer and his unconscious move toward a more concrete ethics, we repeat that the strength of Bonhoeffer's incarnational Christology lies in the paradox of affirming the concrete precisely *because* affirming the transcendence of the God-man Jesus Christ. Bonhoeffer's insistence on an incarnational pattern of Christian life emphasizes the interpretive, concrete embodying of the world's reconciliation to God and of a new humanity: "That is why faith is not a religious relation to God, to a 'highest, most powerful, most good being'—that is not real transcendence—but our relation to God is a new life in 'being-there-for-others,' in participation in Jesus' being. Not the infinite, unreachable tasks, but the respective given reachable neighbour is the transcendent. God in human form! This is what sets Christianity apart from other religions."[69] That too, we add, is what makes Bonhoeffer's theology a humanism.

While by no means excluding social justice from his agenda, Bonhoeffer's Christological humanism is more broadly conceived than Yoder's "Jesulogy" and therefore better suited for constructively addressing current issues regarding the relation of religion, science, and culture. Moreover, Bonhoeffer's indebtedness to patristic Christology is not, as Yoder supposes, a lamentable blind spot leading to a Christology that begins with an abstract conception later filled in with theological content. For the fathers did not begin with a transcendent, Greek conception of a pre-incarnational Word, but their Christology unfolded concretely from the biblical Jesus. Patristic Christology did not talk about "God understood as coming to be man, but about a man coming to be understood as God."[70] Contrary to Yoder's assumption, the church fathers sought to confess "the one who *is* Word and Son in the flesh, and how he is known as such. It is Jesus Christ, the one of Galilee, the one 'descended of David,' who is, in his very humanity, understood to be the Word 'in the beginning with God' (John 1.1.). The starting point is not a dogmatic confession of the Son followed by a description of his human

69. *DBW* 8:558.
70. Steenberg, *God and Man*, 3.

becoming, but the human Christ, who *from* and *in* his humanity is identified with the eternal Son of the Father. One does not begin with the eternal Word, later to take flesh. One begins with the flesh and bones of Jesus of Galilee, and sees in him the eternity of the divine Son."[71] Yoder's attribution of the reverse "logological" approach to Christology may in the end reveal more about his own historical context of fighting rationalist theologies than the church fathers' actual Christology.

In short, Bonhoeffer clearly and rightly affirms the patristic tradition when he writes in *Ethics*, "Christ is the center and power of the Bible, of the church, of theology, but also of humanity, reason, justice, and culture. To Christ everything must return: only under Christ's protection can it live."[72] It is precisely this desire for the unity of reason in Christ, refracted as it necessarily is through the various disciplines of human knowing, that makes Bonhoeffer's theology a Christian humanism.

71. Ibid.
72. *DBWE* 6:337.

3

Bonhoeffer's Theology and Economic Humanism
An Exploration in Interdisciplinary Sociality

Peter Frick

Tatenloses Abwarten und stumpfes Zuschauen sind keine christlichen Haltungen. Den Christen rufen nicht erst die Erfahrungen am eigenen Leibe, sondern die Erfahrungen am Leibe der Brüder, um derentwillen Christus gelitten hat, zur Tat und zum Mitleiden.[1]

Introduction: The Economic Downward Spiral

The aim of this essay is to examine Bonhoeffer's theology vis-à-vis economics. Admittedly, at first glance, this may appear as a rather farfetched idea, since Bonhoeffer was neither trained nor known as an economist and has left us no systematic treatment of his thought on that subject. Yet, there is the curious fact that Bonhoeffer's entire adult life unfolded within an inexorable economic downward spiral. The height of that spiral was for Bonhoeffer in all probability the granting of his doctoral degree in theology in 1927. The bourgeois élan of the Bonhoeffer family, embedded as it was in intellectual elitism and relative economic wealth, had borne another fruit with the legendary academic achievement of the youngest son, at a mere twenty-one years of age. There is little doubt that the prism through which the newly minted Dr. Dietrich Bonhoeffer looked at the world in 1927 was "from above." Yet, from now on, slowly but surely, his vantage point of the world was about to change, and Bonhoeffer was drawn into these changes, not as a spectator, but increasingly as one of the protagonists. The year in Barcelona

---

1. *DBW* 8:34.

(1928–1929) opened his eyes for the social issues of both the business class and those on the margins of society. Then, in 1929, the Wall Street Crash happened, and shortly thereafter Bonhoeffer visited New York City as a post-doctoral student at Union Theological Seminary. During that year, his eyes were opened for the social issues in the United States, most of all the ill of racism and its economic impact on the lives of African Americans. When he returned to Berlin, the economic constraints of the Weimar Republic made themselves felt with his students and society. Germany was plagued with extremely high unemployment, nearly 30 percent by 1932. Even though the rise of Nazism in 1933 temporarily improved economic conditions, as the economy now geared up for the industrial output of war machinery, within the next decade all of Germany was faced with the impending total collapse of its economy. Bonhoeffer himself walked to the gallows with literally no possessions. He, too, had lost everything. His life journey "from above" now ended in the deepest "here below."

Against the foil of Bonhoeffer's own experience of an economic downward spiral, the objective of this essay lies in the exploration of what he had to say of the complex interdisciplinary matrix between theology and economics. What is the relation between these two disciplines? How are the brute realities of economic suffering for the masses to be correlated with the gospel of Jesus Christ? In what manner should theology address economic issues? What is the role of the church between theology and economics? I will examine these questions in several steps. I will first present Bonhoeffer's own pronouncement of the emergence of the humanistic side of his theology, followed by an analysis of his basic theological assumptions in relation to his statements on the questions of economics. I will finally, and more tentatively, sketch a brief outline for the development of a critical theology that provokes the emergence of authentic humanistic economies.

The Humanizing of Bonhoeffer's Theology

Since Bonhoeffer was foremost a theologian, I will correspondingly address our key question of the relation between theology and economics from Bonhoeffer's theological perspective, a path that he himself would have followed. The discipline of theology was the lens through which he analyzed almost all of the spheres around him. That is to say, a theological analysis of the questions of economics would at least have been his starting point in coming to terms with the complex relation between theology and economics.

To repeat what I indicated above, Bonhoeffer's own experience of the downward economic spiral, the descent from a life "above" to the suffering world "below," happened in various stages. Two such crucial stages in this journey were the experiences in Barcelona and New York City. In 1928, Bonhoeffer went for a year to Barcelona in order to be an assistant pastor to a German Lutheran congregation. On his way there, he visited a high mass in Paris that was attended by many prostitutes. The emotional reaction of the young pastor was profound: "It was an enormously impressive picture, and once again one could see quite clearly how close, precisely through their fate and guilt, these most heavily burdened people are to the heart of the gospel."[2] Here we have one of the earliest utterances of Bonhoeffer's emerging social conscience. He speaks of the "most heavily burdened people," whose burdens are often brought about by "fate and guilt." The number of burdened people in his life was to grow steadily, as during the year in Barcelona. There his eyes and heart were opened to the reality of what he termed the "social question."[3]

Interestingly, Bonhoeffer's biographical encounter with the underside of social realities during the Barcelona year had as its correlative a reconception of his theology. In an entry in his diary he notes: "My theology is beginning to become humanistic; what does that mean? I wonder whether Barth ever lived abroad?"[4] Here Bonhoeffer gives us a glance into his theological formation. Prompted by his personal experiences of the "social question," he is thinking about theology in a new key. It is taking shape in a more "humanistic" fashion, even though he does not himself quite know what "humanistic" means. Given his reference to living "abroad," we may surmise that perhaps a "humanistic" kind of theology is one that emerges both in the academy and in the encounters

2. *DBWE* 10:59.

3. Ibid., 62, 69. The social question emerged as Bonhoeffer witnessed the extravagance of the German business community (cf. ibid., 69, 78), human hardship (cf. ibid., 78: financial difficulties), and social marginality (cf. ibid., 110). According to his own description, he encountered globetrotters, vagrants, escaped criminals, hired killers, legionnaires, circus people, dancers.

4. Ibid., 64.

with other human beings and their cultures. Or, more precisely, academic theology is fine-tuned in the academy of life, namely, in the social, political, and economic structures in which people live. Something to this effect Bonhoeffer alludes to in a sermon. Although he does not address the question of theology as such, he ventures a few comments on what we can argue to be one of the goals of theology, namely, the empowering of Christians to live a fully human life. "Christians," he proclaims, "serve *their own time*, and that means they step into the midst of it with all its problems and difficulties, with it seriousness and distress, and there they serve. Christians are people of the present in the most profound sense. Be it *political* and *economic* problems, *moral* and *religious* decline, concern for the present generation of young people—everywhere the point is to enter into the problems of the present."[5] Although Bonhoeffer does not use the word "humanistic" in this sermon, his reflection leaves no doubt: theology is not a mere abstract academic undertaking but must relate in a most concrete manner to the social realities of *human* beings, including the realm of economics.

In New York, we observe a subtle yet important terminological change in Bonhoeffer's characterization of social realities. Whereas in Barcelona he spoke in general terms of the "social question," now, in New York, he speaks of the "social problem."[6] Why this adaptation in expression? Without overstating the case, could it be that Bonhoeffer's exposure to the social realities in Barcelona had still been colored by his life "from above"? While not denying that social issues did exist, the young Bonhoeffer still judged those somewhat disinterestedly, hence the expression "social question." A question does not per se imply an issue. In New York, however, Bonhoeffer took his own sermon from Barcelona to heart, especially in his confrontation with racism[7] in Harlem and the full-fledged economic crisis following the Wall Street collapse a year earlier. Racism and economics were not mere academic issues or neutral social realities. They were concrete social evils and problems. Now Bonhoeffer understood unmistakably: social realities imply tremendous issues, suffering, imbalances, dysfunction, and destruction. What was at stake was not theology but human lives uprooted because of economic

5. Ibid., 529.
6. Ibid., 307.
7. Cf. my essay "Dietrich Bonhoeffer's Theological Anthropology: The Case of Racism."

collapse; hence, theology must address these social issues in a manner such that human life is transformed into new ways of humane and equitable existence.

In the middle of his journey "from above to below," Bonhoeffer penned the now famous recollection for his fellow-conspirators at New Year's Eve 1943, titled "After Ten Years." Even though he had still not arrived at the bottom himself, he ponders: "We have for once learnt to see the great events of world history from below, from the perspective of the outcast, the suspects, the maltreated, the powerless, the oppressed, the reviled—in short, from the perspective of those who suffer."[8]

Economics and Theology: Basic Assumptions

On a global scale, "those who suffer" includes vast numbers of people who suffer because of the negative effects brought about by the economic structures that govern their everyday lives. This is no different in Bonhoeffer's time from our own at the beginning of the twenty-first century. Yet—as we noted already—because Bonhoeffer was primarily a theologian and a preacher and not an economist or a social worker, he was interested in articulating theology and not in advancing economic theories. However, given his own experiences of the economic spiral, it should not come as a surprise that Bonhoeffer did on occasion discuss the questions of economics. Our task is now to articulate the three basic theological and "humanistic" assumptions he brings to bear on his understanding of economics.

Economics as a Reality Dependent on the Reality of Christ

Likely late in the summer of 1942, Bonhoeffer wrote a lengthy review of a monograph by Otto Dilschneider titled *Die evangelische Tat: Grundlagen und Grundzüge der evangelischen Ethik*. According to Bonhoeffer, Dilschneider's was a vintage Lutheran thesis: namely, that Protestant ethics addresses exclusively the question of the personhood of the human being and that all other spheres in the world remain untouched by this key question. Bonhoeffer remarks that "these assertions are intended to prove that Christian ethics does indeed have to do with the Christian businessman, Christian statesman, etc., but not with eco-

---

8. Bonhoeffer, *Letters and Papers*, 17.

nomics, politics, etc."⁹ Dilschneider proposes—by employing the notions of *Personalethos* and *Realethos*—the separation of the person (Christian man or woman) from the realm in which one's personhood (businessperson) becomes actualized (realm of economics). For Bonhoeffer the overarching question thus becomes whether "*in the realm of Christian ethics it is possible to make statements about worldly orders and conditions, thus, e.g., about state, economy, science* ... or whether these things of the world are in fact 'ethically neutral.'"¹⁰

Bonhoeffer places his critique of Dilschneider's basic thesis in the context of liberal theology and religious socialism. The former misread the gospel as a merely religious message mostly irrelevant to social, worldly realities and orders, while the latter emphasized the "social-revolutionary character of Jesus' words about the poor and the rich, about justice and peace." In effect, Bonhoeffer argues, "both have read past the center of the New Testament, namely, the *person of Jesus Christ as the salvation of the world*. The ethical question is resolved in the question of Christ, and the question of the gospel's relation to the worldly orders can be answered only from the New Testament answer to the question of Christ."¹¹ Furthermore, Bonhoeffer argues, "all created things are through and for Christ and exist only in Christ (Col 1:16), i.e., there is nothing that would stand outside the relation to Christ, neither persons nor things; indeed, only in relation to Christ do created things have their being, not only human beings but also state, economy, science, nature, etc."¹²

Bonhoeffer's sentiment expressed in these words takes on an even more crystallized form when placed in the context of his conception of reality (*Wirklichkeit*). One of the most basic presuppositions of all of Bonhoeffer's thought is his critique of what he calls the "pseudo-Lutheranism" of the post-Reformation period, in particular the emphasis on Luther's doctrine of the two kingdoms.¹³ In the section "Christ, Reality and the Good" in his *Ethics*, Bonhoeffer boldly declares: "There

9. *DBWE* 16:540–41.
10. Ibid., 541 (emphasis in the original).
11. Ibid., 542–43.
12. Ibid., 543.
13. In *DBWE* 6:114, Bonhoeffer asserts that Luther's doctrine of the two kingdoms had since the Reformation been misunderstood in that "government, reason, economy, and culture each claimed the right to autonomy."

are not two realities, but *only one reality*, and that is God's reality revealed in Christ in the reality of the world . . . The world has no reality of its own independent of God's revelation in Christ. It is a denial of God's revelation in Jesus Christ to wish to be 'Christian' without being 'worldly,' or to wish to be worldly without seeing and recognizing the world in Christ. Hence there are not two realms, but only *the one realm of the Christ-reality* [*Christuswirklichkeit*], in which the reality of God and the reality of the world are united."[14] Bonhoeffer's view of the Christological unity of reality thus precludes the autonomy of economics. Even though de facto much of our contemporary world functions as if economics is an independent reality, Bonhoeffer's theological premise of the one reality in Christ calls the Christian to be an economic agent within the one structure of reality created and sustained by God.

The Bourgeois Church and the Proletariat

Already in his dissertation *Sanctorum Communio*, the young Bonhoeffer had included a discussion of capitalism, the proletariat, and the church. Reinhold Seeberg, his doctoral supervisor, was rather critical of those pages and wondered if they belonged in the dissertation at all. Not surprisingly, then, those pages suffered the fate of obscurity in the first published editions until the new critical edition of the *Dietrich Bonhoeffer Werke* restored them to their proper place, albeit tucked away in an elongated and tedious footnote.

Bonhoeffer's discussion is framed by Troeltsch's question to what extent the church offers a solution to contemporary social issues. The latter asserts that "the social problem is vast and complicated. It includes the problem of the capitalistic economic period and of the industrial proletariat created by it" but also matters such as the growth of military, super states, colonialism, trade, and the treatment of "people and labor like machines."[15]

As Seeberg correctly detected, Bonhoeffer's discussion of the questions raised by Troeltsch is indecisive as he struggles to do justice to a theology of the church, contemporary social issues, and his own privileged upbringing. Notwithstanding Seeberg's reluctant criticism, it is crucial to keep in mind that here we have one of the earliest in-

14. *DBWE* 6:58.
15. *DBWE* 1:271 n. 430.

dications in Bonhoeffer's work that he clearly perceived the correlation between theology and practice, between the church and society, between the privileged and the unprivileged. How these correlations are articulated theologically and how they actually shape the church or contemporary society is another question. For now, the young doctor of theology wrestles with these issues, and this is to his credit more than it is a criticism. As he matures in age, gains broader theological insights, and experiences the world more and more "from below," the answers to these early questions come increasingly into sharper focus.

The young Bonhoeffer acknowledges that "Christian social work has accomplished admirable things," but the key question for him lies elsewhere. He wonders, "[W]here is the real discussion among gospel, church-community, and proletariat?"[16] The framing of the question with these three nouns is significant. In a nutshell, they represent for Bonhoeffer the pillars of a theology that is based on the Word of God, manifests its power in the church-community, and must concretely shape the world that suffers. Programmatic for his reflection is the acclamation: "No apotheosis of the proletariat! It is neither the bourgeois nor the proletarian who is right, but the gospel alone. Here is neither Jew nor Greek."

This fundamental insight, "the gospel alone," is one of the structural pillars of Bonhoeffer's theological work. The criterion that applies to all his theological decisions is the word of God. A few years later, in his lecture on the history of systematic theology at the University of Berlin in the winter semester 1931–1932, he expresses the same insight most succinctly: "Deus dixit—to recognize this fact is the beginning of all genuine theological thinking, it is the open space for freedom and the living God."[17] Because God has spoken and revealed himself in his word, therefore the word of God stands between what he calls the bourgeois and the proletariat. Bonhoeffer's usage of these two terms is rather interesting. Given his own bourgeois heritage, Bonhoeffer seems hesitant to transgress boundaries that would betray certain sympathies for the proletariat. Yet intuitively he knows that if theology and the church are any good, they must precisely be able to speak to the conditions that divide the masses into bourgeois and proletariat. He never

---

16. Ibid., 272 n. 430.
17. *DBW* 11:199 (my translation).

defines these terms, but it seems that the economic realities and the "class background"[18] attached to either of them would not have escaped his usually lucid perception of reality. He notes that the gospel's proclamation confronts his times with "the problem of the proletariat" in a church that is bourgeois. "The best proof," he argues, "remains that the proletariat has turned its back on the church, while the bourgeois (civil servant, skilled worker, merchant) stayed."[19] For this reason, "sermons are thus aimed at people who live relatively securely and comfortably, in orderly family circumstances, who are relatively 'educated', and relatively stable morally."[20] While Bonhoeffer laments the bourgeois nature of the church, he also thinks that "the coming church will not be 'bourgeois'. How it will look is today still unclear."

Curiously, in that discussion Bonhoeffer also invokes terms such as "working-class people" and "socialist doctrine."[21] It is obvious that while he welcomes the demise of a bourgeois church, he is also reticent about a church with socialist characteristics. "It is incorrect," he remarks, "to think that the idea of socialism as such would sociologically correspond to the Christian concept of community . . . or God's Realm on earth."[22] Bonhoeffer argues that "the socialist idea of equality is theologically and sociologically untenable . . . The Christian community is based on the dissimilarity and inequality of persons."[23] Here then is one of the reasons why Bonhoeffer rejects socialism, at least when it is predicated on equality and placed on the same level as the church. Socialism, he thinks, brushes over human inequality, over each person's uniqueness—in theological language, it does not see that each person bears the unique impression of God's image.

---

18. *DBWE* 1:272 n. 430.

19. Ibid., 273 n. 430.

20. Ibid.

21. Ibid.; On a historical note, however, Bonhoeffer understands why socialism emerged. He is in agreement with Ludwig Feuerbach, who questioned whether religious claims actually correspond to the reality of life. While Feuerbach denies such a correspondence, Bonhoeffer thinks that because theology did not address the matter of correspondence, therefore socialism filled the void and emerged as a social force (cf. *DBW* 11:148–49).

22. *DBWE* 1:274 n. 430.

23. Ibid.

The Value of the Human Being

In accordance with his view that there is only one reality in Jesus Christ, Bonhoeffer contends: "Jesus Christ the human being—that means that God enters into created reality, that we may be and should be human beings before God."[24] In other words, Bonhoeffer's assumption of the unity of reality is not an abstract theological datum, but points to a concrete structure of being in and for the world. "Because, however, the entire new humanity," says Bonhoeffer, "is established in reality in Jesus Christ, *he represents the whole history of humanity in his historical life*."[25] As the context of Bonhoeffer's discussion indicates, this statement is not to be interpreted as a quantitative claim, namely, that the life of Jesus Christ universally subsumes all historical events. Rather, it is a theological statement to the effect that because of the earthly Jesus of Nazareth and the resurrected Christ there is now for humanity as a whole, in the here and now, a new way of being in the world, the new path toward life.

Given that the Christ-reality encompasses all aspects of the world's reality, human life in particular has a unique locus in the world. In Bonhoeffer's own words: "Life created and preserved by God possesses an inherent right, completely independent of its social utility. The right to life inheres in what exists [*im Seienden*] and not in some value or other. There is no worthless life before God, because God holds life itself to be valuable."[26] Just as God pronounced creation itself as good, so likewise is the creation of the human being in itself good. Because all life comes from God, the human being has, as Bonhoeffer says, "an inherent right." This right is completely autonomous. At the same time, while Bonhoeffer grants the autonomy of the value of life independent from "social utility" or any other qualifier, he rejects, as we saw above, the existence of any other autonomous sphere. Concretely, only the human being as such has an inherent and autonomous value. This value is a given, a fact that is grounded in the unity of the Christ-reality; it is one of the inviolable human rights. For this reason, Bonhoeffer boldly but correctly asserts, "[t]he destruction of humanness [*Menschsein*] is sin."[27]

---

24. *DBWE* 6:157.
25. *DBWE* 1:147 (emphasis in the original).
26. *DBWE* 6:193.
27. Ibid., 157.

As an autonomous value embedded as it were in the very existence of a person, the inherent worth of the human being cannot be constructed, or deconstructed, as such. Human worth and dignity may be violated or enhanced, but it cannot be taken from a person. Nevertheless, when Bonhoeffer says that "the destruction of *Menschsein*" is the work of sin, in my view he cannot thereby mean the destruction of the inherent and inviolable value and dignity of a person but only the attacks on a person's dignity. Nonetheless, as we shall see below, such attacks have far-reaching implications on a person's life, not least of which may be the economic one.

At any rate, long after he had joined the conspiracy circle and had come to understand the full measure of Nazi atrocities, Bonhoeffer once again reflected on the value of human life. In "After Ten Years," his New Year's reflection of 1943 addressed to his co-conspirators, he includes a section under the title, "Contempt for Humanity?" "There is the danger," he warns, "that we are drifting into an attitude of contempt for humanity. We know quite well that we have no right to do so, and that it would lead us into the most fruitless relation with other persons . . . The only fruitful relation with other people—especially those who are weak—is one of love, that is to say, the will to have friendship [*Gemeinschaft*] with them. God himself did not hold human beings in contempt, but became human for the sake of humanity."[28]

In terms of the history of theology in the twentieth century, it is the movement known as the "Theology of Liberation" that has most clearly analyzed and articulated what is at stake in a world that has contempt for humanity and a theology that does not refute the dehumanizing effects of economic structures. Many of the founding fathers, such as Gustavo Gutiérrez,[29] Jon Sobrino,[30] and Leonardo Boff,[31] have taken some of Bonhoeffer's ideas—most of all his call to see history "from below"—and have constructed a theology that addresses as a central concern the humanizing of the poor person in the midst of economic oppression. Gutiérrez more than anyone else has painted a disturbing

28. *DBW* 8:28–29 (my translation).
29. Cf. Gutiérrez, *Theology of Liberation*, 24, 42, 119, 227, 253.
30. For example, cf. Sobrino, *Christology at the Crossroads*, 197, 221, 262–63, 274, 308; *Jesus the Liberator*, 2, 56, 232, 250–51; and many of his other works.
31. For example, Boff, *Jesus Christ Liberator*, 245, 320.

picture of what happens to the dehumanized person: those "below," the economically exploited, oppressed, and marginalized, in effect become "*nonpersons*."[32] Their identity as a *human* being is nearly eradicated by economic structures. In this regard, Jon Sobrino very succinctly illuminates the nexus between economics and humanity. He comments on the fact that the economic development of the rich countries has had an almost exclusively negative impact on the humanization of poor peoples. "The civilization of wealth," he laments, "*has failed as a way of guaranteeing the life* of the majorities because its 'quality' of life cannot be universalized, given the universal correlation between resources and population; even if it could be universalized *it would not be desirable* to do so, because it has also failed as a *way of humanizing people and peoples*."[33]

In other words, what Sobrino unmasks as the wide gap between poverty and wealth is not a mere neutral phenomenon or a natural part of our world order. This gap is horrendous not primarily because there are rich and poor persons, but because the existence of wealth implies an inescapable structural consequence, namely, the dehumanization of the poor persons. Poverty is a sin not because money and wealth are evil but because they can potentially destroy the humanity and dignity of human beings. In the words of Sobrino, wealth has "failed as a *way of humanizing people and peoples*."

Economic Systems and Humanity

We are now in a position to examine Bonhoeffer's more concrete statements on economics in relation to the assumptions of his theology in general but also as articulated above in a more particular sense. In order to frame our discussion, we will begin with one of the few passages in which Bonhoeffer addresses the question of economic structures directly. In *Ethics*, he comments:

> There are, for example, certain economic or social attitudes and conditions that hinder faith in Jesus Christ, which means that they also destroy the essence of human beings and the world. It

---

32. Gutiérrez, "Underside of History," 193. For a constructive interpretation of Gutiérrez and Bonhoeffer, see Clifford Green, "Bonhoeffer, Modernity and Liberation Theology."

33. Sobrino, *Where is God?*, 99.

can be asked, for example, whether capitalism, or socialism, or collectivism are such economic systems that hinder faith. The church has a twofold approach here: on the one hand, it must declare as reprehensible, by the authority of the word of God, such economic attitudes or systems that clearly hinder faith in Christ, thereby drawing a negative boundary. On the other hand, it will not be able to make positive contributions to a new order on the authority of the word of God, but merely on the authority of responsible counsel by Christian experts.[34]

The issues raised by these lines that we will now address in more detail are the questions of faith vis-à-vis economics and the broad question of the role of the church in acting as an agent of economic critique.

Faith and Economics

Firstly, Bonhoeffer's words provide an unambiguous indication of the inexorable nexus between economics, sociality, and human life. Economic systems and structures have an inescapable force on "the essence of human beings and the world." Bonhoeffer's view on this matter fits squarely with the theological movement seen from the beginning to the end of his theological oeuvre, namely, to shift the emphasis from the individual (believer) to the (church) community, and, by extension, to the world.

In *Act and Being*, for example, Bonhoeffer attempted to demonstrate that the "transcendental attempt of pure actualism," as also the attempt of ontology "to establish the continuity of the I," failed because of its reference to the individual human being: "In searching for 'reality' it [the transcendental, ontological approach] overlooked the fact that in reality human beings are never individuals only, not even those 'addressed by the You'. Human beings, rather, are always part of a community, in 'Adam' or in 'Christ.'"[35] Even though in this context Bonhoeffer speaks of philosophical and theological baselines, it is one of the bedrocks of his theology that all theoretical notions of these disciplines must find their relevance in sociality. In this sense, the questions of economic systems are also not a primarily individualistic matter but one that is centrally located in sociality. It is noteworthy that the term "economics" etymologically derives from the Greek compound *oikos* (house) and *nomos*

34. *DBWE* 6:361.
35. *DBWE* 2:113.

(law), thus suggesting the governance (law) of the family (house) and by extension the governance of a community, society, nation, and the world. The point is that the very definition of "economy" is social and communal. No one person is a law to her/himself, but, in the Greek sense, law governs the house, hence the family, that is to say, in relation to other people.

Secondly, twice in the above citation Bonhoeffer mentions that economic and social conditions may "hinder faith in Jesus Christ." At first glance, this may come as an unexpected utterance from the very thinker who receives almost iconic esteem for his statements on "religionless Christianity" and so forth. Is he not the man who championed some sort of secular Christianity? Suffice it to say here that not only is there—even still today—an undue and therefore imbalanced weight placed on the raw intuitions penned down in his prison letters; there is likewise in my view an underestimation of Bonhoeffer's deep rootedness in orthodox theological thinking. Even though our pluralistic age prefers a (post)modern Bonhoeffer over a dogmatic one, there is every indication that he espoused a traditional conception of salvation and redemption. Bonhoeffer himself expresses it in this way:

> The kind of thinking that starts out with human problems, and then looks for solutions from that vantage point, has to be overcome—it is unbiblical. The way of Jesus Christ, and thus the way of all Christian thought, is not the way from the world to God but from God to the world. This means that the essence of the gospel does not consist in solving worldly problems, and also that this cannot be the essential task of the church. However, it does not follow from this that the church would have no task at all in this regard. *But we will not recognize its legitimate task unless we first find the correct starting point.*[36]

In a similar, and perhaps even more startling, vein, Bonhoeffer seems very convinced of his position: "The problem of the poor and rich can never be solved in any other way than leaving it unsolved."[37] Whatever Bonhoeffer may have intended with this last citation, it is more important to return to the end of the previous statement. Even though the solving of social issues, including that of poverty, is not the primary task of the church, it does not mean that "the church would have no

36. *DBWE* 6:356.
37. Ibid., 355.

task" in the sociality of the world. What matters in this regard is that the church understands her correct starting point. *In nuce*, the starting point for Bonhoeffer is that "in Jesus Christ God comes down into the very depths of the human fall, of guilt, and of need," and offers "the justice and grace of God." The endpoint is also clear: God's coming "is especially close to the very people who are deprived of rights, humiliated, and exploited."[38]

The context of Bonhoeffer's words is his discussion regarding the dialectic of ultimate and penultimate things in *Ethics*. The coming of the grace of God in the proclamation of his word has an almost irreversible sequence for Bonhoeffer. Coming is preparing; preparing is responsible action: "Preparing the way is indeed a matter of concrete intervention in the visible world, as concrete and visible as hunger and nourishment."[39] Since the word of God is always addressed to the concrete human being who has her/his value independent of any social utility, as we saw above, it follows for Bonhoeffer that "it is hard for those thrust into extreme disgrace, desolation, poverty, and helplessness to believe in God's justice and goodness";[40] "If the hungry do not come to faith, the guilt falls on those who denied them bread. To bring bread to the hungry is preparing the way for the coming of grace."[41]

Bonhoeffer does not address the question of economic systems in this context. His reflections seem to be more on the micro-economic rather than macro-economic level. Yet, just as the theological starting point for social transformation is rooted in the coming of God's grace in the person of Jesus Christ, so likewise the economic starting point for social transformation lies on the micro-economic level of responsible Christian action. For Bonhoeffer such action is not an option of the person who claims to be a disciple of Jesus Christ: "It is, instead, a commission of immeasurable responsibility given to all who know about the coming of Jesus Christ. The hungry person needs bread, the homeless person needs shelter, the one deprived of rights needs justice, the lonely person needs community, the undisciplined one needs order, and the slave needs freedom. It would be blasphemy against God and

---

38. Ibid., 163.

39. Ibid., 164.

40. Ibid., 162. Conversely, "it is hard for the well-fed and the powerful to comprehend God's judgment and God's grace."

41. Ibid., 163.

our neighbor to leave the hungry unfed while saying that God is closest to those in deepest need."[42] To repeat, for Bonhoeffer, the proclamation of the coming grace of God goes hand in hand with social activism for those in need. The two belong together—irrevocably and undividedly. They are the micro-economic preparation for the word of God to bear fruit and not "hinder faith in Christ."

The Church and Economic Critique

The question of the macro-economic task of the church vis-à-vis contemporary economic structures is a far more difficult subject in Bonhoeffer, not least because he rarely touches on this matter. There are, nonetheless, several principles we can discern in his statements.

Firstly, in the above quotation, Bonhoeffer specifically mentions capitalism, socialism, and collectivism (seemingly his way of referring to Marxism) and characterizes them once as "economic systems" and once as "economic or social attitudes." As we noted, Bonhoeffer's primary interest lies in whether they hinder or facilitate a person's coming to faith. Nonetheless, the main point here is that he clearly recognizes that economic structures are systems that play themselves out in the arena of sociality. This is true of all three economic systems mentioned by Bonhoeffer. Be it capitalism, socialism, or Marxism—all of them are more or less rigid structures that prescribe for peoples how they must accomplish their work and be compensated for it and how they are free or repressed to spend those earnings. In other words, there is hardly any person anywhere who is not in one way or another tied to an economic structure. Conversely, every economic system vies to impose its structures on all the people who live within its confines. Bonhoeffer is prudent, however, in that he does not forthrightly declare one system superior over another. For him—and this is decisive—the question he brings to all three of these systems is not in terms of industrial productivity or economic profitability. For example, he does not assume that capitalism is the best and Marxism (collectivism) the worst economic structure. His interest in these economic systems does not lie in the economic realm as such, but on the impact any economic system has on sociality.

42. Ibid.

Secondly, given the above, the task of the church is therefore precisely not in assessing an economic system vis-à-vis its impact on the market, industry, finances, and wealth of a country. Quite to the contrary, the church must be keenly aware of the underside of economic malpractice and draw the "negative boundary." In Bonhoeffer's words, the church has the responsibility to "declare reprehensible" those acts within economic systems that "destroy the essence of human beings and the world." So this is the benchmark by which Bonhoeffer assesses economic systems: it is the question of whether they enhance or destroy the human being. Given Bonhoeffer's theological perspectives, he is not interested in the orthodox economic methods of assessment. The performance of an economic system is for him secondary to its ability to enhance life for the people who live and work within its structures.

As we mentioned at the beginning of this essay, Bonhoeffer's experience of the structures of economics moved more and more on a downward spiral. For him this downward economic spiral was, of course, yoked for ill to the ideology that drove economics forward. Nazist ideology had the unintentional effect that it "destroyed the essence of human beings and the world." The fact that every economic system is predicated on an underlying ideology needs no accounting. This is the case with industrial war economics and Nazism, with Stalinism and Marxist ideology, capitalism and Friedmanian unrestricted-market ideology, and with socialism and its own various ideologies. Bonhoeffer looks at all of these economic structures from the single vantage point of whether they destroy or enhance life.

Suffice to mention here that by current assessments the world as a whole has not done well. A quick look at the statistics of worldwide poverty will preclude any triumphalism in an instant;[43] over one trillion dollars has not helped to improve the overall quality of life in the entire continent of Africa.[44] Rather, the unrestrained, greedy post-World War II capitalism of the wealthiest countries has ruined more nations in the last century than the ordinary person can imagine.[45] The reality for the masses of this world is staggering: millions of refugees and migrant workers, hundreds of millions of malnourished people, scores

---

43. Cf. Schliesser, "Verantwortung nach Bonhoeffer," 297–98.
44. Cf. Moyo, *Dead Aid*.
45. Cf. Klein, *Shock Doctrine*.

of underemployed and unemployed.[46] To be sure, all of these evils are not exclusively the result of an economic structure as such; for, indeed, there is much misuse and corruption among those who are in control of these structures. Nonetheless, it is undeniable that certain forms of capitalistic structures do bring about oppression and contribute to "destroy the essence of human beings and the world."

Conclusion: Toward a Theological "Critical Theory"— And More

Today, it seems to me, one of the most urgent needs for theology is to engage proactively in what Bonhoeffer terms the "positive contribution" with respect to dominant economic systems and structures. How can contemporary theology dare to contribute positively to matters of economics? Are theologians entitled to transgress into the field of other experts? In this regard, Bonhoeffer calls for "Christian experts." Presumably, what he means is not theologians but Christians who are trained as experts in the field of economics. As contemporary theologians, we concede that economic issues are the prerogative of economic experts. Yet, any successful dialogue on economic systems must not only be interdisciplinary and multidisciplinary; it must also include the voice of theologians who will never get tired of promoting humanizing economic systems.

But what may be the contributions of theologians? In his essay on Bonhoeffer, Gutiérrez, for example, cites the famous text from "After Ten Years" that we cited above. "It would be unwarranted," he comments, "to attempt to deduce from Bonhoeffer's use of terms such as 'poor' and 'oppressed' that we are in the presence of a critical analysis of modern society on grounds of that society's injustice and oppression."[47] Even so, Gutiérrez recognizes that "there are weighty indications that Bonhoeffer had begun to move forward in the perspective of 'those beneath'—those on the 'underside of history.'"[48]

As the father of Liberation Theology, Gutiérrez proposes a kind of theology that looks critically at the interplay between theology and

---

46. For a proven approach to reduce poverty on the micro-economic scale, see Polak, *Out of Poverty*.

47. Gutiérrez, "Limitations of Modern Theology," 231.

48. Ibid.

economic structures vis-à-vis the very essence of humanity. Even before him, the Frankfurt School of Critical Theory had addressed very similar questions, albeit from a philosophical, Marxist-oriented perspective. One of its chief architects, Max Horkheimer, unmistakably understood that all "cultural forms which are based on struggle and oppression are not evidence of a homogeneous self-conscious will; this world is not theirs, but belongs to capital."[49] Whatever one may make of the success or failure of the Frankfurt School, one fact remains: the members of the school understood far more clearly than their theological counterparts (there are, of course, exceptions, such as Moltmann, Metz, and others) that culture is largely constructed by economic ideology, which has the potential to destroy humanity at its essence. In the face of contemporary economic crises, post-modern theology must have the courage to articulate a kind of critical theological theory. What shape, what specific tasks, what objectives and desired outcomes such a venture will entail is a matter for this generation of theologians to determine. This is the easy part.

The real question lies completely elsewhere. Even if theologians succeed in articulating a powerful "critical theology," who will subscribe to this kind of theology? Will economists, will the corporate world, will share holders and politicians—in short, the privileged and powerful—really care about a theology that could facilitate a more economically equitable and globally more sustainable world? As long as critical theology is just "public theology" for the sake of theology, it has no sting. A true public, critical theology must aim squarely at real life transformations of those who experience the world "from below." Theology always begins in reflection, but it must end in praxis.

Both Bonhoeffer and Horkheimer experienced the events of world history "from below," as does Gutiérrez in his life with the Quechan people of Peru. Their own *Sitz im Leben* and commitment to the plight of those "below" undoubtedly shaped the contours of their thought and the ways in which they lived. They all understood that "a purely spiritual

---

49. Horkheimer, *Critical Theory*, 207–8. One of the problems today is as follows: the revolutionary working class—or, to use Bonhoeffer's term: the now outdated expression "the proletariat"—exists no longer in a post-Berlin-Wall world, and so there is no longer a dialectical lever to activate the whole or large portions of society. Consumption for the sake of consumption has numbed the social consciousness of the masses, other than charity giving and superficial sympathy with "the less fortunate."

resistance becomes just a wheel in the machine of the totalitarian state. True discipleship, to which many Christians may once again be called, does not lead men back to religion."[50] These words seem as if they could be the prose of Bonhoeffer, but in fact Horkheimer uttered them. For Bonhoeffer, true discipleship leads to the following of Jesus Christ, and, by extension, true critical theology must lead to the equitable economic life of those "below." Not a single person in this world is excluded from what Bonhoeffer declared:

> God
> wants us to be wholly
> what we are.
> Be men and women,
> both wholly
> and in their essence
> as created by God.
> Be human beings
> with your own wills, with your own passions
> and your own concerns,
> your happiness and your distress,
> your seriousness and your frivolity,
> your jubilation and your misery.[51]

Such wholeness of humanity is not merely a matter of an inner strength or fundamental disposition toward life. A person's wholeness is critically shaped by the structures of economic systems within which he or she lives. As such it is the task of every good theology to work with other disciplines toward economic structures that make possible a life of human dignity by providing work, education, health, food, clothing, and whatever else is necessary for the livelihood of every people in our world. This journey is a long one, and possibly a rocky one, but theology has to become a leader on that path—and not miss this obvious challenge. The goal is nothing less than humanity's life and experience of genuine economic sociality.

---

50. Horkheimer, "Thoughts on Religion," in *Critical Theory*, 130–31.
51. *DBWE* 10:530.

PART TWO

Bonhoeffer on Sociality and the Church

4

Sociality, Discipleship, and Worldly Theology in Bonhoeffer's Christian Humanism

Clifford J. Green

A STRIKING PHENOMENON OF THE VAST SECONDARY LITERATURE about Dietrich Bonhoeffer is that so little of it tries to address his theology as a whole. What are its fundamental patterns of thought? What are their enduring characteristics? What are new developments? What drives its movement? When we look at Bonhoeffer's older contemporaries in Protestant theology in the twentieth century—Barth and Tillich, for example—there is a fairly broad consensus about their work read as a whole. There is no such consensus about Bonhoeffer. Indeed, while early interpreters were bold to advance theses about the nature of Bonhoeffer's theology as a whole and what drove its development,[1] more recent scholarship has tended to focus on specific topics and texts.

This article is a contribution to addressing the question of Bonhoeffer's theology as a whole. At the 2008 Prague International Bonhoeffer Congress, I suggested that the quest for an authentic Christianity is an appropriate description for the movement of the whole.[2] But that is a very general summary and, while I discussed some significant details about Bonhoeffer's biblical hermeneutics, his Christian

---

1. See for example Hanfried Müller, whose thesis was summed up in his title *Von der Kirche zur Welt*. See also Godsey (*Theology of Dietrich Bonhoeffer*, 265), who held that Bonhoeffer's "*understanding* of the revelation of God in Jesus Christ . . . develops and thus provides the clue to the development within the theology itself." Ernst Feil (*Theology of Dietrich Bonhoeffer*, 84) argued "that there is continuity in the structure and central ideas of Bonhoeffer's theology and that all of these ideas are increasingly grounded in Christology."

2. See Green, "Bonhoeffer's Quest."

peace ethic, and his critique of religion, I did not venture a characterization of the whole, even a partial one. This article does not propose a comprehensive answer either. But by looking again at the movement from *Sanctorum Communio* to the prison theology and *Ethics*, I want to highlight one major theme, or better, orientation, that I believe is characteristic of the whole. This is finally epitomized by Bonhoeffer's word "worldliness," in its positive and polemical import, as it comes to clarity in the prison letters. Given that aim, I will first revisit my own work of nearly forty years ago, my argument about Bonhoeffer's theology of sociality, adding now a new perspective about its fundamental orientation. Then I will look at the turn to *Discipleship*, again considering a new ingredient—the Sermon on the Mount and commandments of Jesus—that appears in Bonhoeffer's theology in 1931. Finally, in light of the above, I will examine the meaning of "worldliness" in the prison letters, concluding that it is a fundamental orientation of Bonhoeffer's theology as a whole. Given the theme of this volume, "Being Human, Becoming Human," moreover, this essay can also be read as a case study of how one Christian theologian thought about the meaning of being human, and of his own pilgrimage to enter into what he called the new humanity of the God who became human, to live into that faith by which, as he wrote, one becomes human and Christian.[3]

Theology of Sociality

Sociality in Bonhoeffer is a complex conceptuality with several components. It is not just a general idea of relationality, sociability, and community in human existence. Nor is it reducible to and exhausted by Bonhoeffer's focus on the church, the *sanctorum communio*. Rather, it is a set of clear, coherent, and interrelated theological convictions about the human person in both intersubjective encounters and in the corporate relations of human communities. My argument in 1971[4] was that this conceptuality, this dynamic pattern of thought, was programmatic for Bonhoeffer's whole theology: that it informed his thinking from the doctoral dissertation to Tegel, and that one cannot fully understand

---

3. Bonhoeffer, *Letters and Papers*, 370, in the fateful letter of July 21, 1944.
4. The work published in 1975 by Scholars Press, and by Eerdmans in a second edition in 1999, was a dissertation completed in 1971.

Bonhoeffer's theology without knowing this conceptuality. I will now present a summary, drawn from Bonhoeffer's first presentation of it.[5]

Central is what Bonhoeffer calls "the Christian concept of person." Perhaps to resist the pervasive individualism of contemporary Anglo-American culture, one should begin here and now with the assertion that, in the Christian understanding, human beings are essentially, intrinsically, and unavoidably communal creatures. It is in communities that range from the family to humanity-as-a-whole that human persons, individuals to be sure, come into being and flourish. Bonhoeffer, however, begins his exposition of the person with a paradigm of interpersonal encounter, and then moves to communities. Formally defined as a self-conscious and willing being, a person is a socio-ethical historical being living always in relation to others. Specifically the I-you relationship[6] is an ethical encounter of wills in which the self meets the encountering will of the other, experiencing the will of the other as limit and barrier. That is, the otherness, the contrariness, the resistance of the will of the other, puts the self in an ethical situation. The encountering will of the other calls forth the response of the self, thereby putting the self in the ethical position of responsibility. Indeed, the person as an ethical self is created precisely in such encounters with the other. Accordingly, the historicity of the self is constituted not primarily by the temporality of such encounters, but by their call for ethical decision.

Theoretically, this phenomenology might be inferred by observing and construing human behavior and relationships generally. But for Bonhoeffer, of course, it is a theological construct. For the presupposition of all Christian thinking is that human existence is existence *coram Deo*, existence before God as the ultimate "Other." Accordingly, the paradigm of transcendence for Bonhoeffer is sociality. It is not only that the other person in his or her otherness "transcends" one's own self, and that the other is therefore an analogy, or image,[7] of the otherness of God. God is simultaneously beyond the self *and* present to the self. God

---

5. See *Sanctorum Communio* (*DBWE* 1:21), where Bonhoeffer deals with "the social intention of all the basic Christian concepts"; see also Green, *Theology of Sociality*, ch. 2.

6. Bonhoeffer is not drawing on Martin Buber here; see my "Editor's Introduction" in *DBWE* 1:5.

7. For more exact detail on Bonhoeffer's understanding of the image of God, see pp. 88–89 below.

"establishes" the other as inviolable you, and God is present as divine You in the you of the other person. In this aspect of his "Christian social philosophy" we see already an axiom of all Bonhoeffer's theology: the relationship with God is embedded in human sociality. God's "otherness" is not in absence, but in presence. Negatively put, there is no access to God apart from and outside of human sociality.

Everything that has been said so far about relationships between individuals can now be transferred to, or restated in terms of, the corporate dimension. There is no need here to review again the typology of social forms that Bonhoeffer developed in debate with the systematic sociology of the time, and which he used to make the argument that the church is a unique social form that reflected its nature as a reality of revelation.[8] Rather, I turn to his understanding of community. Defining community (*Gemeinschaft*) after Ferdinand Tönnies as the social form that arises when people will one another and their common life as ends in themselves, Bonhoeffer asks: What conceptual model is appropriate to interpret the social spirit of communities? Given the various models available (e.g., a familial or tribal model, a Marxist class model, a capitalist market model), Bonhoeffer answers with his concept of the person, now in the form of "collective person" (*Kollektivperson*). This does not mean divorcing a community from the individual persons and wills that compose it, thereby creating a "super-person" that dominates its members, demeaning and exploiting them. On the contrary, it is precisely designed to confer on corporate communities the ethical status intrinsic to individual persons. But if communities are construed as "ethical collective persons," how is one to understand an ethnic community, a gender community, or the community of a nation—let alone the worldwide community of nations—as having personal ethical status? Does this not devolve back to the individual ethical persons who comprise the community, thereby atomizing it and effectively denying such a thing as corporate ethical responsibility?

Communities are responsible, parallel to the ethical responsibility of individual persons, through the actions of people who represent the community and act on its behalf. This is the process Bonhoeffer calls *Stellvertretung*, vicarious representative action, giving the biblical example of the prophets of Israel. The prophet, on the one hand, repre-

---

8. Here Bonhoeffer is appropriating the German systematic sociology of the early twentieth century on a Barthian basis.

sents Yahweh—he encounters the people as a whole with God's word of justice and judgment; the prophet also acts vicariously in repenting as a representative of the people. In our own time we can see public leaders like Martin Luther King Jr. and Nelson Mandela embodying such prophetic encounter and judgment; and certainly Dietrich Bonhoeffer, both in his roles in the church and in the conspiracy, understood himself to be acting in repentance as a vicarious representative of his people. If we understand society to be composed not of atomistic individuals but of jostling communities—racial and ethnic communities, gender communities, economic interest groups, parties of competing political philosophies—Bonhoeffer sees them as engaged in moral encounter with dynamics that are illuminated by the ethical encounter of the I-you encounter of persons. (A clear example of this is his view in *Ethics* of the mandates of family, labor, state, and church, which exist in relationships of being with each other, against each other, and for each other.[9])

The communal-corporate life that has been described here in a somewhat formal phenomenological way is filled with concrete theological content when Bonhoeffer describes the encounter of God and humanity-as-a-whole (*die Gesamtgemeinschaft*) according to his model of personal, ethical encounter. Adam is the *Stellvertreter* of the old fallen humanity; he is its *Kollektivperson* who personally embodies its sinful mode of being in relation to God; but Christ is the *Kollektivperson* of the new humanity, whose concrete social form is the *sanctorum communio*. Grounded in Christ, *Stellvertretung* "is the life-principle of the new humanity,"[10] the Christological basis of that "being with one another" and "active being for one another" that are the constitutive acts of the *sanctorum communio* as community of love: "The sociality of Christ and his love for humanity personifies and creates the sociality of the new humanity."[11]

If the foregoing is at least the skeleton of the conceptuality of sociality in Bonhoeffer's dissertation, it is possible now to point briefly to its presence and theological employment in successive writings. Not every part of this complex conceptuality will always be in the foreground of every text. Rather than spelling out many details I will simply mention

9. Of the several discussions of the mandates in *Ethics* see *DBWE* 6:388–408, esp. here 393.
10. Quoted in Green, *Theology of Sociality*, 56; see *DBWE* 1:147.
11. Green, *Theology of Sociality*, 58.

some examples concisely, referring in the footnotes to more expansive expositions.

In *Act and Being* revelation is understood as a social reality. Christ, encountered in the social reality of the church-community, is the "collective person" of the new humanity. The revelation of God in the community is a revelation of God as person. Central to the argument, and enduring throughout Bonhoeffer's theology, is the understanding of God's freedom: "God is not free from humanity but is *free for humanity. Christ is the word of God's freedom.* God *is* present . . . 'haveable,' graspable in the Word within the church."[12] Consequently, "the being of revelation 'is' . . . the being of the community of persons that is constituted and formed by the person of Christ."[13] Sociality establishes the personal character of Christ's presence as an "other," outside the self, but not an entity, an extant thing;[14] sociality is the form of the presence of transcendence. The presence of Christ in word and sacrament in the life of the church exposes and judges the violated sociality and isolation of the person "in Adam," but also frees people from their self-enclosed isolation and allows them to enter into genuine community and authentic selfhood with others.

I also argued that in *Act and Being* the distinctive anthropological-soteriological problem in Bonhoeffer's theology, namely, the problem of power, came to the fore and persisted in subsequent writings. Power, insofar as it led to violated sociality, is a crucial problem for a theology of sociality since the exercise of power, and the misuse of power, is an intrinsically social problem.

In his university lectures of 1932–33, the theology of sociality is the basic conceptuality with which Bonhoeffer deals with both Christology and theological anthropology. This can be illustrated briefly with a couple of examples. Striking in *Creation and Fall* is the interpretation of *imago Dei* as *imago relationis*. That is, creaturely likeness to God is not an individualistic attribute possessed by a self-contained individual; rather it involves a relationship, and a specific one at that. Bonhoeffer begins with his previously stated understanding of God's freedom as a "being-free-for," specifically God's being-free-for-humanity. By analogy,

---

12. *DBW* 2:90–91 (translation and emphasis mine).
13. *DBWE* 2:113.
14. Green, *Theology of Sociality*, 88–89.

human freedom that in some way images God is also a freedom-for, a relational freedom, a being-free-for-God and being-free for the neighbor. But it is not just relatedness per se, but among humans as with God, a freedom of love[15]—this specific relation is the image of God.

In the 1933 Christology lectures[16] the person concept of the theology of sociality plays a central role. The Christological question is properly the "Who?" question concerning the person of Christ, not a "How?" question about the union of two reified "natures." And, like God's freedom and relation to creation, Christ's person and being is his freedom and presence as a being-*pro-me*, being-for-me. Hence "I can think of Christ only in existential relation to him and, at the same time, only within the church-community."[17] Since the *Personstruktur* of Christ is ontologically related to humanity, it has a necessary anthropological component and is developed in the threefold *Gestalt* of Christ as word, sacrament, and church-community; these in turn are related to the anthropological categories of history, nature, and society. Further elaboration of the Christology deals with the new humanity, transcendence and revelation in the Christian community, the sociality of word and sacrament, and Christ as the Mediator—all treated in terms of sociality.[18]

Looking at the theology of sociality as a whole now, I want to gather together all the foregoing details, all the trees so to speak, in order to ask: what sort of forest are we looking at here? What is the presupposition of all these details, and what is their cumulative effect? I have spoken of sociality as a theological conceptuality. It is that, and more— more than a set of ideas, beliefs. It is a fundamental orientation. And it is simultaneously a polemic. Positively it is an orientation to life *in the social, historical, natural-physical world*, theologically understood. The reality of which the Christian gospel speaks is, according to Bonhoeffer, embedded in this social, historical, sensual world. The reality of God, of

---

15. For a more detailed exposition see ibid., 190–97. See also the discussion of "Sin and Sociality" (200–203) and the discussion of orders of preservation (203–5).

16. While the Christology lectures in *DBWE* 12 are not only a new translation but also a new reconstruction of the lectures from student notes, the theological argument is essentially unchanged.

17. *DBWE* 12:314.

18. In Green, *Theology of Sociality*, see "The Sociality of the Present Christ" (211–20) and "Christ as Mediator" (220–33).

Christ, of the Spirit, is embedded in human historical sociality, above all (but not exclusively) in the community of faith and discipleship. Christ is present in the midst of this community. Negatively it is a polemic against any attempt, desire, or wish to find God, Christ, Spirit "outside" or "behind" this social, historical, natural nexus. Later in the article I will explore two writings where this "worldly" orientation is abundantly clear: first, in Bonhoeffer's polemic against "otherworldliness" in the 1932 address, "Thy Kingdom Come: The Prayer of the Church-Community for God's Kingdom on Earth," and second, in the prison letters where "worldliness" is constitutive of the nonreligious interpretation of biblical and theological concepts.

Transition to Discipleship

The thesis that Bonhoeffer's writings can be described as a "theology of sociality" and that this conceptuality is characteristic of his theology as a whole, notwithstanding the later developments in his thinking in the 1930s and especially in Tegel prison, was received favorably and appears to have gained wide acceptance. Having briefly reviewed the origin of this conceptuality in the dissertation and its articulation in following years, the question must now be posed: how does it relate to what comes later, particularly the "turning away from the phraseological to the real" that occurred in 1931–1932?[19] In 1971 I argued as follows. In his first writings, especially in *Act and Being*, Bonhoeffer reveals his preoccupation with a soteriological problem that is characteristically modern, the problem of power, that is, sin manifested in the exercise of power both personal and societal. This contrasts with the focus of soteriology in the medieval period,[20] and in Luther, which in shorthand can be called sin as guilt. Furthermore, the problem of power was not only an intellectual preoccupation for Bonhoeffer; it was also profoundly personal. Candid personal revelations matched with theological, philosophical, and ex-

---

19. Letter of April 22, 1944, Bonhoeffer, *Letters and Papers*, 275 (*DBWE* 8:358; translation mine). Cf. Green, *Theology of Sociality*, ch. 4.

20. Green, *Theology of Sociality*, 111. Soteriology is considered here from a psychological perspective. In Anselm, who formulated the classical medieval soteriology, the emphasis is objective, sin as objective offense to the honor of God, and the moral and spiritual necessity of either compensation (satisfaction) or punishment. The subjective manifestation as guilt grows out of the penitential piety as practiced both in the monastery and in parish life.

egetical texts disclose the autobiographical dimension of Bonhoeffer's theology. To summarize the personal aspect of the soteriological problem of power I spoke of the power of the dominating ego,[21] intending thereby to distinguish this characteristically modern phenomenon from its medieval-Reformation antecedent of guilt, especially in Luther.

In Bonhoeffer's academic and autobiographical texts the problem of the power of the ego has four main facets. The person he describes is first—and here I use the masculine intentionally—creator, interpreter, and ruler of his own world of which he is the center. Second, he dominates others, treating others as things and God as a "religious object." Not mutuality and self-giving but demanding and competition are typical of this person. Third, human sociality is violated, breaking community with God and others, throwing the self into "bleak isolation" and "eternal solitude." Fourth, conscience, rather than leading to a change of life, is *self*-accusation and *self*-exhortation and thus a means of self-assertion and self-justification.[22] In the autobiographical mode Bonhoeffer expresses all this as making the cause of Christ a vehicle for his own ambition, that is, using theology and the church to pursue a successful academic career that would meet personal goals and familial expectations.[23]

While I continue to hold that the portrait that Bonhoeffer draws in his discussions of sin has an autobiographical dimension, I want to stress here that my intention is certainly not psychological speculation or judgment about Bonhoeffer personally. My concern is theological, interpreting the cultural and psychological analysis presented in his writing. So I prefer to treat this portrait as a figure, an "ideal type," especially a type characteristic of modernity, just as Luther was characteristic of a late-medieval person.

So, how did I understand Bonhoeffer's "turning away from the phraseological to the real"[24] in light of his theology of sociality? The

21. For the definition of "ego" here see ibid., 109.

22. Ibid., 113–15. For the evidence in Bonhoeffer's texts summarized here, see 111–25.

23. Ibid., 141.

24. Bonhoeffer's phrase in his letter of April 22, 1944, "eine Abkehr vom Phraseologischen zum Wirklichen" (*DBW* 8:397); I use this phrase as the title of chapter 4 in *Theology of Sociality*, which interprets the phrase and assembles the evidence for the interpretation.

crux of my initial interpretation is that the isolated, dominant ego is simply at odds with the understanding of person and community set forth in Bonhoeffer's theology of sociality. To be sure, that conceptuality gives a central place for "sin and the broken community," but its theology of creation describes personal relations and community of mutuality, love, and freedom for others; and its presentation of the church is the new humanity that the Holy Spirit creates as a community of love (*Liebesgemeinschaft*) in which the members live in "active-being-for-one-another."[25] Therefore, what Bonhoeffer reveals of himself in his dissertations and autobiographical writings, let us say, is a person in contradiction of his own teaching. This I took as the impetus toward what Bonhoeffer retrospectively called "a great liberation."[26] Furthermore, I saw Bonhoeffer's resolution of the soteriological problem of power, theologically and personally, in two steps: initially in the book *Discipleship* and then in the prison letters. In both cases I spoke of a "Christological answer to the soteriological problem of power."[27] In *Discipleship*, I argued, "the predominant strain of the Christology . . . is the power and *authority* of Christ."[28] By submission to Christ Bonhoeffer sought to control and rein in the power of his own ego.[29] Concomitantly the book advocates the suppression of ego autonomy. But in the prison theology the Christology is a *theologia crucis*, stressing the weakness of Christ, and in those writings we find an affirmation of ego autonomy. Along these lines my interpretation highlighted problems in *Discipleship* such as the dominating figure of Christ, submissiveness urged on the disciples, contradictions in the Christology and anthropology, and violent language.[30]

Years later, however, a second and closer look at Bonhoeffer in the period beginning in 1931 led me to new insights about what he retrospectively called "turning away from the phraseological to the real."[31]

---

25. Ibid., 55; *DBWE* 1:178, 182.

26. Letter to Elizabeth Zinn, 1936 (*DBW* 14:113); quoted in Bethge, *Bonhoeffer: A Biography*, 205.

27. Green, *Theology of Sociality*, 138.

28. Ibid.

29. See the retrospective judgment in Bonhoeffer, *Letters and Papers*, 369, about "trying to live a holy life."

30. Green, *Theology of Sociality*, 170–79.

31. Bonhoeffer, *Letters and Papers*, 275.

That a closer look is necessary was perceptively suggested by George Hunsinger as early as 1980 in a review of the first edition. Hunsinger wrote: "It is one thing to argue, however, that the theme of sociality is 'presupposed' by *Nachfolge*, and quite another to contend that it is 'indispensable' to that work."[32] In other words, there is something else going on in *Discipleship* that cannot be deduced from or predicted by the theology of sociality—though it is not unrelated to it.

In this second look the focus falls more sharply on the integration of faith and life, the reciprocity of belief and behavior, and the personal authenticity and theological innovation this entails. One revisionist investigation of the year 1930–31 is Hans Pfeifer's essay about Bonhoeffer's postdoctoral year at Union Theological Seminary.[33] I have also examined this transition in the broader context of the surrounding years, 1928–1932, in my introduction to volume 10 of the *Dietrich Bonhoeffer Works*,[34] which confirms Pfeifer's interpretation.

Two very personal letters to intimates in which Bonhoeffer refers to the change in his life and theology that occurred in 1931–32 can serve as a focus. The first is his letter to Elizabeth Zinn in January 1936, in which he looks back to the years before Hitler. In this letter he speaks of the ambition that drove his work "in a very unchristian way." He had made into an opportunity for his own advancement the "cause of Jesus Christ"—theology, the church. He was liberated from this, he tells us, by "the Bible, especially the Sermon on the Mount." Consequently he committed himself to the church, which had formerly been a subject for academic discourse, so that from then on "the renewal of the church and the pastorate" became his passion. Significantly, for what in the thirties was central to his ecumenical work, he also explains that "Christian pacifism . . . suddenly became self-evident."[35]

The second letter is to Eberhard Bethge on July 21, 1944, the day after the final failed attempt to kill Hitler. This letter is intrinsically connected to the one a decade earlier that had mentioned both the

---

32. Hunsinger, Review. I still contend that it is indispensable, but it is more evident in the latter part of the book on the Pauline corpus than in the predominant section on the Sermon on the Mount and related Synoptic texts.

33. Pfeifer, "Learning Faith and Ethical Commitment."

34. See the "Editor's Introduction" in *DBWE* 10.

35. *DBW* 14:112ff.; quoted in Green, *Theology of Sociality*, 141. On "pacifism," see inter alia Green, "Pacifism and Tyrannicide."

Sermon on the Mount and his vocation in the church. In his 1944 letter Bonhoeffer refers to a conversation he had with Jean Lasserre in New York at Union Seminary in 1931, the second semester of the academic year.[36] Their discussion was about what they wanted to do with their lives. Bonhoeffer said that he "would like to learn to have faith."[37]

All the evidence about what learning to have faith meant points to discussions among the friends at Union about the Sermon on the Mount. What is the relation of faith and the commandments of Jesus?[38] Bonhoeffer goes on in the letter to say that he thought he could acquire faith by trying to live a holy life, and that he wrote *Discipleship* during that stage of his life. While that book, together with its companion *Life Together*, which reflects the practices of Finkenwalde, certainly includes the spiritual practices of biblical meditation and prayer, this does not minimize the Sermon on the Mount. It dominates the book. There we find detailed exposition of what it means to obey the commandments of Jesus in the Sermon on the Mount. And here the relation of faith and life, theology and ethics, gospel and commandment, is summarized in the axiom: Only the one who is obedient believes, and only the one who believes is obedient.[39] From 1931 through 1932 Bonhoeffer addressed his students in these terms and said that they could learn to have faith ("recognize Christian truth") by basing their lives completely on the word of Christ,[40] living a communal Christian life based on the Sermon on the Mount.

"Learning to have faith," then, is defined as learning to follow Jesus, *Nachfolge Christi*—that is, committing one's life to the way of Jesus and living by the Sermon on the Mount and his commands. It is striking

---

36. For one who was not always careful about dates and similar matters, it is significant that he bothers to say specifically "in America thirteen years ago." That means 1931. At the end of his first semester at Union, December 1930, he wrote to his friend Rössler that he was very depressed, saying that the church situation is desperate, and that his hope of finding a "cloud of witnesses" (Heb 12:1) in America has been "bitterly disappointed" (*DBWE* 10:261). The second semester—1931—brought a breakthrough.

37. Bonhoeffer, *Letters and Papers*, 369: "ich möchte glauben lernen" (*DBW* 8:542).

38. When Bonhoeffer reports Lasserre as saying he would like to become a saint, I take that as a reference to sanctification by Lasserre. He later said that he always wanted his life to accord with his convictions (cf. *DBW* 10:40–2). Lasserre wanted belief and behavior, faith and ethics, to be integrated.

39. *DBWE* 4:63; cf. esp. n. 16.

40. *DBWE* 10:36.

that faith here is not defined in the first place as justification by faith and forgiveness of sins. It means committing one's life to following in the way of Jesus.[41]

The liberating and formative new element that emerged in 1931–32, then, was Bonhoeffer's theological and personal wrestle with the question of the nature of faith, particularly the integration of belief and behavior, theology and ethics, gospel and commandment, as that confronted him above all in the words of Jesus in the Sermon on the Mount. This was fundamental to his theology during the Church Struggle and the Finkenwalde seminary. Retrospectively, and without being too precise as to date, Bonhoeffer was to look back from Tegel after his years in the conspiracy and say that the book *Discipleship*, published in 1937, marked the end of this stage of his life.[42]

Transition to the Prison Theology

As a transitional step at this juncture from what Bonhoeffer called the *Discipleship* period, and looking ahead to *Ethics* and especially the Tegel letters, it is revealing to examine the address "Thy Kingdom Come . . . on Earth"[43] that was given in November 1932. This means it was given within days of the address "Christ and Peace," the piece that presented in nuce the central ideas of *Discipleship*. If many readers for more than seventy years have read *Discipleship* as a call to scripture and personal piety, perhaps even as a call to a sectarian separation of the church from the world, "Thy Kingdom Come" is provocative because of its vigorous polemic against otherworldliness and its advocacy of a Christian

---

41. See Bonhoeffer's letter to Karl Barth of September 1936 reporting that he is working "above all on the interpretation of the Sermon on the Mount and the Pauline doctrine of justification and sanctification" (*DBW* 14:235–36). This is a fascinating letter, the first since receiving Barth's letter in London insisting he return to Berlin, and written some months after the letter to Elizabeth Zinn. He refers to his current work on *Nachfolge*, and says that he is wrestling with questions raised by the Bible that have been bothering him and that he is probably approaching them differently from Barth. "The whole period [the two years since he went to London]," Bonhoeffer tells Barth, "was basically a constant, silent controversy with you, and so I had to keep silent for a while" (Bonhoeffer, *Testament to Freedom*, 430).

42. Bonhoeffer, *Letters and Papers*, 369.

43. *DBWE* 12:285–97. The subtitle, rarely cited, is important especially for its concluding words, quoted from the Lord's Prayer: "The Prayer of the Church-Community for God's Kingdom on Earth."

worldliness over against a secularized Christianity. There must be, then, a prima facie compatibility between *Discipleship* and "Thy Kingdom Come ... on Earth."

Even more provocative is the fact that Bonhoeffer starts "Thy Kingdom Come ... on Earth" by an allusion to Nietzsche's polemic against otherworldliness in *Thus Spake Zarathustra*.[44] Beginning by accusing Christians of being either secularists or otherworldly, the word Bonhoeffer uses for "otherworldly" is Nietzsche's neologism "*Hinterweltler*." It is found in the section Kaufmann translates as "On the Afterworldly." While this invokes the English meaning of "afterworld," an attenuated world after death, it does not fully communicate Nietzsche's meaning. For he not only assembled a word that sounds like the German word for "back-woods people" (*Hinterwäldler*); above all, he is writing polemically about a "behind-world," an illusory world "behind" the real world. Bonhoeffer, who was well read in Nietzsche, picks up this polemical word and makes it his own.

One additional contextual point: this address is given during the time in 1932, in his second year of teaching and chaplaincy in Berlin, when Bonhoeffer is talking with his students about a residential community trying to live a Christian life guided by the Sermon on the Mount. In April he had said to his students at the Technical University that the way to recognize Christian truth is "solely through the free experiment in living, in once just basing one's life completely on the word of Christ, just to live totally with it, to live by it, to hear it, to obey it."[45] Now in November he addresses another group of students on the church's prayer for God's kingdom on earth. This is an interpretation of a prayer that such a community would pray.

---

44. Bonhoeffer's words here are Nietzsche's neologisms "*Hinterweltler*" and "*Hinterweltlertum*." See *DBW* 12:264–67; *DBWE* 12:285ff. translates "*Hinterweltler*" as "otherworldly," which is not incorrect but not as colorful as Nietzsche's allusion to "backwoods people." See Nietzsche, "On the Afterworldly," (in *Thus Spake Zarathustra*) cited in a different translation in *DBWE* 12:385 n. 2. For comment on the language see the German editors' afterword for *Creation and Fall* (*DBWE* 3), 164 nn. 69 and 70. When Kaufmann's version of Nietzsche earlier (p. 125) uses "otherworldly" to translate "*überirdischen*," it reminds one of how frequently Bonhoeffer uses the word "earth" in the sense of "loyalty to the earth," in "Thy Kingdom Come!"

45. *DBW* 11:415–16 (translation mine); Sermon at the Technical University at the opening of the semester, ca. April 15, 1932.

Bonhoeffer's targets are Christians: otherworldly Christians and secular Christians, and his polemics are aimed at both. Against both parties he asserts that belief in God's kingdom means loving "the Earth and God as one."[46] Consistently he states that God's world is dawning in *this* world, and that those who pray for the coming of God's kingdom do so only "as those who are wholly on the earth ... [in] the most profound solidarity with the world."[47] Even though both types of Christians, secular and otherworldly, are criticized by Bonhoeffer, nevertheless the otherworldly Christians who lust for the eternal hereafter come off worse in the polemics. At least the secularists are devoted to the world, even if they do not believe and pray, as Christians should, for "God's kingdom [which] is the *kingdom of resurrection* on Earth."[48] Bonhoeffer concludes by directing his hearers away from Nietzsche's "afterworld" to the twofold form of God's kingdom on earth, church and state as orders of preservation.

From this analysis I draw several conclusions. First, Bonhoeffer rejects otherworldliness in favor of faithful Christian life in loyalty to the world and the cultivation of an authentic Christian worldliness. Second, secularism, for Bonhoeffer, even Christian secularism, is not an appropriate form of Christian worldliness. Third, since these sentiments are contemporaneous with the germination of *Discipleship*, they should be read as compatible with it. The theology of the latter should not be read as otherworldly, escapist, or divorced from concern with the National Socialist context,[49] but should be understood as forming a strong Christian identity—ecclesial and personal—for nurturing faithful life in the political and ecclesial world in which Bonhoeffer lived. Finally, this address prepares the way for a full-blooded affirmation of a Christian worldliness implicitly in *Ethics* and explicitly and programmatically in *Letters and Papers from Prison*.

---

46. *DBWE* 12:286.
47. *DBWE* 12:288–89.
48. Ibid., 291 (Bonhoeffer's italics).
49. See the article of Martin Onnasch arguing that *Discipleship* should be understood as responding "much more strongly to the challenges from the national socialist ideology than is often assumed" ("Zeitgemässe Theologie?," 218).

Worldliness in *Letters and Papers from Prison*

The topic of "worldliness" or "worldly," normally expressed in the words "*Weltlichkeit*" and "*weltlich*," really comes to the fore in the prison theology.[50] While over the years there has been much discussion about what Bonhoeffer meant by "religionlessness" and "non-religious," as in "religionless Christianity" and "non-religious interpretation," far too little attention has been paid in the English literature to what he meant by "worldly" and "worldliness." In the first place, this is because the German word "*weltlich*" was wrongly translated by "secular," and everybody thought they knew what that meant and interpreted Bonhoeffer accordingly.[51] But in fact Bonhoeffer hardly mentioned the word "*säkular*" in *Letters and Papers from Prison*,[52] and he never used it to describe his proposal for a "non-religious interpretation of Biblical and theological concepts." This is consistent with the fact that in his 1932 address, "Thy Kingdom Come," he clearly distinguished his own orientation to the world from Christian secularists.

---

50. In an early comment on Genesis 1:28, Bonhoeffer says that God's blessing and command to fill the earth and rule it "affirms humankind wholly within the world of the living ... It is humankind's whole empirical existence that is blessed here, its creatureliness, its worldliness [*Weltlichkeit*], its earthliness" (*DBWE* 3:68). This is consistent with major points in his theological anthropology, which stresses, within sociality, both the historicity (temporality, living through time, and decision) and the natural-bodily character of human existence.

51. The *DBWE* edition of *Letters and Papers from Prison*, published in 2010, has corrected this grave misinterpretation of Bonhoeffer. The old English edition repeatedly used the word "secular" to translate "*weltlich*." For example: "How do we speak ... in a 'secular' way about 'God'? In what way are we 'religionless-secular' Christians ... ?" (Bonhoeffer, *Letters and Papers*, 280; *DBW* 8:405). Again, "it's time to say something concrete about the secular interpretation of biblical concepts" (ibid., 346; *DBW* 8:512). Or again, the first section of Chapter Two of his "Outline for a Book," on "Weltlichkeit und Gott," is translated "God and the secular" (ibid., 381; *DBW* 8:558). In every one of these cases, and others, Bonhoeffer's own word is "*weltlich*," "worldly," or some variant of it. For more comment on this translation problem and its problems in its historical context, see my "Bonhoeffer's Quest for Authentic Christianity." In that essay I also comment on the distinction between Bonhoeffer's attitude to secular developments in a "world come of age" and his proposal for "non-religious interpretation"—the latter does not entail the secularization of Christianity.

52. The word "*säkular*" appears in only one paragraph, where Bonhoeffer speaks of existentialists and psychotherapists as "the secularized offshoots of Christian theology" (Bonhoeffer, *Letters and Papers*, 326; *DBW* 8:478).

In fact, the idea of "worldliness," or "the worldly," is a crucial part of Bonhoeffer's post-religion project in the *Letters and Papers*.[53] Indeed, he uses the term explicitly to describe his proposal, sometimes speaking of *non-religious* or *religionless* interpretation and other times simply of *worldly* interpretation.[54] Significantly, the adjective "worldly" is used almost as often to describe the project as the word "non-religious." Even more revealing, on two occasions he hyphenates the two words, showing that they are equivalent: on one occasion the phrase is "religionless-worldly Christians" and in the other "worldly-non-religious interpretation."[55]

Careful comparison of these two phrases reveals another important insight about Bonhoeffer's project. The adjective "non-religious" is his negative and polemical description of it, while "worldly" is the positive and affirmative description. In the very first sketch of his project, the letter of 30 April 1944, Bonhoeffer asks: "In what way are we 'religionless-worldly' ['*religionslos-weltlich*'] Christians . . . ?"[56] Here the negative and positive equivalence of the two terms, the two sides of the one thing, is self-evident.

What then does "worldly" mean? Clearly not the "shallow and banal this-worldliness [*Diesseitigkeit*] of the enlightened, the busy, the comfortable, or the lascivious, but the profound this-worldliness, characterized by discipline and the constant knowledge of death and resurrection."[57] The profound Christian worldliness, grounded in the

---

53. Another term Bonhoeffer used to mean the same as "worldly" is "*Diesseitigkeit*," which is rightly translated "this-worldliness" since its literal emphasis on "this-sidedness" is a polemic against otherworldliness (Bonhoeffer, *Letters and Papers*, 369–70; *DBW* 8:541–42). Cf. also *DBW* 8:501; Bonhoeffer, *Letters and Papers*, 337, here translated "this world."

54. For "religionless" or "non-religious" see Bonhoeffer, *Letters and Papers*, 282, 285, 328, 362; for "worldly" see ibid., 280, 286, 346, 379.

55. Ibid., 280, 379; *DBW* 8:405 ("'*religionlos-weltlich*' *Christen*"), 546 ("*weltliche nicht-religiöse Interpretation*").

56. Ibid.; *DBW* 8:405. The same double formulation is also found in *Letters and Papers*, 379 (there translated correctly for once as "worldly, non-religious interpretation"); *DBW* 8:546. In the latter (and also in *DBWE* 8:490), an editorial note reveals how Bonhoeffer unintentionally stressed the equivalence of the two terms by first writing "worldly interpretation of Christian concepts" and later after "worldly" inserting "non-religious."

57. Bonhoeffer, *Letters and Papers*, 369.

gospel of Christ, is contrasted to an otherworldly type of Christianity. This is clearly evident in the *Letters*, as in statements like the following:

> I am thinking about how the concepts of repentance, faith, justification, rebirth, and sanctification should be reinterpreted in a "worldly" sense—in the Old Testament sense and in the sense of John 1:14.[58]

> God's "beyond" is not the beyond of our cognitive faculties. The transcendence of epistemological theory has nothing to do with the transcendence of God. God is beyond in the midst of our life.[59]

> Unlike believers in the redemption myths, Christians do not have an ultimate escape route out of their earthly tasks and difficulties into eternity ... This-worldliness must not be abolished ahead of its time; on this the NT and OT are united.[60]

> Christianity has always been regarded as a religion of redemption. But isn't this a cardinal error, which separates Christ from the Old Testament and interprets him along the lines of the myths about redemption? ... The redemption myths try unhistorically to find an eternity after death ... Redemption in that case means redemption from cares, distress, fears, and longings, from sin and death, in a better world beyond the grave. But is this really the essential character of the proclamation of Christ in the gospels and by Paul? I should say it is not. The difference between the Christian hope of resurrection and the mythological hope of resurrection is that the former sends people back to their life on the earth in a wholly new way.[61]

Probably the sharpest statement about worldliness qua "*Diesseitigkeit*" is found in the letter of May 5, 1944, where Bonhoeffer asks about God's righteousness and the Kingdom of God on earth:

> Does the question of saving one's soul even come up in the Old Testament? Isn't God's righteousness and kingdom on earth the center of everything? And isn't Rom 3:24ff. the culmination of the view that God alone is righteous, rather than an individualistic doctrine of salvation? What matters is not the beyond

58. *DBWE* 8:373, cf. *Letters and Papers*, 286.
59. Bonhoeffer, *Letters and Papers*, 282.
60. Ibid., 337, in the translation of *DBWE* 8:447–48.
61. Ibid., 336; translation revised.

[*Jenseits*] but this world, how it is created and preserved, is given laws, reconciled, and renewed. What is beyond this world is meant, in the gospel, to be there *for* this world ... in the biblical sense of the creation and the incarnation, crucifixion, and resurrection of Jesus Christ.[62]

This is a powerful statement about the presence and activity of God *in the temporal, historical, social, physical world*. It slams the door on pious otherworldly escapism.

In sum, the prison theology carries forward and elaborates the polemic against religious otherworldliness that was so vigorous in the address "Thy Kingdom Come ... on Earth" in 1932. From the passages cited above we have to conclude that this polemic is intensified in the letters so that the alternative Christianity Bonhoeffer is advocating, the non-religious Christianity, is radically intra-worldly, embedded in the social, historical, natural world.

I suspect that there are at least two reasons why worldliness and the attack on otherworldliness in *Letters and Papers from Prison* have not been recognized in their full radicality. The first is the problem of translation, already mentioned. The words "worldly" and "worldliness" simply disappeared when they were translated by "secular" or some variant of it. The second is that, because everybody noticed that a critique of otherworldliness was part of Bonhoeffer's critique of religion, attention was not given to the problem of otherworldliness as a theme in its own right; it was subsumed under the discussion of religion and religionless Christianity and thereby blurred and obscured.[63]

Certainly there is a need to parse more fully the different dimensions in the meaning of "worldly." That has not been undertaken here. Important in that task is public theology, especially as practiced in *Ethics*; those issues of history, society, natural rights, culture, law, and goodness discussed in *Ethics* accompanied Bonhoeffer to prison and

---

62. Translation in the forthcoming *DBWE* 8:372–73 (Bonhoeffer's italics). Cf. *Letters and Papers*, 286; *DBW* 8:415. The reference to Romans 3:24ff. is provocative since this is the passage Luther understood as the *locus classicus* for the doctrine of justification by faith and therefore as a doctrine of personal salvation. For comparisons of Bonhoeffer and Luther see the index in Green, *Theology of Sociality*, and my essay "Bonhoeffer in the Context of Erikson's Luther Study."

63. It may also be that debate about the topic "world come of age" confused the discussion of what Bonhoeffer meant by a "worldly" interpretation of biblical and theological concepts.

were not abandoned when he took up his new theological project.[64] But first it has been necessary to address the polemic against otherworldliness in its own right, and likewise to recognize that worldliness—not secularity—is the positive category in that project.

Looking now at the whole, from the first articulation of the theology of sociality in the dissertation to the radical worldliness of the letters, another result comes into focus: the theology of sociality and the affirmation of worldliness are two ways of making the same point. Worldliness is the explicit content and the implicit polemic in the theology of sociality. Sociality is about worldliness: God encountered in human relationships and communities—not anywhere else—as spelled out in the theological paragraphs above.[65] Another way to say it: the theology of sociality requires the polemic against otherworldliness; the polemic against otherworldliness protects the theology of sociality.

In conclusion I must emphatically point to the theological ground of this worldly sociality: *the Christology of the God who became human in Jesus Christ, the Menschgewordene.* For Jesus Christ is the name of the God whom Bonhoeffer described in *Act and Being* as "free for humanity."[66] Bonhoeffer is not talking about a secularized Christianity, or the triumph of Feuerbach and Nietzsche. Ever since his 1933 lectures on Christology he had consistently used the terms *Menschgewordene* and *Menschwerdung*,[67] stressing that God had become not only truly flesh and blood but really, fully, and truly *human*. And that human Jesus, of whose freedom for others he wrote in his last writings, is the paradigm and promise of authentic human being and sociality. At the heart of Bonhoeffer's Christian humanism and his worldly, non-religious Christianity is John 1:14.

---

64. I have discussed this briefly in "Bonhoeffer's Quest," 348–49. It should be emphasized that Bonhoeffer regarded the Tegel project of religionless-worldly interpretation of biblical and theological concepts as a "prelude" and "anticipation" of *Ethics*; cf. *Letters and Papers*, 394 and *DBWE* 8:518.

65. See above, 88–89, esp. the summaries about Christology, creation, etc.

66. See above, 88.

67. God "become human," God's "becoming human." These terms are preferred to "*Fleischwerdung*," "becoming flesh," and "*Inkarnation*."

5

Community Turned Inside Out

Dietrich Bonhoeffer's Concept of the Church and of Humanity Reconsidered

Kirsten Busch Nielsen

THE BACKBONE OF DIETRICH BONHOEFFER'S THEOLOGY IS CHRISTOLOgy. If one sees Bonhoeffer's writings as the attempt to unfold, in a contemporary context, the meaning of believing and confessing the lordship of Jesus Christ, undoubtedly one has a good grasp of the core intention of his theology.

But it must be added that more specifically Bonhoeffer—without separating the person of Christ from the work of Christ—lets Christology take its point of departure in soteriology. Paul's words in 2 Corinthians that God reconciled us to himself through Christ and gave us the ministry of reconciliation (2 Cor 5:18–19) play a central role in Bonhoeffer's writings. Bonhoeffer emphasizes that it is God who reconciles the world to himself and that, as a consequence, "[n]ow there is no longer any reality, any world, that is not reconciled with God and at peace. God has done that in the beloved son, Jesus Christ."[1] That reconciliation *has* taken place and that this must throw light on every part of theology is a strong conviction in Bonhoeffer's own theology, which has Christology as its center.

Further, Christology in Bonhoeffer's theology is surrounded by an ellipse. One focus of this ellipse is anthropology, which must ask: "Who is the human being?" The other focus is ecclesiology, which has to ask: "What is the church?" Bonhoeffer relates these questions and his answers to them to each other. That Bonhoeffer combines his understand-

---

1. *DBWE* 6:83.

ing of the human being and his understanding of the church should not surprise anyone. Of course theology's interpretation of the human being in creation, fall, and reconciliation must be related to the church as the community of believers.

What is surprising in Bonhoeffer is the very strong interest he has in ecclesiology and the way his understanding of the church is influenced by his anthropology (including his understanding of sin). Historically, Bonhoeffer's doctoral dissertation, *Sanctorum Communio* (1927/1930), marks a milestone in Protestant ecclesiology of the early and mid twentieth century. Bonhoeffer not only aimed at studying the sociology of the church theologically, in itself an innovative step. But at the same time he also claimed that "it would be good for once if a presentation of doctrinal theology were to start not with the doctrine of God but with the doctrine of the church."[2] In a way, this is how the argument of *Sanctorum Communio* is actually arranged. With its main chapters on "The Primal State and the Problem of Community," "Sin and Broken Community," and "Sanctorum Communio," the concluding part of which is called "Church and Eschatology," the book presents itself as Bonhoeffer's own presentation of doctrinal theology, his own "church dogmatics," in the sense that the book is formed as a brief but comprehensive exposition of Christian doctrine. That this exposition of Christian doctrine is to a large extent specifically an exposition of a theological anthropology is clear already from the wording of the headings, which stress concepts such as "community" and "sin."

Bonhoeffer scholarship has paid extensive attention both to his ecclesiology and to his theological anthropology.[3] What I aim at here is to give an account of the relationship between the two. In order not to lose myself in details, I shall restrict myself thematically to a very brief outline of both Bonhoeffer's understanding of church and his understanding of humankind, leaving aside the theological and philosophical complexity of his argument. Furthermore I shall for the sake of clarity limit myself almost exclusively to Bonhoeffer's first book, *Sanctorum Communio*. What I want to focus on is the interrelatedness of the no-

---

2. DBWE 1:134.

3. See, e.g., Soosten, *Die Sozialität der Kirche*; Gutter, *Innerste Konzentration*; Gerlach, *"Bekenntnis und Bekennen der Kirche"*; Class, *Der verzweifelte Zugriff*; Nielsen, *Syndens brudte magt*.

tions of church and of humankind in Bonhoeffer's theology as put forward in *Sanctorum Communio*.

In his theological argumentation, Bonhoeffer undertakes a double move. First, we shall see how Bonhoeffer's ecclesiology leads to anthropology; second, how his anthropology leads back to his understanding of church.

From Bonhoeffer's Ecclesiology to His Anthropology

Bonhoeffer's proposal that one should "start with the doctrine of the church" reveals the maximalism (rather than minimalism) of his ecclesiology—as does his conviction that "the church is God's new will and purpose for humanity."[4] But Bonhoeffer's maximalist ecclesiology is balanced by his strong critique of church and of religion, which shows his profile as both a traditional and a modern Protestant theologian.[5]

This balance (or better perhaps: this tension) in Bonhoeffer's understanding of the church has to do with the relation between what is traditionally considered the church's visibility and its invisibility, a concept also used by Bonhoeffer.[6] For Bonhoeffer, the "invisible" church *is* at the same time the "visible" church. It is of great theological importance, he thinks, to consider the outward and thus visible form of the church as a necessary part of the church as such. The church as an organization, i.e., "the empirical church," and the church in its being, "the essential church," is inseparable.[7] This does not mean that the church is not an invisible being, too. As the body of Christ it is invisible: "The church is visible as a corporate social body in worship and in working-for-each-other. It is invisible as an eschatological entity, as the 'body of Christ.'"[8] And yet, on the other hand, invisibility is too much for the Christian, as Bonhoeffer explains in a letter to a friend in 1931. He nearly sighs, this statement shows, for a not-only-invisible content of faith and theology: "The invisibility is destroying us . . . This crazy, relentless being thrown

---

4. *DBWE* 1:141.

5. Cf. my article "Critique of Church."

6. Cf. ibid., 330–31. My rather positive assessment of visible-invisible in Bonhoeffer is contradicted by, e.g., Hegstad, *Den virkelige kirke*, 91–93. For a recent discussion of visibility-invisibility as a still promising challenge to ecclesiology, see Grosshans, *One Holy, Catholic and Apostolic Church*.

7. *DBWE* 1:217.

8. Ibid., 141.

back to the invisible God himself—no human being can endure that any longer."[9]

The tension between visible and invisible is the background against which Bonhoeffer explains how he understands the church. Over the years, he describes in slightly differing ways the church as God's revelation in the world—i.e., as the revelation of Christ—or as the place of God's revelation in the world. He focuses on baptism, the Word, and the Eucharist (in this very order) as *notae ecclesiae*. He underlines that the church is *sanctorum communio*. Through the notion of vicarious representative action (German: *Stellvertretung*), he ties ecclesiology and Christology so closely to each other that one cannot but consider it an identification—an *asymmetric* identification, but nevertheless an identification.[10] Combining such dogmatic understandings of the church with social philosophy and sociology of the 1920s and applying insights from both Martin Luther and Friedrich Schleiermacher, Bonhoeffer argues that the church more than anything else must be seen as a community. Community is not just inward and invisible. Any theological interpretation of the church as a community, he claims, has to include the actual, empirical, outward, and visible structures of community. The church is neither *just* invisible nor *just* a visible religious community or public organization.

According to Bonhoeffer, the church considers "the fact of Christ, or the 'Word'" to be constitutive for itself in its self-understanding, namely, as a visible-invisible community.[11] The Word establishes "the logical and sociological unity . . . of the essential and the empirical, 'invisible' and 'visible' church."[12] Thus, the church is in all of its dimensions created by the Word—the church both as the invisible body of Christ and as a social community. In short, that the church is a community and therefore must be interpreted in the category of sociality is due to the Word. Bonhoeffer's ecclesiology in this way leads to and implies a theory of human sociality as well as an anthropology.

---

9. Letter to Helmut Rössler, October 10, 1931, in *DBW* 11:32–34; 33 (my translation).
10. Cf. Abraham, "Wort und Sakrament," 150.
11. *DBWE* 1:126.
12. Ibid., 220–21.

From Bonhoeffer's Anthropology to His Ecclesiology

In his exegesis of the Biblical account of creation and fall and his understanding of humankind as created in the image of God and as fallen (whatever that means) into sin, Bonhoeffer consistently stresses the category of sociality. What it means to be created in the image of God and what it means to be a sinner can, according to Bonhoeffer, most adequately be understood through the category of human sociality.[13]

Bonhoeffer claims not only that human beings are created into community with God and with each other. He also understands these two dimensions of what it means to be human to be simultaneous. Neither one of them precedes the other: "Community with God by definition establishes social community as well. It is not that the community with God subsequently leads to social community; rather, neither exists without the other."[14]

This strong underlining of community in Bonhoeffer's anthropology, however, is not at the sacrifice of individuality. On the contrary, Bonhoeffer considers individuality and community as interdependent in the way that being an individual person implies being a person in relation to others and vice versa: "[I]n some way the individual belongs essentially and absolutely with the other, according to God's will."[15] In Christian theology, Bonhoeffer argues, the notion of personhood is not a notion of individual subjectivity, but of intersubjectivity and sociality.[16]

This applies not only to Bonhoeffer's account of creation, but also to his account of sin. After the fall, the original relations of creation between "I" and "you" and between "I" and humankind as such are changed. As a consequence of sin or as an expression of sin, love is replaced by egoism. An originally "giving" relation between human beings has been superseded by a "purely demanding" relation.[17] Conscience—which according to Bonhoeffer's negative interpretation belongs more to fallen humankind than to creation—has made its entry.

---

13. For a detailed account of Bonhoeffer's understanding of sin in both early and late writings, see my *Syndens brudte magt*.

14. *DBWE* 1:63.

15. Ibid., 56.

16. Cf. ibid., 45–46, 50.

17. Ibid., 108.

In many respects, Bonhoeffer's interpretation of creation and sin is quite traditional. Fundamentally, sin is unbelief, Bonhoeffer claims. This notion of sin is one of the constants in Bonhoeffer's theology from *Sanctorum Communio* to *Letters and Papers from Prison*. In the early writings, Bonhoeffer's linking together of sin and unbelief manifests itself in his interpretation in *Act and Being* of Martin Luther's statement "sola fide credendum est nos esse peccatores."[18] With Luther, Bonhoeffer claims that human knowledge of sin is a matter of faith: "Only to faith, in revelation, do we have access to the knowledge that we are sinners in the wholeness of our being."[19] Thus, Bonhoeffer's different definitions of sin are congruent with unbelief in the sense that they have to do with the relation between the human person and God.[20] At the same time, these definitions do express the changes and movements in Bonhoeffer's writings through the years. One of these definitions is sin as loneliness and isolation. Bonhoeffer translates his traditional Lutheran understanding of sin into this specific interpretation of sin that is based on his understanding of the human person as a social being, someone whose identity is bound to his or her relation to other human beings.

This train of thought provides the background for Bonhoeffer's effort to understand together "the culpability of the individual and the universality of sin."[21] According to Bonhoeffer, the conceptual connection between individual guilt and universal sin must, however, also include universal *guilt*, i.e., "the culpability of the human race."[22] Not only sin is universal; guilt is, too. The idea that "the individual culpable act and the culpability of the human race"[23] are related to each other is, Bonhoeffer claims, one of Luther's hamartiological convictions. Luther, Bonhoeffer says, "maintains that sin is simultaneously inexcusable and

---

18. Cf. *DBWE* 2:136–37, 143–44. Cf. Luther, *Lectures on Romans*, 215.

19. *DBWE* 2:137.

20. Without claiming that the list is complete, I would suggest that Bonhoeffer through the years defines sin as unbelief, disobedience, breach of the law, self-justification, idolatry, godlessness, and perversion (cf. *curvatio*)—with unbelief as the most basic definition. Cf. my *Syndens brudte magt*, 159–74.

21. *DBWE* 1:110.

22. Ibid.

23. Ibid.

universal [. . . whereas] Protestant orthodoxy [. . . did] not succeed in preserving this."[24]

The universality of sin and thus its unavoidability has been dealt with in tradition by means of the doctrine of original sin, *peccatum haereditarium* or *peccatum originale/peccatum radicale*—the latter term being the one preferred by Protestant theology because it stresses that sin influences all human beings universally, while also influencing each individual deeply and radically. Bonhoeffer underlines that the universality of sin in the first sense should not excuse or explain the sin and guilt of the individual, i.e., sin in the second sense.

Thus, in order to cover the issue of sin, as Bonhoeffer must do since he designs his ecclesiology in *Sanctorum Communio* as an exposition of Christian doctrine from creation to eschaton, he has to "expose the new social basic-relations between I and You, as well as between I and humanity."[25] The new social relations bring along the perversion or distortion of the original social relations. Community collapses. The individual becomes totally isolated. But since personal sin is both individual and universal, Bonhoeffer must conclude that "recognition of one's *utter solitude* leads to the other insight, namely the *broadest sense of shared sinfulness*, so that by our very nature the 'one' is led to the 'other.'"[26] It is of great importance, then, how the social dimension of human identity is reflected in Bonhoeffer's notion of individual, personal sin. According to Bonhoeffer, the doctrine of original sin is simply the theological elaboration of "the social significance of sin."[27]

Bonhoeffer underlines that "the social element [. . . is] not excluded, but posited simultaneously" with the individuality of the sinner.[28] When the individual person turns himself or herself against God in the sinful act, this is simultaneously an unexplainable and inexcusable act of the individual *and* an act of humankind. Humankind is present in the individual. It is, as Bonhoeffer suggests, a matter of representation. This is how the individual, personal guilt and the universality of sin are related to each other. The stronger the presence is of the

---

24. Ibid., 113.
25. Ibid., 107.
26. Ibid., 109.
27. Ibid.
28. Ibid., 114.

individual in the act of guilt, the stronger is also the presence of humankind. It applies to Adam as well as to anybody else that "[w]hen, in the sinful act, the individual spirit rises up against God, thus climbing to the utmost height of spiritual individuality ... [,] the deed committed is at the same time *the deed of the human race ... in the individual person.*"[29] The individual person's experience and awareness of oneself as *peccator pessimus* is closely related to his or her "experience of ethical solidarity."[30] Thus, the subject of sin is both the individual and "the human race,"[31] but the latter only "'in' individuals."[32] Just as an individual is a person in the strict sense of the word, a community of subjects, according to Bonhoeffer, can be a person. A people, a married couple, a family, a friendship, and the church can be looked on as a "collective person," with whom "there is a will of God ... just as with individuals."[33] Also humanity in its sinfulness must be regarded as a collective person. This notion, collective person, has to solve the problem that was left unsolved by the doctrine of original sin in its traditional form, namely, how to encompass two points: (1) that sin is universal and (2) that sin, in its universality, is connected with guilt.

One may consider the representation Bonhoeffer aims at here a turned-inside-out-representation. It is a turned-inside-out-representation when the individual sinful person recognizes himself or herself as sinful humanity, a non-community. For one of the consequences of sin is that the individual is isolated from others and that his or her relation to others is perverted. So, one must ask Bonhoeffer, how is it possible that the individual sinful person in his or her loneliness can represent the others, and how is it possible that the community of sinners can be just that: a community? Bonhoeffer has an open eye for this paradox. He does not dissolve the paradox but leaves it as it stands with the following commentary: "The structure of humanity-in-Adam is unique because it is both composed of many isolated individuals and yet is one, as the humanity that has sinned as a whole."[34]

29. Ibid., 115.
30. Ibid., 116.
31. Ibid., 118.
32. Ibid., 119.
33. Ibid.
34. Ibid., 121.

Humanity-in-Adam is unique because of its self-contradiction: a personal community of isolated individuals.[35] Both *because of* and *in spite of* the sinful perversion of human relations and the isolation of the individual, humanity-in-Adam is a collective person. This only makes sense under the circumstance of sin.

Our considerations have come full circle. It is time to turn again to Bonhoeffer's ecclesiology. His interpretation of humanity-in-Adam lays the foundation of the interpretation of the church as "the humanity of the new Adam,"[36] i.e., as a new community of human beings. It was God's reconciliation in Christ to himself of the world that brought about this new humanity. What is important to bear in mind is that the humanity-in-Adam lives on in this new humanity of the new Adam. There is a simultaneity, a *simul*, between the humanity-in-Adam and the humanity-in-Christ.

The church as the new humanity is founded or, as Bonhoeffer says, *established* through Christ's vicarious representative action: "In vicarious representative action for all he fulfils the law by love,"[37] and the "person of Christ must ... unite all individuals in himself, and act before God as their vicarious representative."[38] Furthermore, the mutual vicarious representative action of the members of the church according to Bonhoeffer *actualizes* the church as a "community of spirit" (German: *Geistgemeinschaft*).[39] The close connection between Christology and ecclesiology is still maintained at this point in the argument. Thus, the traditional interpretation of the community and of the church as the body of Christ is echoed. It is as the body of Christ that the community and the church are involved in the representative vicarious action.

---

35. For a critique of Bonhoeffer's use of the concept of the collective person about humanity-in-Adam, see Brandt, "'Christus als Gemeinde existierend'?," 173–75. Brandt's specific critique is relevant. But in itself it is also a demonstration of the remarkable and almost self-contradictory character of the sinful humanity-in-Adam; cf. the quotation above about the unique structure of humanity-in-Adam (*DBWE* 1:121). Christiane Tietz-Steiding has mentioned a similar critique of Bonhoeffer's notion of the individual person (Is the *homo peccator* to be considered a *person*?) in *Bonhoeffers Kritik der verkrümmten Vernunft*, 165, 269.

36. *DBWE* 1:142.

37. Ibid., 148.

38. Ibid. For the relation between Christology and ecclesiology, see also Bonhoeffer's Christology lecture in *DBW* 12:239–303, 266–69.

39. *DBWE* 1:178–92, 261.

How Bonhoeffer understands this is evident not only in *Sanctorum Communio* and other early writings, but also in *The Cost of Discipleship* from 1937. Here Bonhoeffer states that "[s]uch vicariously representative action and suffering, which is carried out by the members of the body of Christ, is itself the very life of Christ who seeks to take shape in his members (Gal 4:19)."[40]

Concluding Remarks

One of the challenges or provocations of Bonhoeffer's theology is that, through his theological ellipse, anthropology and ecclesiology, he makes visible some aspects of Christian theology that are often just assumed and not spoken of and not thought through. Bonhoeffer's double move has consequences for both anthropology and ecclesiology. In these concluding remarks, however, I shall only focus on ecclesiology.

Bonhoeffer's understanding of the church is sophisticated and marked by tension. It reflects the twofold idea of the church as *sanctorum* community and *peccatorum* community, both aspects encompassing the so-called visibility as well as the invisibility of the church. And furthermore, it includes Bonhoeffer's account of the Christian doctrine of man, i.e., his claim that there is an interdependence between the human person's individuality and his or her sociality, an interdependence that plays a role in creation, sin, and reconciliation and thus in both aspects of the church. Bonhoeffer recognizes, however, that this role is played out in different ways in creation and reconciliation and thus also in different ways in the church as *sanctorum communio* and *peccatorum communio*. Should *peccatorum communio* be thought of as a community or shouldn't it rather be conceived as a community turned-inside-out? For the sake of clarity I shall venture to sketch the outline of Bonhoeffer's ecclesiology in *Sanctorum Communio* as follows, even if I run the risk of simplifying matters and leaving out of consideration important questions (especially concerning Bonhoeffer's notion of faith, of knowledge of sin, and of forgiveness of sin):

---

40. *DBWE* 4:222.

Sanctorum Communio	*Peccatorum Communio*
The church as community	The church as community turned-inside-out
The individual person	The sinful individual person
The personality of the individual in interdependence with sociality	Perversion of the relation between individual personality and sociality
Community with other human beings/ community with God in Christ	Isolation from other human beings/ isolation from God
The reconciled individual person/the reconciled humanity, humanity-in-Christ	The turned-inside-out community of sinful individuals as humanity-in-Adam

Any contemporary systematic reflection on the identity and the task of the church must take into account other and more questions and issues than Bonhoeffer does in his writings on the church, including *Sanctorum Communio*, and must of course also choose other philosophical and sociological sources of inspiration than those chosen by Bonhoeffer in the late 1920s. Thus, today, not many will dispute a claim like Bonhoeffer's that the individuality and sociality of the human person are in some way or other interwoven. But, theologically, the possibilities offered by Bonhoeffer's early ecclesiological works are still promising. Bonhoeffer succeeds in putting forward a theory of the church that holds together both negative and affirmative aspects. Retaining the notion of sin that he does, namely, sin as unbelief manifesting itself in the isolation of the individual and thus perverting the relation between individuality and sociality, Bonhoeffer is able to work together in a coherent whole the church in its empirical or visible and its essential or invisible form. Thus, Bonhoeffer does *not simply exclude* from ecclesiology what the church is not or what it should not be (although his theology at the same time does imply such a critique of the church), *nor* does he *simply repeat* the *simul justus et peccator* (which on the other hand certainly is an important part of Bonhoeffer's theological background and horizon). Not many Protestant ecclesiologies are as complex as Bonhoeffer's and thereby as well protected "from inside" against sliding into one-sidedness.

6

The Narrow Path

Sociality, Ecclesiology, and the Polyphony of Life in the Thought of Dietrich Bonhoeffer

Barry Harvey

DIETRICH BONHOEFFER CONCLUDES THE PREFACE TO *DISCIPLESHIP* with a comment which, though in its immediate setting refers to the decision of the Confessing Church to resist incorporation into the Reich Church, sets the appropriate context for assessing the contribution of his theology to the question of sociality: "Today it seems so difficult to walk with certainty the narrow path of the church's decision and yet remain wide open to Christ's love for all people, and in God's patience, mercy and loving-kindness (Titus 3:4) for the weak and godless. Still, both must remain together, or else we will follow merely human paths."[1] From *Sanctorum Communio* to his prison writings, Bonhoeffer presupposes an ecclesial locus when reflecting on the social nature of human beings. To be sure, his understanding of the essential character of the church changes over time in response to extraordinary circumstances, but to the last it remains central to his thinking about the social character of human existence before God.

In what follows I argue, first, that from beginning to end, ecclesiology is at the heart of Bonhoeffer's social thought and can in no wise be viewed as dependent on a prior theory of sociality per se, especially in the sense that most of what can be known about social processes in general, or the social and historical aspects of the church in particular, must first be gleaned from the social sciences or social philosophy, and only then can theologians work out whatever questions or problems

1. *DBWE* 4:40.

remain.[2] When we look closely at Bonhoeffer's writings, beginning with *Sanctorum Communio*, we see that it is the concern with a proper understanding of the church that generates the need, first, for the theological concept of sociality and, second, for an inquiry into the relationship of theology to social philosophy and sociology, resulting finally in a theology that positions the deliverances of these disciplines in relation to basic Christological and eschatological concerns. The church is thus the interpretive context for Bonhoeffer's social thought. Simply put, the church is not an instantiation or illustration of a prior concept of sociality per se but instead forms the hermeneutical standpoint from which he interprets human words and actions, both personal and social, as either open to or closed off from the coming of Christ, a position that he consistently maintains throughout his career.

Second, I dispute the contention of some that Bonhoeffer relaxes the connection between Christ and the church in his later prison correspondence in order to embrace completely and unreservedly a world come of age. This position does not accurately reflect the fullness of Bonhoeffer's own statements on this subject; moreover, it is theologically unsound, reflecting the recurring temptation in modern theology to "naturalize the supernatural,"[3] or as Bonhoeffer might put it, to erase the distinction between the penultimate and the ultimate. Among its many problems, such a move gives rise to the specter of a renewed supersessionism.

Finally, I argue that in a world that presumptively compliments itself on having brought the human species to maturity, Bonhoeffer is correct to hold to the centrality of the church in the construction of a coherent and credible theological concept of sociality. Moreover, the picture of the church that emerges over time gestures toward an alternative mode of sociality that bears striking similarities to the forms that Jewish life took following the Babylonian Exile.

The Church and the Theological Concept of Sociality

In the editor's introduction to the English edition of *Sanctorum Communio*, Clifford Green states that for Bonhoeffer, "Ecclesiology is

---

2. See Milbank, *Theology and Social Theory*, 1–6.
3. Ibid., 207.

set in the midst of a 'theology of sociality.'"[4] This way of putting the matter is not so much incorrect as it is misleading, for it can leave the impression that ecclesiology is properly a function of a more basic conception of sociality and thus leaves it in jeopardy of being positioned by secular social science and social theory, or at least by conceptions of humankind's social nature that see the church as one particular species of a more generic conception of human community.

It is possible to approach the church in this manner, says Bonhoeffer, looking at it "from the outside" as a "religious community" or "public corporation." Nevertheless, when viewed from the outside, that is, from the perspective of sociology and social philosophy, we miss the essence of the church, which is compounded of its empirical form and the new social basic-relations that constitute the reality of revelation. Our real relationship to other persons (which of course is the principal reference of the concept of sociality) is properly oriented to our relationship with God: "*But since I know God's 'I' only in the revelation of God's love, so too with the other person; here the concept of the church comes into play.*"[5] Indeed, according to Bonhoeffer, anything that we could say about the possibility of social being as such, that is, in its primal state, is predicated on our understanding of the church as set forth in revelation.[6]

Bonhoeffer does not deny that the church takes an empirical form, which, when viewed from the outside, can become the object of a sociological morphology. But to take this approach, he quickly demurs, would render "all theological reflection . . . superfluous." The reality of the church is finally that of revelation, a reality that must either be believed or denied. An adequate measure for assessing the claim of the church to be God's church-community (*Gemeinde Gottes*) can only be found "by stepping inside it, by bowing in faith to its claim."[7] The church thus constitutes the hermeneutical standpoint from which he interprets human sociality Christologically and eschatologically, or, as he puts it in a prison letter, from the standpoint of the gospel and of Christ.[8] I therefore contend (*pace* Green) that Bonhoeffer does not first

---

4. DBWE 1:1. Green is here drawing on his insightful work *Bonhoeffer: A Theology of Sociality*.
5. Ibid., 56 (emphasis in original).
6. Ibid., 65.
7. Ibid., 126–27.
8. *DBW* 8:482.

develop a theology of sociality as such and then set ecclesiology within it. Instead the theological concept of sociality is a function of ecclesiological reflection.

We should remember that this idea of sociality (*Sozialität*) is an abstract concept denoting the condition in which the body of institutions and relationships are formed, within which a relatively sizeable group of people live, move, and have their being.[9] From Bonhoeffer's perspective there is no such thing as sociality as such, because it can refer to two very distinct sets of conditions: in Adam and in Christ. By itself, then, the concept has no content, and must be explicated "within a real historical dialectic."[10] The form this dialectic takes in Bonhoeffer is surprisingly similar to that exhibited in the writings of many of the church fathers.[11] He denies, for example, that unaided human reason can truthfully speak about humankind's "primal state" unaffected by sin. The logic of theology from beginning to end is eschatological and is therefore dependent on revelation, and thus any theologically coherent reflection on the primal state can only take the form of "hope projected backwards."[12] Projected, that is, from the interpretive standpoint of the church, a claim that Bonhoeffer emphasizes even more forcefully in the introduction to *Creation and Fall*: "Only the church, which knows of the end, knows also of the beginning."[13]

9. See Williams, *Keywords*, 291.

10. *DBWE* 1:62. It is interesting to note that though the term *Sozialität* appears multiple times in *Sanctorum Communio*, Bonhoeffer uses it only one other time, in *Act and Being*, and then only in passing (Cf. *DBWE* 2:120).

11. Bonhoeffer erroneously asserts that little attention was paid to community with God and social community prior to Schleiermacher and then cites Augustine's *City of God* as a case in point: "In speaking of the church in Adam's time, writers were in no way thinking of any sort of relationship in community, but only of the preaching of God's word already at the beginning of human history, in the sense of Augustine's sentence, for example: 'ecclesia, quae civitas dei est . . . cuius ab initio generis humani non defuit praedicatio' ('[Christ's] church, which is the city of God, proclaimed from the very beginning of human history. . . .') (*De Civitate Dei*, 16, 2)" (*DBWE* 1:64 n. 1). What Bonhoeffer is attempting to articulate with the abstract concept of sociality was most certainly addressed by the fathers, though admittedly in terms of the conceptual resources available to them. In Book XIX of *City of God*, for example, Augustine says that every good act that the city of God directs toward the attainment of that peace which it possesses in faith while on its pilgrimage is performed either for God, "or—since the city's life is inevitably a social one—for neighbour" (XIX.17).

12. *DBWE* 1:61.

13. *DBWE* 3:22.

The primary assumption that the early Bonhoeffer shares with the fathers with regard to sociality is that human community in its primal state must be thought of in connection with community with God. According to Henri de Lubac, the church fathers taught that the unity of the mystical body of Christ presupposes a previous natural unity of the human race as created in God's image: "[T]he divine image does not differ from one individual to another: in all it is the same image. The same mysterious participation in God which causes the soul to exist effects at one and the same time the unity [i.e., the sociality] of spirits among themselves." As a result of the infidelity to the divine image, says Lubac, "every breach with God . . . is at the same time a disruption of human unity." Maximus the Confessor, for example, wrote of original sin as a separation, a breaking up or "individualization" in the pejorative sense of the word, such that the one nature shared by all was shattered into a thousand pieces.[14]

In like fashion Bonhoeffer states that community with God and social community presuppose each other, such that neither exists without the other. As a result, "even the formal concept of person can be conceived only in terms of community. Thus unbroken social community belongs to primal being [*urständliches Sein*], in parallel to the eschatological hope we have for it in the church." But with the act of disobedience against God a rupture occurs within the unbroken community, and with the loss of direct community with God, human beings also lose unmediated human community. Sin imposes itself between human beings and God, and between human persons.[15]

Bonhoeffer recognizes with Augustine that ecclesiology, in order to be done properly, can only be attempted in juxtaposition to the social order of Adam, that is, of fallen humankind.[16] Indeed, owing to God's activity in Christ, made manifest to all in and through the church, there now exists in the world two distinct kinds of human sociality.[17] In place of Augustine's two cities typology, however, Bonhoeffer distinguishes between the broken community in Adam, in which human beings "are

---

14. Lubac, *Catholicism*, 25–33.
15. *DBWE* 1:63.
16. Augustine, *City of God*, I. Preface.
17. "[D]uo quaedam genera humanae societatis existerent" (ibid., XIV.1; cf. XV.1).

bound together in status corruptionis [state of corruption]," and the *sanctorum communio* of the church in Christ.[18]

There are, to be sure, important differences that should not be overlooked. Bonhoeffer, as is to be expected, works with a concept of the person that was unknown to Augustine, as well as with the modern distinction between community (*Gemeinschaft*) and society (*Gesellschaft*). With respect to the latter, however, Bonhoeffer ultimately refuses to draw the bright line one might attempt to draw between these aspects of sociality: "[I]t must be emphasized that no pure type exists in concrete form. There is no community without the connection of wills that exist in a society; but even more certainly, there is no society without the connection of wills existing in a community, because society [*Gesellschaft*] is essentially rooted in community [*Gemeinschaft*]."[19]

In other words, people can only go about their business on the tacit assumption that error, deception, self-deception, irony, and ambiguity, though everywhere present in these interactions, will not finally render reliable reasoning and coherent action impossible.[20] These assumptions are formed and sustained by the stock of activities, stories, habits, and institutions that fosters a common life and language, i.e., by a particular mode of sociality. These practices and habits provide the conventions that enable the members of a community to engage each other in meaningful transactions by making inferences about future behavior and present intentions from premises about past behavior. This includes our transaction with God, for, as Bonhoeffer's contemporary Hans Urs von Balthasar puts it, "the personal in Christ can only confront the personal in the individual Christian in union with what appears to be impersonal, the church and the sacraments."[21]

This hermeneutical standpoint in the church, as I have called it, is carried forward by Bonhoeffer into his later writings, up to and including his prison correspondence. There are developments, to be sure,

---

18. *DBWE* 1:109, 145–57.

19. Ibid., 91. One way that Bonhoeffer tries to distinguish between a community and a society is that in the former the relations are "direct" or unmediated (*Unmittelbarkeit*) and in the latter "mediated" (*Mittelbarkeit*) (ibid.), which is unsustainable, since even the most intimate of relationships are dependent on, and thus mediated by, a variety of societal practices and institutions (e.g., marriage).

20. MacIntyre, "Epistemological Crises," 139.

21. Balthasar, *Theology of History*, 81.

having principally to do with an increasing sense of church-community and world working at cross-purposes. In his 1935 lecture on the interpretation of the New Testament, for example, he states that the church must be a community that sets limits, expels false teaching (perhaps even disassociating itself from the authorities), and is in a position to hear the Apocalypse. For such a community, bearing witness as aliens in the world, not friendship with it, is the norm.[22]

Bonhoeffer makes a similar claim in *Discipleship* in language that again is strongly reminiscent of Augustine's *City of God*: "Here on earth, the church-community lives in a foreign land. It is a colony of strangers far away from home, a community of foreigners enjoying the hospitality of the host country in which they live, obeying its laws, and honoring its authorities. With gratitude it makes use of what is needed to sustain the body and other areas of earthly life." It participates in the life of the host country, prays for those in authority over it, and offers the best service it can, but in the end "it is merely passing through." At any given moment it might hear the call to move on, and then "it will break camp, leaving behind all worldly friends and relatives, and following only the voice of the one who has called it."[23]

There remains, of course, the disputed question of the church's status vis-à-vis a world come of age in his prison writings. Ralf Wüstenberg sees a sharp contrast between Bonhoeffer's view of the world in *Ethics* and that found in his prison correspondence: "Whereas in a manuscript from the *Ethics* the world, which is in the process of 'coming of age', was regarded negatively in terms of 'nihilism', in the prison letters Bonhoeffer reflects positively on the autonomy of the world, humanity, and life." What caused this change? "Between the *Ethics* and these positive statements in the *Letters and Papers from Prison*, Bonhoeffer had read Wilhelm Dilthey."[24]

---

22. *DBW* 14:420–21. The editors rightly reference Heb 11:13 in connection with this statement: "They confessed that they were strangers and foreigners on the earth" (Cf. ibid., 461–62).

23. *DBWE* 4:250–51. The editors of the English language edition try to mitigate the sharpness of the German terminology (*Fremdling, Fremdlingschaft*) by stating that Bonhoeffer uses it in the sense of "transients" (250 n. 88), citing for support his pastorates in expatriate churches in Barcelona and London. But just a few years prior to the publication of *Discipleship*, the anti-Semitic theologian Gerhard Kittel, in a book entitled *Die Judenfrage*, used *Fremdlingschaft* to denote the status of Jews in Germany. See the review of Kittel's book by Mathilde Steckelberg (84).

24. Wüstenberg, "Philosophical Influences," 147–48.

I contend that Wüstenberg over-reads the influence of Dilthey and therefore the degree to which Bonhoeffer embraces the world's coming of age, neglecting in the process other passages that give a very different impression of Bonhoeffer's estimation of the world and of the church's role in engaging it.[25] In his letter of July 18, 1944, for example, he states that human beings are called to suffer with God in a godless world, and that they must live in this world without somehow trying to conceal or explain away its godforsakenness.[26] In addition, he continues to insist that those who wish to affirm life must do so through their participation in the incarnation, crucifixion, and resurrection of Christ,[27] and thus they affirm life that is natural, open to Christ.[28] In so doing they expose the godlessness of the world to an unexpected light and thus can expect to suffer as in Christ they too seek to sanctify the unutterable name of God.[29] Whatever else might distinguish a world come of age from previous historical periods, then, it is clear that Bonhoeffer thinks that unjust suffering and death as a consequence of conduct outside the accepted boundaries are still an integral part of it.

These statements strongly suggest that what Bonhoeffer says about the last things and the things before the last in *Ethics* is still in force: "Christian life neither destroys nor sanctions the penultimate. In Christ the reality of God encounters the reality of the world and allows us to take part in this real encounter. It is an encounter beyond all radicalism and all compromise. Christian life is participation in Christ's encounter with the world."[30] Living unreservedly in a world come of age does not mean that one endorses it or accepts without comment its own self-understanding. In the important letter of April 30, 1944, for example, Bonhoeffer asks whether the difference between things before the last and the last things takes on a new significance in connection with his assertion that Christ should no longer be regarded as an object of religion but as the Lord of the world.[31] He thus goes to considerable lengths

25. For a more nuanced interpretation of Dilthey's influence on Bonhoeffer's prison writings, see Feil, *Theology of Dietrich Bonhoeffer*, 178–85.

26. *DBW* 8:535.

27. Ibid., 381, cf. 415.

28. *DBWE* 6:163.

29. *DBW* 8:226.

30. *DBWE* 6:159.

31. *DBW* 8:405–6.

to articulate the points of pressure, tension, and conflict that occur precisely at the center of life between a world that no longer considers itself under the tutelage of "God" and those who through prayer and acts of justice share in the messianic suffering of God.[32]

Such statements presumably reaffirm Bonhoeffer's contention in *Ethics* that the Incarnation can never serve as God's affirmation of the world in abstraction from Good Friday and Easter. There can be no greater error, he writes, than to separate the three elements of the event of grace: "In the becoming human we recognize God's love toward God's creation; in the crucifixion God's judgment on all flesh; and in the resurrection God's purpose for a new world."[33] The humanity of Jesus does not ratify the established world and human life as it exists in a fallen world. In Christ, God judges our conceptions of what it takes to make and to keep human life human and offers in their place the decisive definition in Jesus's life and passion.[34]

We should therefore interpret the phrase "a world come of age" as Bonhoeffer's way of specifying more precisely the nature of the penultimate realm at this particular point in history and not as an abandonment of the eschatological distinction between last things and things before the last. He wants to affirm life in such a world, to be sure, but his comments should not be read as an uncritical endorsement of its relationships and institutions. His contention that the world's coming of age should not be treated as the subject for either polemics or apologetics is instead a call for a better interpretation of its basic features than it supplies for itself, namely, from the standpoint of the gospel and of Christ.[35]

Ecclesiology, *Vita Christiana*, and a World Come of Age

Another point of contention has to do with the continuing significance of the church in Bonhoeffer's later writings. Wüstenberg, for example, states that in the prison writings Bonhoeffer develops his understanding of Jesus as the one for others "initially without any connection to the

---

32. Ibid., 435.
33. *DBWE* 6:157.
34. Cf. Yoder, *Politics of Jesus*, 99.
35. *DBW* 8:482.

church."[36] And in what is otherwise an insightful essay on Bonhoeffer's Christology, Andreas Pangritz concludes with a similar (and equally problematic) claim. He cites a well-known passage from a letter to Eberhard Bethge in which Bonhoeffer states that the undivided love that God desires from us is nonetheless intended to provide a type of *cantus firmus* around which our worldly loves constitute the counterpoint. Like the relationship between the two natures of Christ in the Chalcedonian formula, the love of God and our earthly love are undivided and yet distinct (*ungetrennt und doch geschieden*).[37] Pangritz, attempting to explicate Bonhoeffer's desire to articulate a "this-worldly" and "religionless" understanding of faith in a world come of age, states that in this formulation his "earlier, sometimes almost compulsive identifications of Christ and community, Christ and peace, Christ and David, are relaxed and finally liquefied by a new conception, in which 'divine and human nature', love of 'God and his eternity' and 'earthly, erotic love' can communicate with consummate ease in a Christological interplay."[38] In effect, Pangritz moves to naturalize the supernatural, that is, to assert that the Incarnation essentially erases the distinction between penultimate and ultimate, and thus to imply that the social institutions and relationships of a world come of age, from the intimate to the global, already belong substantially to the realm of last things.

At no time in his earlier works, however, does Bonhoeffer ever simply identify Christ with community, peace, or David. Moreover, the nature of these relationships differs substantially. The relationship of Christ to the character of David is typological in nature, whereas the relationship of the figure of Christ to the concept of peace is that of (ultimate) cause to (penultimate) effect, as described in the Epistle to the Ephesians: "[Christ] is our peace . . . [creating] in himself one new humanity in place of the two, thus making peace" (2:14a, 15b).[39] As for the relationship of Christ to the concept of community, Bonhoeffer does hold them together throughout his work, but never is there

36. Wüstenberg, *Theology of Life*, 150.

37. *DBW* 8:440–41.

38. Pangritz, "Who is Jesus Christ, for Us, Today?," 151. One wonders whether Pangritz would regard the identification of Christ with the Jewishness of Jesus as compulsive.

39. Unless otherwise indicated, all biblical citations are from the New Revised Standard Version.

an identification of the two. And though in his later writings he does propose a rather substantial reconfiguration of the church, there is little or nothing to suggest that he regards his earlier work that links together Christ and the church, or Christ with specific figures or events in the Old Testament, as "compulsive" or in any way misconceived.

On the contrary, like a musical performance that moves incessantly toward its final cadence, Bonhoeffer's reflections on a world come of age and related notions in his prison letters invariably lead him to talk about the church. In the letter of April 30, 1944, for example, in which he introduces the concept of a religionless understanding of Christianity,[40] Bonhoeffer concludes that the time of interiority and conscience, and thus of religion in general, is over, and states that the religious a priori of humankind that had constituted the Western form of Christianity for its entire nineteen-hundred-year history has been taken away. Christians are thus left with the question of how Christ can become the Lord of the religionless.[41] He then asks what religionless Christianity might look like, and how Christians, as those who belong entirely to the world, might talk in a "worldly" sense about "God." He moves immediately to a series of questions that focus on the life and mission of the church, beginning with: What does it mean to be the church, the *ek-klesia*, the called-forth ones, when we no longer see ourselves from a religious point of view as a people uniquely favored by God, but as those who belong fully and completely to the world? In these circumstances, what is the place of worship (*Kultus*) and prayer (which I take to mean, what would it mean to think of these activities as nonreligious in nature)? Does the ancient tradition of the arcane discipline have a role to play here? And finally, what light does eschatology, and specifically the difference between the categories of last things and things before the last, shed on a religionless situation?[42]

---

40. This concept does not, however, appear *ex nihilo* in the prison correspondence. In the *Ethics* manuscript, Bonhoeffer states that the first concern of the church "is not with the so-called religious functions of human beings, but with the existence in the world of whole human beings in all their relationships. The church's concern is not religion, but the form of Christ and its taking form among a band of people" (*DBWE* 6:97).

41. *DBW* 8:402–4.

42. Ibid., 405–6.

Bonhoeffer expands on these same themes a week later in a letter dated May 5, 1944, in which he declares all religious concepts problematic. He credits Karl Barth with beginning the criticism of religion as an a priori category for theology, though he does take him to task for installing a positivist doctrine of revelation. In spite of Barth's lapse in judgment on that point, Bonhoeffer goes on to commend Barth for replacing the concept of religion with the church, which was the biblical (that is, the correct) move to make. He then once again mentions the role that the arcane discipline could play in the reinterpretation of the central concepts of repentance, faith, justification, rebirth, and sanctification in a "worldly" sense.[43]

What is most troublesome about Pangritz's desire to loosen the connection between Christ and the church-community, however, is the implicit supersessionism. A polymorphous phenomenon within the Christian tradition, supersessionism has historically come in at least two different forms. In the older and more familiar type dating back to the post–New Testament period, the church replaces the Jewish people as God's chosen nation. According to this picture, the church alone wears the mantle of "Israel," and the Old Testament promises and prophecies are fulfilled not only in Jesus, but also in the church, such that it is now the "New Israel" (an expression not found in the New Testament) and thus sole heir to the rights and privileges of Israel's heritage. This form of supersessionism nonetheless remained tightly linked both to concrete history and to the church as in some sense Israel.[44]

Pangritz's statement certainly does not perpetuate this earlier type of supersessionism, but it is related to new forms that, in the opinion of George Lindbeck, began to emerge in the sixteenth century in connection with the debate over how and when the church was founded. Catholics uniformly cited Jesus's comment to Peter, "On this rock I will build my church" (Matt 16:18), whereas Protestants pointed to a variety of events—Jesus's baptism, the call of the apostles, Pentecost—as their candidate for the point of origin. Regardless of how one resolved this matter, a profound shift in ecclesiology had occurred, as the resulting conceptions of the church were no longer connected in any substantial and historical way to the peoplehood of Israel. Add to this the theo-

---

43. Ibid., 414–16.
44. Lindbeck, "What is the Future?," 358–60.

logical innovations that came about during the Enlightenment, which shifted attention away from the church and Israel as bodies of people "to Judaism and Christianity conceived of as religions that individuals believed in and/or practiced."[45]

These shifts of attention gave rise to the theologies of replacement that did more than neglect the church as connected in some sense to Israel; they discarded it. The concept of fulfillment continued to be promoted, says Lindbeck, but with a radically different meaning: "Fulfillment is no longer conceptualized in terms of the biblical narratives of God keeping and confirming promises and prophecies to persons and groups, but in terms of the impersonal patterns and evolutionary progress according to which one religion provides the conditions for the emergence of a better and higher one. Fulfillment now applies to religion, not peoples."[46] All those who continued to hold on to outdated rites and practices (one thinks here of the numerous polemics against Judaism that dot the intellectual landscape of Germany in the eighteenth and nineteenth centuries)[47] were thus dismissed as allochronic, "belonging to a different time, and surviving into the present on false pretenses . . . merely relics doomed to extinction."[48]

By disassociating the polyphony of life from the life and language of the church, Pangritz simply takes this newer type of supersessionism a step further. The *vita christiana* is no longer conceived in terms of the biblical story of God remaining faithful to his covenant community, or of the supposedly universal property of "religion," but in terms of individuals enjoying an amorphous "interplay" between "love of God and his eternity" and "earthly, erotic love" detached both from the practices and institutions of the church-community and from David (and presumably from his people, the Jews). Ironically, in Pangritz's hands the church suffers the same fate that befell Israel in the original version of supersessionism.

---

45. Ibid., 360.

46. Ibid.

47. See, for example, the dismissive treatment of Judaism in Kant, *Religion Within the Boundaries of Mere Reason* 6:125–36, and in Hegel, *Lectures on the Philosophy of Religion*, 357–75. For a thorough and incisive analysis of the treatment of Judaism by a representative sample of European and North American intellectuals from the seventeenth to the twentieth centuries, see Carter, *Race: A Theological Account*.

48. Bauman, *Postmodern Ethics*, 36.

The Continuing Significance of the Church in a World Come of Age

Dissolving the connection between Christ and the church does not yield the kind of social concreteness that Bonhoeffer always desires but leads instead to a conception of the polyphony of life that is "strange, vague, or merely sentimental."[49] I am convinced that Bonhoeffer would share Paul Ramsey's amazement that there are so many "post-Constantinians" who (1) proclaim with joy the end of that era, yet (2) never hesitate to issue advice to states as if they were Christian kingdoms, and (3) continue to applaud the destruction of the remaining "social space" that sustains the independence of educational and other church institutions that will be needed if the church is to be even an effective sect in today's world, capable of conveying Christian ethos, faith, and practice to our children's children.[50]

The question remains, however: How are we to think about the church as a social body in relation to a world that compliments itself on having come of age?[51] Here we need to expand upon Bonhoeffer's statements, some of which are explicit (e.g., his comments about the church as a colony of foreigners in *Discipleship*), others put more implicitly, which suggest that the church forms an alternative mode of human sociality, that is, a distinctive condition or social context that gives rise to a set of institutions and relationships within and through which a group of people are formed (or more precisely, within and through which Christ takes form in them). Among the most intriguing are passages in his prison correspondence in which he cites or refers to Old Testament texts. Scholars often comment on what he says *about* the Old Testament in these letters, but few examine the specific passages that he refers to *in* it. These references provide us with important clues to the meaning of concepts such as a world come of age, religionless Christianity, and living unreservedly in this world, but equally important, to the need of our own time for an understanding of the church that can live faithfully and

---

49. See Underhill, "Future of Mysticism," 66.

50. Ramsey, *Speak Up for Just War*, 125.

51. There is no necessity in taking that claim at face value, for, as Terry Eagleton asks, "Can a world incapable of feeding so many of its inhabitants really be described as mature?" (Eagleton, *Reason, Faith, and Revolution*, 89).

truthfully while simultaneously living fully and completely in a world that no longer pays lip service to the God of Jesus Christ.[52]

When discussing a world come of age, religionless Christianity, and living completely in this world, Bonhoeffer refers almost exclusively to exilic and post-exilic texts in the Old Testament. In the much-discussed letter of April 30, 1944, for example, after stating that God would shortly accomplish something that could only be received with the greatest wonder and awe "for those who have eyes to see," he says that Psalm 58:11b ("surely there is a God who judges on earth") and Psalm 9:19–20 ("Rise up, O Lord! Do not let mortals prevail; let the nations be judged before you. Put them in fear, O Lord; let the nations know that they are only human") will be seen as true. As though to confirm the apocalyptic tone of these passages from the Psalter, Bonhoeffer then says that we shall need to repeat Jeremiah 45:5 to ourselves daily. This verse reads, "And you, do you seek great things for yourself? Do not seek them; for I am going to bring disaster upon all flesh, says the Lord; but I will give you your life as a prize of war in every place to which you may go."[53] This is one of five times in the prison correspondence in which he either cites or alludes to this short chapter in Jeremiah, more often than any other biblical passage. Moreover, it is not just the frequency of citation that makes this particular verse significant, for he often refers to it at critical points in his letters to Bethge.

In the letter dated July 16, 1944, Bonhoeffer suggests seven biblical passages that Bethge might use as sermon texts, of which only one is from the New Testament (Matt 28:20b, "And remember, I am with you always, to the end of the age").[54] Of the other six, three are from the Psalter, all of which, in one way or another, exhort the soul to look to God for salvation (Pss 62:1; 119:94a; 42:5). Of the remaining passages, one is from Jeremiah, the other two from the later chapters of the Book of Isaiah. In the passage from Jeremiah God comforts the remnant of Israel that had survived the sword and found grace in the wilderness: "[T]he Lord appeared to him from far away. I have loved you with an everlasting love; therefore I have continued my faithfulness to you" (31:3). The first verse from Deutero-Isaiah reads: "[D]o not fear, for I

---

52. For a more detailed explication of these texts, see my essay "Life in Exile," 227–41.

53. *DBW* 8:401–2.

54. Ibid., 529.

am with you, do not be afraid, for I am your God; I will strengthen you, I will help you, I will uphold you with my victorious right hand" (Isa 41:10). The second also addresses Israel, the people whom God had formed and knows by name, exhorting them not to fear, for God has redeemed them (43:1). Bonhoeffer then recommends that Bethge confine himself to a few essential and simple thoughts, above all that a person must live for a time in a community to grasp the way that Christ takes form in it.[55]

He returns to the book of Isaiah in a letter written two days later, in which he states that participating in the messianic event constitutes the fulfillment of Isaiah 53 (the last of four so-called suffering servant songs). He unpacks what this fulfillment looks like by referring to a series of events—table-fellowship, healing stories, the shepherds in Bethlehem, the centurion in Capernaum, the rich young man, the encounters with the eunuch and Cornelius—in the gospels and the book of Acts. None of these events, he notes, is a "religious act." The faith that shares in God's suffering is instead something whole, namely, the act of life itself. Jesus therefore does not summon human beings to a new religion, but to life.[56]

The largest concentration of citations from the Old Testament in Bonhoeffer's prison correspondence is found in the letter that he writes on the occasion of his godson's baptism. He once again cites Jeremiah 45, with its emphasis on not looking to do great things but simply receiving one's life as a prize of war. The task of his generation would likewise be not to seek great things but to rescue and preserve their souls out of the chaos and to recognize that this is the only spoil that they could carry out of the burning house. He then quotes a proverb about preserving the integrity of one's heart, saying that he and his generation would have to sustain their lives rather than shape them, to hope rather than plan, to hold out rather than advance, in the hope that they would preserve what later generations would need to plan, build up, and shape a new and better life.[57]

---

55. Ibid.; In light of such a statement one wonders how Pangritz can sustain his contention that in the later prison writings Bonhoeffer relaxes and liquefies the link between Christ and community.

56. Ibid., 535–37.

57. Ibid., 432–33.

Later in the sermon he quotes three more passages from the Old Testament, all of which either presuppose or are set in the exilic and post-exilic periods. The first comes from a statement that Jeremiah addressed to the last king of Judah, warning him that those who resist the rule of the Babylonian king will be punished by war, famine, and pestilence, but God would leave on their own land those who willingly serve Nebuchadnezzar (Jer 29:7). The second comes from the so-called Isaiah Apocalypse: "Come, my people, enter your chambers, and shut your doors behind you; hide yourselves for a little while until the wrath is past" (Jer 26:20). The final Old Testament quotation comes from a psalm connected to the dedication of the rebuilt Temple, reminding the one who worships the God of Israel, "For his anger is but for a moment, and his favor is for a lifetime. Weeping may tarry for the night, but joy comes with the morning" (Jer 30:5).[58]

In the last paragraph of the meditation he once again quotes a passage from the book of Jeremiah, this one looking forward to the time when God will restore the chosen people in the promised land: "[T]hey [the nations] shall fear and tremble because of all the good and all the prosperity I provide for it" (Jer 33:9b). Until then the Christian movement will be a silent and secret affair, as women and men pray, live justly, and wait for God's own time. He concludes with a benediction from the book of Proverbs, in which he prays that it might be said of his godson one day that "the path of the righteous shines like the light that shines forth ever brighter until full day" (Prov 4:18).[59]

The fact that Bonhoeffer refers time and again to Old Testament texts drawn almost exclusively from exilic and post-exilic books when discussing a world come of age, religionless Christianity, and living completely in this world suggests that a typological connection is starting to take shape for him between the fate of the people of Israel during and after the Babylonian exile and the church's mode of sociality in a world come of age. If this figural link points us in the right direction with respect to the question of sociality, then the common history and heritage that Christians share with the Jewish people may teach us something of what it means to live by faith in a world come of age. David Novak observes that in situations where Christian spiritual and

58. Ibid., 434–35.
59. Ibid., 435–36.

even physical survival is at stake, there is much to be learned from the fact not only *that* the Jews have survived but also *how* they survived, both physically and spiritually (which, as Novak observes, are two sides of the same coin, a point that Bonhoeffer also emphasizes in his discussion of the *anthropos teleios*).[60] Novak writes, "Learning how God has not abandoned us to oblivion can greatly help you appreciate how God has not abandoned you to oblivion either. Learning what God has done for us in the past enables us to have faith in what God is yet to do for us in the future. By doing that for you, we Jews can fulfill God's assurance to Abraham that he and his progeny will 'be a blessing' (*berkhah*) for the other peoples of the world (Gen. 12:3)."[61]

I do not claim that Bonhoeffer's prison correspondence contains a fully developed ecclesiology explicitly fashioned around these typological links between his time and circumstance and those of the Babylonian exile in the sixth century BCE. Faithfulness to an author demands that we not attribute something to her or him that she or he does not say, but it does not mean we can never push forward with her or his ideas and images in order to see where they might lead us. Bonhoeffer understands that the activity of reading and deciphering texts is more than a simple "archaeological expedition" in which we try to unearth a mysterious property called "meaning" from beneath the surface of a text (its graphic symbols), deposited there by an author sometime in the past. He even labels as unbiblical this concept of "meaning" (*der Sinn*) and suggests that if it is used at all it should be read as a translation of what the Bible calls "promise."[62] Interpreting a text, an event, even the entire life of a person, is on this view a performative exercise oriented toward the future, particularly if we see, as Bonhoeffer does, our lives as existing finally only in Christ and thus in the life of the triune God.

A good reading, then, may make interpretive moves that neither the author nor those who first received it ever anticipated but to which they may have responded positively. In the words of Aristotle, events

---

60. Ibid., 511.

61. Novak, *Talking with Christians*, 12–13.

62. *DBW* 8:573; According to Herbert McCabe, for something (a thing, a sign) to have meaning is for it to have a role in the business of living, and to communicate is to share a common world of meanings, which in the case of Bonhoeffer means to be snatched up into the messianic event of Jesus Christ (McCabe, *God Matters*, 120); see *DBW* 8:535–36.

in a good story "occur unexpectedly and at the same time in consequence of one another."[63] Good interpretations, I would argue, exhibit something of the same character. What his prison letters provide are certain semantic trajectories that I propose to take up and take further, for they may well teach us something of what it means for the church to be the church in a world come of age. What follows, then, is a constructive proposal that builds upon the assumptions, descriptions, and assertions about religionless Christianity, a world come of age, and the Old Testament that appear in these letters.

What characterizes the post-exilic or diasporic existence of Israel as a distinct form of sociality? Due to space limitations I can only touch on a few of its more salient features. Post-exilic or diasporic Judaism was founded on a common memory of shared space and the hope for a return to that space.[64] Orientation in time thus characterizes its distinctive polyphony of life. Shared memory inscribed the meaning of particular events and places within a narrative that relativized (though not completely severing) the "natural" connection between life in a particular plot of land, on the one hand, and on the other, what it means to be a nation or people. Every place they settled, every people with whom they interacted, became a sign of a past that is not over and done with and of a future that remains to be realized.

Because they lived predominantly in lands ruled by other nations and peoples, their lives were permeated with tensions and ambiguities. In their synagogues and homes they praised the God of their ancestors: "the Lord, the Most High, is awesome, a great king over all the earth . . . God is the king of all the earth" (Ps 47:2, 7a). In such a setting worship was not a "religious" act but, as William Stringfellow asserts in terms that are very reminiscent of Bonhoeffer, a political event.[65] And yet everywhere they looked in their daily lives they saw a vast array of authorities claiming what scripture reserved for God alone. To use

---

63. Aristotle, *Poetics*, 1452a. Interpretive disagreements may therefore have more to do with the assumptions that the various participants bring to the conversation than with what is indicated or implied in a text.

64. Boyarin, *Radical Jew*, 245.

65. "The liturgy . . . whenever it has substance in the Gospel, is a living, political event. The very example of salvation, it is the festival of life which foretells the fulfillment and maturity of all of life for all of time in *this* time. The liturgy *is* social action because it is the characteristic style of life for human beings in this world" (Stringfellow, *Dissenter in a Great Society*, 154; emphasis in the original); cf. *DBWE* 4:261–62.

Bonhoeffer's terminology, they were compelled to learn how to live without God, before God.[66]

Fidelity to God in exile and dispersion thus took the precarious form of following a communal way of living that, on the one hand, distinguished them in crucial ways from the peoples in whose midst they lived, touching on every aspect of life, and on the other, set forth the ways they could cooperate with their Gentile neighbors. Over the centuries, then, Jewish communities have cultivated the difficult and precarious art of living in between competing interests and demands on their loyalty. They have worked diligently to develop practices and habits of living as set forth in the Torah and Talmud, while at the same time seeking to foster working relationships with their hosts, to work whenever possible for the common good.

Above all, the specter of suffering and death never seemed to be far away for the Jewish people. According to Michael Wyschogrod, two themes coalesce in this regard around the motif of Abraham's election. The first is that to be elected by God is to be reassured by God's power and to share in that power as God secures a future for the chosen people: "There is no nation with a greater feeling of self-worth than the Jews. It feels itself loved as no other people. This gives it its will to live under the most adverse circumstances." The second theme is that "to be near God is to become a friend of death because of the terrible danger that surrounds all human intimacy with God." To be loved by God requires the willingness to accept death at the hand of God and thus to suffer "for the sanctification of God's name." This is a dreadful truth to contemplate, writes Wyschogrod, "and it is not at all certain that it is a truth Israel should know."[67]

What would it mean for the church to cultivate such a mode of human sociality in a world come of age? First, as Bonhoeffer has already suggested, it would be to take a communal form of existence that neither seeks to withdraw from the mode of sociality fostered by the world

66. *DBW* 8:533.

67. Wyschogrod, *Body of Faith*, 24; According to Wyschogrod, the existence of the Jewish people is the earthly abode of God, "among or in whom God dwells." It is vital that this people live ethically, and if not God severely punishes them. Their sin does not drive God out of the world completely, however, for that would happen only with "the destruction of the Jewish people." Wyschogrod then states that Adolf Hitler understood this: "He knew that it was insufficient to cancel the teachings of Jewish morality and to substitute for it the new moral order of the superman. It was not only Jewish values that needed to be eradicated but Jews had to be murdered" (223).

nor sanctions its conceptions of power, status, or legitimacy. It looks instead to develop a *modus vivendi* that is capable of preserving its identity and integrity while pursuing the goods of everyday life it shares with the penultimate social order. Christians must therefore forego the privileges the church enjoyed within the framework of Christendom past, when its wishes and rights took center stage, and acknowledge the justice of history and submit willingly to God's judgment, participating broadmindedly and unselfishly in the entire existence of their fellow women and men, and especially in their sufferings, and thereby prove themselves worthy to survive.[68]

In chapter three of his "Outline for a Book" Bonhoeffer discusses the form of communal life the church should adopt in a world come of age. He states that it must take part in the day-to-day tasks of life together, not as those in authority but as those who help and serve.[69] In particular, the church will have to confront the roots of evil: hubris, the adoration of power, envy, and self-deception. To do this, Christians will need a very special set of dispositions, among which he lists moderation, purity, trust, faithfulness, steadfastness, patience, discipline, humility, modesty, and frugality.[70] These are not the traits normally nurtured by the powerful and the well-established, but they are irreplaceable to those who lack the wherewithal to plan strategically their goals and methods, who must know how to play on a terrain not of their own choosing, controlled by forces that do not take their wishes into account. Their actions will unfold in fragments, taking advantage of whatever opportunities present themselves at particular times and in concrete circumstances.[71]

In closing, I return to the Bonhoeffer quote with which I began this essay. As the one in whom the individual, the particular, and the universal are united, Christ alone is the center into which "the whole reality of the world has already been drawn . . . and . . . held together."[72]

68. *DBW* 8:434–45.

69. Ibid., 560.

70. Ibid.

71. See Certeau, *Practice of Everyday Life*, 37. Bonhoeffer concedes in the letter to his grandnephew that his generation spent too much time cultivating a type of reasoning that assumes that a rational person, from the privileged standpoint of "the onlooker," can weigh the possibilities of action and then execute the desired action (*DBW* 8:432).

72. *DBWE* 6:58.

This includes our identity as subjects, since it is only as we are addressed by and then taken up by God's love that both I and my neighbor truly become human subjects, persons related to each other in Christ (regardless of whether my neighbor is also a believer), and it is precisely here that the life of the church comes into play. Far from constricting the polyphony of life, it is only through Christ's ecclesial body that his universal significance, to quote Balthasar, "is 'liquified' and rendered accessible to all times and places, without forfeiting his uniqueness."[73] It is in and through the church-community, gathered together in the power of the Holy Spirit, that the historical particularity of Christ is universalized and his universality made particular in an actual, concrete mode of sociality in which every person receives her or his gift, a unique identity and calling in a world that prides itself on having reached human maturity.[74] Though it seems difficult to travel the narrow path of the church's decision and yet remain open to Christ's love for all people and to have mercy for and show loving-kindness to the weak and godless, both must remain together, for all other concrete modes of sociality fall short of the human race and thus of God's love.

---

73. Balthasar, *Theo-Drama*, 284.
74. See Buckley, "Field of Living Fire," 91.

PART THREE

Discipleship, Conformation, and Responsibility

7

The Christological Presuppositions of Discipleship[1]

John H. Yoder

THE BODY OF TEACHING AND PRACTICE AMONG THE EARLIEST ANAbaptists that we have come to call "discipleship" had at least three kinds of rootage, of unequal genetic immediacy. There was the heritage of late-medieval Jesus-legalism,[2] which had been espoused most widely in Franciscan and Waldensian forms, most recently and firmly among the Czech Brethren. Here the accent lay upon determining the status of Jesus's teachings, especially in the Sermon on the Mount, with the clear understanding that, if they have the status of law, they then are to be obeyed.[3] A direct and causal linkage of this tradition with the Zurich beginnings remains to be traced, but certainly the Waldensian-Moravian underground was widely represented and was taken up into Anabaptism as it spread.[4]

---

1. [Editors' note: The following is a previously unpublished essay from 1987. Due to the condition of the original manuscript, this essay has been altered slightly for publication in this volume. These alterations include minor typographical and grammatical corrections, updated and corrected citations for Bonhoeffer's works, and the deletion of a couple of footnotes containing untraceable references.]

2. The term "legalism" here is used descriptively, not pejoratively. Its almost exclusively pejorative use in Protestant circles is derived from certain polemic preoccupations of magisterial Protestantism and may not properly be presupposed in historical analysis. Properly to understand either Bonhoeffer or the Anabaptists, as we here hope to do, demands openness to the importance of a healthy "nomic" element in any serious ethic.

3. A very fitting example is the *Probacio preceptorum minorum* of Martin Lupáč (d. 1468), 55.

4. The debate about Anabaptist origins has traditionally opposed the concept of a

More directly visible is the second kind of rootage, the incorporation of mysticism. It shows through in Anabaptist vocabulary (*Gelassenheit, Nachfolge, Kreuz*), even though the meaning of these terms shifts as Anabaptism assimilates them. To this we shall return in the form it takes for Hans Denck. Yet this dimension cannot explain the breakthrough of Anabaptism as a visible movement in history.

For the most visible genetic rootage we therefore properly turn to Huldrych Zwingli, with his powerful fusion of Erasmian humanism and the preaching of a rediscovered Bible, from which he expected the ineluctable renewal of God's people. The first, and the clearest, definition of the "discipleship" with which the Anabaptists began was therefore Zwingli's. It grew from his beginnings in Erasmian humanism: by his own testimony, Zwingli experienced a kind of conversion to a Christ-centered, biblically informed, ethically earnest vision of the renewal of the church.[5] By mid-1520 this thrust had been deepened within Zwingli's growing awareness—as he moved beyond Erasmus—that a politically and personally costly conflict would have to be faced. His courage to face this eventuality was nourished by the deepening of his Christ-centered ethic to include the cross as an experience in the life of the church. To Oswald Myconius in catholic Luzern he writes of the persecution and excommunication he expects: "Born in blood, the church I think can be restored in no other way than again in blood."[6]

Like the cross of Christ, the suffering of the church is far more than her fair share of the inevitable suffering to which all men are heir in a fallen world. It is a necessary mark of the working of God—it is a working of God—for the restoration of his people. It carries already the characteristics we shall watch for as our study moves along:

---

pre-reformation continuity of believers' church dissent (van Braaght, Gottfried Keller, Ludwig Keller, E. H. Broadbent, more recently Delbert Gratz, Alexander Rempel, and Hans Hillerbrand) to the datable Zurich origins (John Horsch, Fritz Planke, H. S. Bender). The debate is largely semantic, depending on whether "origin" is meant in terms of genetic personal and institutional connections or in terms of *Ideengeschichte*.

5. Farner, *Huldrych Zwingli*, 3; Rich, *Theologie Zwinglis*, 10, 12, 14 et passim.

6. Zwingli, *Sämtliche Werke* 7:341ff. Very similar phrasings occur in Zwingli's "Auslegung der Schlussreden" of May 1523—an indication that it must have been a part of his familiar preaching repertory (ibid., 2:288). [Editors' note: Yoder does not specify which edition of Zwingli's *Sämtliche Werke* he is citing from. Although it is not always stated, it may be assumed that translations from German editions are the author's, unless otherwise noted.]

- a parallel between the human fate of Jesus and that of his disciples, the rootage of this parallelism not in legalism nor in proof texts but in the disciple's participating in the nature of Christ, and
- the linkage between this suffering and the renewal of the church.

What needs to be clarified, according to this vision, is not (as with the Waldensian-Moravian heritage) whether God's rules are rules, or whether He is to be obeyed, but rather the substantial question of what God calls us to do and the moral question of whether we are ready to suffer.

One further thrust became visible as Zwingli unfolded his preaching from the Gospels; the concepts of "cross" and "discipleship" were spread back out over the pre-passion life and teachings of Jesus: "To be a Christian is not to chatter about Christ, but to walk as He walked";[7] "This is what it means, 'following after Him,' when we do as He did."[8]

Like so much of the rest of early Anabaptism, the concept of discipleship is thus a part of the inheritance received by the Swiss Brethren from Zwingli. Although, as things finally worked out, Zwingli did not apply his criterion of conformity to Christ[9] to the details of political ethics, his preaching 1519–1524 must by all accessible testimony have been full of the imagery of "doing as Jesus did."

This vision of discipleship is not a mere external mimicry, for it can also be stated in terms of participation in the same body: "And if you have to suffer for it you know it cannot be otherwise. Christ must suffer still more in his members. But he will strengthen and preserve them steadfast, even unto death."[10] By the time of the writings of Michael Sattler this "body" vision was more fully developed still.

The first testimony to the specific shape of Michael Sattler's thought is the letter he left with Martin Bucer and Wolfgang Capito on his leaving Strasbourg in late December 1526 or early January 1527.[11] The bulk of the letter is twenty-one theses, distilled out of as many biblical texts:

---

7. Ibid., 3:407.
8. Ibid., 2:130; other parallels cited in Yoder, *Täufertum und Reformation*, 187.
9. Zwingli's term was *glychförmigkeit*.
10. Wenger, *Conrad Grebel's Programmatic Letters*, lines 184ff and 308ff.
11. Krebs and Rott, *Quellen zur Geschichte der Täufer*, 68; cf. "Michael Sattler" in the *Mennonite Encyclopedia* 4:427–34 (esp. 428).

4. Baptism incorporates all believers into the body of Christ;

5. Christ is the head of His body,[12] i.e., of the believers or the congregation (Eph 2:22);

6. As the head is minded, so must its members also be (1 Cor 12:26);

7. The foreknown and called believers shall be conformed to the image of Christ (Rom 8:29).

The lengthy article VI of the Schleitheim "Brotherly Understanding" repeats most of these allusions and shapes its entire argumentation around the Gospel accounts. Should the Christian be a magistrate?[13] Jesus disappeared when they wanted to make him king. Should a Christian be a judge? Jesus refused to decide between two brothers in the matter of an inheritance. He refused (John 8) even to share in the sentencing of a woman clearly guilty of the capital offense of adultery.[14] "As Christ, our head above us is minded[15] just thus[16] should the mem-

---

12. Franklin H. Littell, in "Some Free Church Remarks on the Concept, The Body of Christ" (in Skydsgaard et al., *The Church*, 127), affirms that Anabaptists and radical Puritans "shunned the imagery of the body of Christ." The point Littell is making is theologically proper, if by "body of Christ" we mean the concept being talked about in a largely catholic symposium. But the Anabaptists, leaning on Zwingli, did, as we are observing, use the term in a very central place. Its meaning is not institutional-sacramental but ethical. It is in the Müntzer letter and in Schleitheim. It comes to the fore later in the connection Menno makes between incarnation and church discipline. It places ethics within Christology and is thus functionally parallel to the "following-after" imagery of "discipleship."

13. Any effort to understand the Anabaptist attitude to "the sword" must begin by setting aside modern concepts of the state as welfare agency, as organ of the self-expression of "the people," and as agency of "responsibility." The "sword" of which Anabaptism speaks is the concrete set of governments which by this time are already actively persecuting religious dissent, in which there were no welfare functions except such as were being taken over from the monasteries, and no democratic process except for a few guild members in a few cities. The late feudal lord whom "the sword" in Anabaptist usage speaks of most typically is less like the concept of the state which modern protestant social ethics presupposes than he was like a Cosa Nostra chief. Modern use of these Anabaptist texts as "ideal types" for a generalized commitment to social irresponsibility is thus irresponsibly anachronistic.

14. The question really being put to Jesus considers him more as a rabbi than as a judge.

15. "Minded" is a reference to Phil 2:5.

16. Literally "all that"—a concern for thoroughness in the disciple's reflection of varied dimensions of Jesus's posture.

bers of the body[17] be minded through Him, so that there be no division in the body, whereby it would be destroyed."[18] The unity of the body of Christ is the identity of the church's behavior now with Jesus's behavior then. If we share in his "mindedness," this will issue in deeds like his.

The second source of discipleship language, we said above, is mysticism, whose most representative witness within Anabaptism is Hans Denck.[19] Denck's initial locus of concern is the authenticity of personal faith, which is reached by a path of struggle and suffering, reaching finally a state of yieldedness (*Gelassenheit*), which is the central meaning of faith.

In this perspective, the central concern of Denck's two main writings[20] is not ethical or ecclesiastical but speculative: how can the Law of God be conceived as that which condemns men, without releasing the believer from the obligation to obey it (as a kind of popularized Lutheranism seemed to him to be doing)?

This orientation leads to a rejection of infant baptism, not (as with the Zwinglian radicals of September 1524) because the infant cannot commit himself to the rule of Christ of binding and loosing,[21] but because there is no inner spiritual purification to which the outward water baptism of the child could correspond.[22] This same mystical concern leads Denck to reject violence and political sovereignty as well—more because they are compulsive, unyielded, than because of any particular

---

17. In modern English the word "members" has two meanings, with belonging to a group ("membership") being more current than belonging to a body. In the German the contrary is the case; the only meaning is the anatomical one.

18. [Editors' note: Yoder did not supply a reference for this quote; however, cf. his own English translation of the Schleitheim Articles in Koop, *Confessions of Faith*, 25–33.]

19. Denck is genuinely an Anabaptist in the institutional sense, forming the link in the succession of baptisms from Zurich (via Reublin and Hubmaier) to southern Germany (Hut). Much of his thought was, however, solidified before his own baptism and most of his extant writings are pre-Anabaptist.

20. "What is meant when Scripture says that God does and makes good and evil" and "On the Law of God; how the law is dissolved and yet fulfilled"; Fellmann, *Hans Denck*, 27ff.

21. Wenger, *Conrad Grebel's Programmatic Letters*, 194ff.

22. Fellmann, *Hans Denck*, 24. This is a year before his baptism. The rejection of infant baptism does not itself entail the mandate for baptism upon confession.

command of Jesus.[23] The example of Jesus[24] is that of his condescension or his yieldedness,[25] that of the divine renunciation of vindication which his work represents, rather than any events from the Gospel biography.[26]

The widely quoted word of Denck, "*Nachfolge*,"[27] is far less focal for him than modern use of it would make it seem. He uses the word only twice,[28] although of course the concept of conformity to Christ occurs in other wordings. The topic at issue here is not ethics at all, but theodicy. Men who blame God for evil (as those do who say they cannot keep from sinning) thereby lay an automatic, unconditional, and unmediated claim on His grace, i.e., a claim which can bypass the need for Christ as medium (or means: *mittel*):

> If it were true, what he [who wants to excuse himself before God] ascribes to God, then God could and would chastise no one (for He is just and chastises no one who is not guilty) and all creatures would already be reconciled ["at rest"—*in der ruw*],[29] which is not yet [the case], but rather one must come therein [into rest] by the medium. But the medium is Christ, whom no one can verily know, unless he follows Him with his life. And no one can follow Him, unless he first know Him. He who knows Him not, does not possess Him, and cannot come to the Father without Him. He who knows Him and does not testify by his walk [*wandel*], He will judge together with all the wicked, regardless [of the fact] that he was previously called and received into the fellowship of the Gospel.[30]

The necessity of Christ for reconciliation is affirmed, as is the necessity of obedience, or "*Nachfolge*," for knowing Christ. But what "*Nachfolge*" means the passage simply presupposes. The clearest approx-

---

23. Ibid., 84. The command of Christ in question is not the rejection of killing or hatred, but the "binding and loosing" mandate of Matt 18:15ff.

24. Ibid., 47.

25. Ibid., 40.

26. Ibid., 84.

27. [Editors' note: To avoid confusion, when *Nachfolge* is being referred to as a term, it is placed in quotation marks, but left open when referring to Bonhoeffer's book of that title.]

28. Fellmann, *Hans Denck*, 46 and 54; the comparable *schuler* occurs on 58 and 84.

29. "Rest" (Hebrews 4) is a favorite mystical image of atonement.

30. Fellmann, *Hans Denck*, 45.

imation to an affirmation that the believer must be "like Christ" is found in Denck's probably pre-Anabaptist *Was geredt sei*.[31] Here the believer recapitulates not Jesus's earthly choices but the metaphysical kenosis of Philippians 2, the renunciation of godlikeness and sovereignty.

With this capsule summary of the vision of the rootage of Anabaptist discipleship in a specific attitude to Jesus and to the renewal of the church, we cannot help observing a marked parallelism between this and some of the most widely received themes in the work of Dietrich Bonhoeffer. This is what the present study is seeking to test. Two prefatory remarks are needed here to identify, and to set aside, what we do not intend to deal with.

Here I am going to ask how the Anabaptists understood discipleship. We have not asked how important it was for them, whether they all used the concept, or whether they themselves thought it was more central than several other of their concerns. That modern scholarship considers "discipleship" a central or representative theme in Anabaptist self-understanding is largely the product of the flash of creative synthesis that led Harold S. Bender, without extensive inductive source study,[32] to identify discipleship as one of the three marks of the "Anabaptist Vision." Might Bender have been moved toward this analysis by reading Bonhoeffer? If so, he may have been one of the very first North Americans to appreciate, years before its first appearance in partial translation, something of the creative originality of *Nachfolge* and something of its promise as beginning a recapitulation of the radical reformation.[33] Yet the modern Mennonite reception of Bonhoeffer cannot be my theme here.

We must set aside any trust in the adequacy of the *word* "*Nachfolge*" as a handle for our theme. Not only are "*Nachfolge*" and "discipleship" not etymological equivalents; neither has a clear biblical equivalent. We do not therefore ask how the Anabaptists used the word "*Nachfolge*," which they did not all use and which even then had several sources

---

31. Ibid., 37.

32. Bender, "The Anabaptist Vision," 3, and esp. 13ff.

33. At that time Prof. Bender was teaching a course named "Discipleship" at Goshen College. There is ground for hope that enough of the notes from that course may be found to enable some clarification of genetic relations.

and several shades of meaning. We should rather deal with a pattern of thought for which "discipleship" is *our* word.[34]

Thus as the first focus of our concern is to be discipleship-as-interpreted-by-the-Anabaptists, we need not seek to analyze the various verbal constructions for "following after" (like the German usage or that of the Gospel texts), which could conceivably mean less than the Christological definition of ethics that we have seen to be at the center of radical Zwinglianism. It is after all possible for an admirer to "follow after" a great man without affirming any commitment to a quality of life that could be described as acting as a member of his body or doing as he did. Likewise, we may set aside any concentration upon the analysis of the ontological status of being a disciple, an emphasis toward which an English noun ending in "-ship" tends to predispose one. This slant would be reinforced by certain understandings of regeneration or sanctification. We are free, for our present purposes, to stay with the simplicity of the phenomenon observed above, "an ethic for which the concrete humanity of Jesus, in his social decisions, provides the model."[35]

As we move to Bonhoeffer as the other focus for comparison, we are therefore not asking whether he talks about Christ or about discipleship; of course he does. The question we bring with us is focused much more narrowly. How does the Christ of Bonhoeffer's call to discipleship relate to the lifestyle of the man named Jesus? What is it that the disciple is called to do, for which he forsakes other loyalties? Is it centered upon his subjective loyalty and disposition to obey—something that, as we saw, could be a minimal verbal meaning of "following after"? Is it the adoption of a stance or a status, whether a traditional one like "regeneration" or a modern one like "openness to the future," without specific behavioral content? Or is it in some serious sense a sharing in the sober social reality of the Messiah's cross through that instrumentality of his body, i.e., of a community projecting into its present the meaning of his past servanthood?

---

34. In New Testament usage as well there is a unity of substance broader than any one set of terms. The roots and images "follow," "learn," "imitate," "indwell," "take the place of" can all be used to say more or less the same thing. Cf. Schulz, *Nachfolgen und Nachahmen*.

35. [Editors' note: A reference for this citation does not appear in the original manuscript.]

The present study pretends neither to precision nor to completeness. Its intent is achieved if it can characterize an issue and identify an interpretative hypothesis for more thorough testing. The stance of Bonhoeffer will be lifted out of the most familiar and accessible sources and further checked by sketchy cross-references to his major Anglo-Saxon interpreters.

The Shape of the Pacifism of the Early 1930s

The clearest social-ethical commitment of the "ecumenical Bonhoeffer" was probably his participation in the (1934) Fano Life and Work conference and the related ecumenical youth conference. Editor Robertson says that Bonhoeffer's address "The Church and the Peoples of the World" was "a call to peace, but not to pacifism."[36] Such a sweeping distinction is hardly helpful, if by "pacifism" and "not pacifism" are meant any of the options traditionally available as Christians face the challenge of war. Bonhoeffer's position may not be what, without defining it, Robertson calls "pacifism," but when taken at face value (and when illuminated by his project of visiting Gandhi), it cannot well be called anything else.

Bonhoeffer's address at Fano is not prescriptive. He repeatedly asks "How does peace come about?" without giving an operational answer. He largely contents himself with the language of open-endedness and risk-taking: "Peace must be dared. It is the great venture." Yet he links this "faith" language with concrete illustration: he asks what might happen "if one nation should meet the aggressor, not with weapons in hand, but praying, defenceless, and for that reason protected by 'a bulwark never failing'?" He calls upon "one great Ecumenical Council of the holy church of Christ over all the world" so to speak that all peoples will know that "the Church of Christ in the name of Christ has taken the weapons from the hands of their sons, *forbidden war*, proclaimed the peace of Christ against the raging world."[37] Vague this is, and homiletically overblown, but, Robertson notwithstanding, it is pacifism. But what kind of pacifism? In what Christology is it rooted?

Three strands of the answer stand out. One is what today would be called "just war pacifism." The Youth Conference resolution character-

---

36. Bonhoeffer, *No Rusty Swords*, 289.
37. Ibid., 291 (my italics).

izes conscientious objectors as "young people who take the doctrines of these [i.e., ecumenical mainstream Life and Work member] churches, as they understand them, seriously enough to follow them to their ultimate implication."[38] What were "the doctrines of these churches"? Since they were not the historic peace churches, their doctrine on war was the just war tradition, holding creedal status for most Protestants, which rejects war not always and everywhere but as an "ultimate conclusion" in particular situations where the criteria of cause, authority, means, and intention are not met. Emil Brunner had just given the name "genuine pacifism" to the view that says that the advent of modern political and weapons techniques of total war should lead to the rejection of any thinkable all-out modern war as never able to meet these criteria.[39]

A second strand in Bonhoeffer's thought is a proof text from the Psalms: "I will hear what God the Lord will speak: for he will speak peace to his people, and to his saints" (Ps 85:8). This word, says Bonhoeffer, is a binding command[40] "that we shall obey him without further question, this is what he means."[41] But why choose precisely this word? Why give it just this meaning? The least we must say is that here is no explicit Christological foundation.

The third basis is the unity of the church as a bond transcending other loyalties: "They cannot take up arms against Christ himself—yet this is what they do if they take up arms against one another."[42] Christ existing as human community is here at the center, but not Jesus the prophet or Jesus the king. The cross is not in the picture.

We conclude that where Bonhoeffer's ethical commitment was nearest in shape to that of Anabaptism, namely, in his pacifism in the mid-30s,[43] the rootage is not the same. The natural-theology shape of just war thought, the cosmic theocracy of the Psalm word proclaimed prophetically with sovereign unconcern for whys and hows, and the

---

38. Ibid., 293.

39. Brunner, *Divine Imperative*, 470ff.

40. In a sense Bonhoeffer's question is that of the pre-Reformation dissenters: is the law binding? (cf. note 3 above).

41. Bonhoeffer, *No Rusty Swords*, 290.

42. Ibid.

43. By this time Bonhoeffer was already clearly committed to the church struggle against Hitler. His "pacifism" should thus not be thought of as an early liberal stage of his thought.

church commitment of ecumenical internationalism carry the weight: Jesus is not needed or named.

The Subjacent Christology of *Nachfolge*

Discipleship begins with the denunciation of cheap grace and proceeds by way of the demand for simple obedience. At the core, the issue put to a person by the "call to discipleship" is a concern not first of all with how he will behave if he follows Jesus, but with the renunciation of self-determination and of one's own reasoning. That I must obey without questioning and that in order to be ready to obey I must have renounced self-will are demands which could be made of me by any moral teacher or any lord; they are not intrinsically linked with how that particular master himself behaved, or with whether what he asks of me is the same as his own behavior.

The exposition proceeds, however, immediately to "discipleship and the cross." Here the correspondence between the disciples' path and that of the master becomes decisive. The suffering of Jesus is the suffering of one who is rejected, and his disciple will take upon himself this same suffering and rejection. Here we have a close analogy to the renunciation of self that was for Hans Denck the precondition of a true knowledge of Christ and fellowship with Him. Yet (as with Denck), the language is weak in concreteness. The focus is upon existential self-understanding and on the readiness of the disciple to bear the strain of enmity; there is no description of how he behaves differently or what decision or behavior on his part it is that brings upon him the cross.

It is affirmed that the Christian somehow also bears the sins of others:

> Since he has suffered for and borne the sins of the whole world, and since the burden of guilt fell on him, he shares with his disciples the fruit of his suffering; the Christian also has to undergo temptation, he too has to bear the sins of others, he too must bear their shame and be driven like a scapegoat from the gate of the city. Thus the Christian becomes a bearer of guilt and sin for other men. He would certainly break down under this burden, but for the support of Him who bore the sins of all. Thus in the power of the suffering of Christ he can bear the sins that fall upon him, overcome them by forgiving them. The Christian

becomes a burden-bearer—"bear ye one another's burdens, thus ye will fulfill the law of Christ" (Gal. 6:2).[44]

Here the careful interpreter encounters one problem atop another. What does it mean that sin and shame are piled on the disciple and drive him out the gate of the city? Does it mean anything specific in terms of social ethics? Or is it a symbolic description of existential inwardness?

The latter part of the passage would seem to give it a distinct social meaning, within the context of the congregation. The reference to Galatians 6:2 is unclear because one cannot tell whether it means to refer straightforwardly to the process of "restoring the brother in the spirit of meekness," i.e., to a concrete social process of fraternal discipline within the Christian congregation, or whether it is in some less literal sense conceived of as the believer's bearing the hostility of the world. How suffering in rejection and being reconciled with the brother are identical the passage does not tell us.

The chapter on the cross has thus added the conception of conformity with the master in his suffering, yet has not included within that conformity anything of precise ethical meaning. The center of Jesus's own acceptance of his cross being seen in his abandon of self-will, the same is the meaning of the call to the follower. But it is not yet said that someone who has abandoned self-will in following Jesus should be expected to act the way Jesus did. Will he be a monk or a politician? An emigrant or a conspirator? Or does the meaning of bearing the cross exist on a level unrelated to such concrete decisions?

Increasing concretion comes as the exposition moves to the Beatitudes. This is certainly a step toward what we have identified as the Anabaptist model, but it is still clearly not the same thing. The Beatitudes deal not with behavior but with disposition. There is some doubt as to whether the liberal Protestant assumption that these are ethical guidelines at all can be sustained on the basis of the original context.[45] If it can be done at all, then it can only be done as Bonhoeffer does, by describing an orientation of the spirit, which still leaves open how one thus oriented will actually behave.

---

44. My translation from Bonhoeffer, *Nachfolge*, 43; cf. *DBWE* 4:88.

45. The "makarisms" (Greek: *makarios*, "blessed") do not say "it will go well in general for people who behave thus" but rather "the coming of the Kingdom is good news for those who are already thus."

It is perhaps significant that whereas the Beatitudes are stated in affirmative form, Bonhoeffer translates them into negations: the renunciation of honor, of power, of violence. This is somewhat parallel to the mystical meaning of *Gelassenheit*, but distinguishable from its ethical meaning.[46]

The concentration upon an attitude, the negative form into which the Beatitudes are recast, and the absence of specific examples leave us again at a loss for a precise interpretation. Perhaps, in line with his other practically pacifist commitments of the 1930s, Bonhoeffer here was taking for granted a renunciation of violence so concrete as to exclude war, participation in the police function of the state, and tyrannicide. Or perhaps he was clearly not making that assumption. Or perhaps it did not occur to him right at this point that in order to understand his message there might be any need to know which of these contradictory assumptions he was making. The text itself in any case does not enable us to decide. The most significant thing Bonhoeffer has to say about the Beatitudes is the reorientation of all values which they proclaim, the renunciation (*Verzicht*) of self-concern of which they are the testimony, and not the concreteness of a new lifestyle that (as he takes for granted but does not spell out) will need to follow.

One more step toward concreteness is taken in the exposition of the renunciation of retaliation: "With this word Jesus frees his church out of the political and juristic order, out of the national form of the people Israel, and makes her what she truly is, namely, a politically and nationally unbound congregation of believers."[47] He thus goes beyond the Matthean text itself in drawing its negative implication not simply for retaliation but for political order that (he assumes) rests upon retaliation or the threat thereof. This negation is further reinforced by the express rejection of the mainstream Reformation distinction between the private person who is thus freed from national solidarity and the social or official personage who continues to carry the responsibilities of political power: "This distinction between me as a private person and as bearer of an office which is normative for my behavior is foreign to Jesus. He says not a word about it. He addresses His disciples as those

---

46. Although the mystical meaning prevails in Denck, the ethical meaning is present in Sattler's earliest writing (see note 11): "Christians are fully *gelassen* and have placed their trust in their Father in Heaven without any outward or worldly arms."

47. My translation from Bonhoeffer, *Nachfolge*; cf. *DBWE* 4:132.

who had forsaken everything to follow Him. Both private and official should be completely subjected to the command of Jesus. His word lays claim upon them without distinction. The obedience He demands of them is without distinction."[48]

This rejection of violence for the disciple is not equated with a liberal, humanistic hope for the healing of society through the generalized renunciation of force. That such a renunciation could become a general program for society at large Bonhoeffer rejects as fantasy or pure fanaticism.

If we juxtapose these three affirmations:

a. That the disciple of Jesus is called to renounce not only retaliation but therefore also national solidarity;

b. That there exists no exempt status for the Christian as official personage which would not be subject to this call; and

c. That the world cannot be governed by this pattern,

it would seem to follow logically that the disciple would need to renounce participation in the governing of the world, to the extent to which its characteristic retaliation and violence limit his participation, and therefore he could accept not being qualified to serve as a magistrate.[49] It is not possible to discern in logic what it is that would keep Bonhoeffer at this point from accepting such a conclusion. Yet he does not state it as being evidently implied. He goes on without explaining what alternative stance toward the social structure would follow from the observations he has just made. As before, he makes no effort to illuminate what discipleship means for the disciple by reference to any events in the pre-passion ministry of Jesus.

This is as far as *The Cost of Discipleship* can bring us. Together with the mystical strand of Anabaptism, *discipleship* expresses itself in *Gelassenheit*, renunciation, in a posture which has no reason to do other than implicitly obey whatever the master says. Parallel to the "moralistic" strand of Anabaptism, the issue is stated simply as whether we are willing to obey without questioning. But we do not find the picture

---

48. Bonhoeffer, *Nachfolge*, 87; cf. *DBWE* 4:134–35.

49. The double negative phrasing is important here. The disciple does not withdraw from society, as Jesus did not. He accepts the way society excludes people like him. Cf. note 13 above.

completed by what we observed to be the most original, socially most realistic strand of Anabaptism, that which began to perceive already in late 1523 that the testing of this whole approach would come at the point of the readiness of the church to give up her control over society. This realism perceived that the model of Christian social participation is not simply the cross of Christ in some symbolic or emotional sense, but also the attitude toward political office that helped to bring him, the Jesus of the Gospels, to the cross. Both the logical realism that would have seen this question arising out of the points already made by Bonhoeffer concerning retaliation and the New Testament realism that would have expected the humanness of Jesus to be part of the picture are missing in *The Cost of Discipleship*. Bonhoeffer does not focus upon these issues and reject the Anabaptist response to them; they simply have not yet come to a head in his thinking.

Discipleship in Ethics[50]

The *term* "discipleship" is no longer significant in *Ethics*. To know just what has become of its meaning and how and why would demand chronological analysis on the basis of the re-ordering of the materials in the sixth German edition and in correlation with other contemporary witnesses—an effort beyond our present intent. We must limit ourselves to the surface of the materials and to the pursuit of those strands of thought which we have identified before.

Early in the 1955 translation we encounter a brief section on "conformation"[51] very much in the spirit of Hans Denck. The Christian is not to seek to transform himself by following Christ's teachings; yet the form of Christ will, of its own power, take form in man, namely, in the church as Christ's body. Yet the desire to avoid self-saving works-righteousness is much stronger in this prefatory treatment than any concern for ethical concretion. Thus we are left up in the air epistemologically. The body of Christ is the church; but what church? Or what kind of church? What does it do to the individuality, the historic specificity, the "Jesus-ness" of Christ that His "form" is rather communal than personal? "To be conformed with the Risen One—that is to be a new

---

50. [Editors' note: This subheading is not in Yoder's manuscript but was added by the present editors for clarity.]

51. Bonhoeffer, *Ethics* (1955 ed.), 80ff; cf. *DBWE* 6:92ff.

man before God."[52] But what does a Risen One do? What ethics fits His "form" and what ethics would not? He "lives in the world like any other man. Often there is little to distinguish him from the rest. Nor does he attach importance to distinguishing himself, but only to distinguishing Christ."[53] But what is it that distinguishes Christ?

Thus *Ethics*, now more afraid of moralism than of cheap grace, does not identify *formally* the problem of how the shape that Christ takes in the church is related to Jesus; nor does it answer the problem *substantially*, as *Nachfolge* had done. The result of this lacuna is then naturally that one's clues about the meaning of Christ will be taken from elsewhere than Jesus. One source—surprisingly for such a late date in Bonhoeffer's career—will be the cultural establishment: "The form of Christ is the unity of the western nation ... [T]o take a wider view would be to overlook the mysterious fact of the self-containedness of the western world."[54] An ethic of nature is affirmed in the name of incarnation[55] as the basis (for instance) of the affirmation of the right to life, rather than rooting that right in covenant (as would K. Barth), or in the quality of the Father's grace (as Matt 5:48 and Luke 6:35-36), or in the subjective authenticity of love (Matt 5:21-22). When the theme of government is treated, Christ is related to it as cosmic Lord[56] and as innocent victim[57] but not as messiah, lawgiver, priest, or prophet. Government's task is affirmed as knowable apart from revelation although revelation confirms it. Government should support the practice of religion[58] and keep differences between religions from endangering public order.[59]

The centrality that government has here, in contrast with the other orders or "mandates," would seem to belie the claim of some in-

---

52. Bonhoeffer, *Ethics*, 82; cf. *DBWE* 6:95.

53. Ibid. [Editors' note: It is interesting to note that in the new *DBWE*, the term is "promote" rather than "distinguish."]

54. Ibid., 87; cf. *DBWE* 6:101.

55. Ibid., 145-46, 155-66; cf. *DBWE* 6:174, 185-96.

56. Ibid., 336-37; cf. *DBWE* 16:511 [Editors' note: The passages Yoder refers to here are from Bonhoeffer's theological position paper "State and Church," which is appended to earlier editions of *Ethics*, but is now collected in *DBWE* 16.].

57. Ibid., 337; cf. *DBWE* 16:511.

58. Ibid., 348; cf. *DBWE* 16:523.

59. Ibid., 349; cf. *DBWE* 16:524.

terpreters that the plurality of the "mandates" was intended to reduce the dominance traditionally given to government in Lutheranism or the privileges given the church by Lutheran governments. Even though government's job is a secular one that other persons can discharge and not a religious function, still only Christians really know its true meaning and its divine authority. Jesus was related to government, we noted, as an innocent victim; but from this no ethical conclusions are drawn about how or when Christians should probably be innocent victims. Christ is related to government in the same way that, as creator, He is related to the entire cosmos; there is thus no substantial distinction between an ethic of the orders of creation and a Christological ethic, for all that is Christological about this ethic is the confession of cosmic lordship.

Thus in ways the inexpert reader cannot untangle, the form of Christ may be the cosmic orders, the unity of the western world, or the church; how these three interrelate is not said. In any case we need not relate them to the words or the earthly work of Jesus, which do not contribute ethical substance.

Bonhoeffer's Interpreters

As typical for a wide stream of Bonhoeffer interpretation we might take the capsule statement of John Godsey in his *Preface to Bonhoeffer*:[60] "[J]ust as in Christ the reality of God entered the reality of the world, so the sacred is to be found only in the secular, the revelational only in the rational, the supernatural only in the natural, the Christian only in the worldly." Godsey is quite right in going on to assert that there is no direct contradiction between the discipleship and community life books of the 1930s and the "worldliness" of the prison letters. But this affirmation does not make it easier to see how the definition of how the supernatural was in the natural, the divine in the human, could so consistently pay so little attention to the human shape of Christ as Jesus. To leap as does the credo and as does Bonhoeffer from the crib to the cross[61] is precisely to leave out of one's Christology the substance of ("secular") social living in occupied, rebellion-torn Palestine. Thus we can partly understand how the concreteness of our ethics must be drawn not from

60. Godsey, *Preface to Bonhoeffer*, esp. 7ff. and 13.
61. Ibid., 12.

Jesus but from the four "mandates" of labor, marriage, government, and the church—the four most evident dimensions of the sociality of man in which, as far as the record shows, Jesus was less involved than other men. What does it mean to affirm incarnation and yet not to make Jesus the criterion of the will of God for these realms? The mandates "function conjointly under the commandment of God revealed to Jesus Christ, which embraces the whole of life, namely, the permission to live as men before God."[62] But how is the command of God to be married or to be a king or to be a citizen sharing in government revealed in Jesus? Certainly only in some indirect and abstract way, over some such bridge as "be loving" or "be responsible."

Godsey's summary is typical of the concern of Bonhoeffer's interpreters to focus the Christological problem on the metaphysical issue of history and transcendence or of godhood and manhood, rather than (with *Discipleship*) on Jesus the authoritative teacher or (with the Anabaptists) on Jesus the revelatory man. This preoccupation with the thinkability of Chalcedon is justified by the early Christology lectures, but it is foreign to the movement of Bonhoeffer's thought from there on. We may nonetheless make of it a fitting and fundamental paradigm for the Christological clarification we are seeking here.

There are, it turns out, two operational meanings of the word "incarnation." Appealing to the same creedal rootage and echoing the same body of hallowed phraseology, the two meanings nonetheless rely upon fundamentally different, even contradictory, approaches to the meaning of our humanity. Often without being aware of it, one or the other option will be taken for granted, with the effect that whereas what one thinks one is arguing about is the affirmation of incarnation, what is really at stake is the clash of two contradictory meanings of that term or concept. We might call one "Jesulogical" and the other "logological." The root of the difference may fairly be described as epistemological, taking that term in its broader sense as pointing not merely to the question of how we know what we know, but rather to a concern for naming the source of the substance of what we assume we know. For eastern Orthodoxy and Anglicanism, in different ways, and likewise for some recent mainstream styles of social ethics in western Protestantism, the word "incarnation" serves as the label for a commitment to the sweep-

---

62. Ibid., 19.

ing acceptance of things as they are. We know things by observing their obvious "nature." Since God chose to take upon Himself the reality of humanness, nothing that is human must be alien to our concern. Thus such slogans as "presence," "involvement," or "responsibility," expanding to include more precisely ethical categories such as "power" or "compromise," all are baptized or given a mandate which can claim to hark back all the way to Chalcedon. When you want to know what it is like to be human, you go out and look at how humans behave; that is what God assumed in taking on humanity. The concept of incarnation serves to support the claim that God asks us to behave that way (the way humans do) for the sake of His presence in the world, presence for which the name of Jesus is a symbol. To know what it is that God became when He became man, we do not look at Jesus but at "man." Jesus (not the man of Galilee but the God-assuming-manhood of Chalcedon) is the accreditation of this affirmative and accepting approach to man as he is. The problem of Christology is how the transcendent Logos could thus take on humanity; what humanity is or should be is not the problem, since we know thereby the self-evidence of "nature."

The alternative conception of incarnation, which we may call "Jesulogical," has already been suggested backhandedly by my schematic way of characterizing the mainstream approach. It would be to say that in Jesus Christ God did not become mankind in general, or all men, or humanity as such, or common humanity. He entered in the story of His people in the form of a particular man who was named Jesus and not Judas, who was a Jew and not a Greek, a man and not a woman. When confronted with the choice, this particular man took the path of the cross rather than that of the crown, which was offered to him by the other versions of "humanity" that prevailed in the setting where he found himself. Not "becoming man" but "becoming *that* man" is then the wonder and the scandal of the incarnation.

Then the epistemological approach will be just the reverse. "Jesus as the Christ" means that the words and work of that man are not only our way to know God but also the only true way to know Man. The definition of "man" we find in the streets or in sociology or in Heidegger or Husserl is not that manhood which God willed, created, restored, assumed. The problem of Christology is not whether or how God could or did become man, but what kind of man He chose to be.

The "logological" preoccupations of Bonhoeffer's interpreters[63] thus tend to move Bonhoeffer away from any similarity to Anabaptism's respect for the historicity of Jesus, and away as well from the posture of Bonhoeffer's own ethical writings. Thus Robertson informs us that the "history" of which Christ is the center is more related to Teilhard de Chardin than to the historicity of the man Jesus.[64]

The Christology lectures begin[65] by affirming that the *geschichtlich* Christ is the same person as the *historisch* Jesus of Nazareth; the announced intention is to avoid taking over the dichotomy of event-versus-meaning or *Historie*-versus-*Geschichte* that was characteristic of liberalism. But once historicity is affirmed, the historical details turn out to be unimportant after all. The history/faith dialectic, as classically exposited in the ancient Christological debates, fills the agenda. The concern for working out the logical implications of incarnation as a metaphysical paradox even resurrects the orthodox Lutheran/Reformed debates about the mode of the Eucharistic Presence:[66] "Revelation becomes the act in which Christ, who comes to me in the Word, sacrament, and community, the humiliated God-Man whose total existence is for me, is confessed as God."[67]

To describe in another way what is happening here: the problems which the "logological" kind of incarnation puts to modern man is whether he can believe it—whether he can accept, emotionally, logically, and reasonably, confessing such an idea. The problem of faith is a problem in the mind of the believer. "Revelation is the act in which Christ is confessed," we just read; revelation is located in the mental actions of believers, and the Christ of whom this confession is spoken

---

63. Each chapter in Martin Marty's *The Place of Bonhoeffer* is introduced by editorial comment interpreting that segment of Bonhoeffer's writings as an aspect of the search to understand Jesus Christ. The preoccupation is uniformly "logological." Jesus of Nazareth, Jesus of history, Jesus the moralist of the Mount, Jesus the crucified King of the Jews, does not appear. *Ethics* can be described in the chapter by George Forrell (203ff), for example, without any need for back-reference to *Discipleship* and its treatment of the Sermon on the Mount.

64. Bonhoeffer, *Christ the Center*, 21.

65. Ibid., 69–73.

66. Ibid., 55: "That Christ will be present in the Church as man, he has said in the words of institution of the Eucharist."

67. Phillips, *Christ for Us*, 83.

is the one borne by the liturgical actions of preaching, sacrament, and community.

For the "Jesulogical" vision of incarnation, on the other hand, the revelation happened before and outside the believer, in Jesus of Nazareth, and in the apostolic church's appropriation of him in her believing testimony, so that the Gospel events retain a categorical priority over the church's reflection and confession of them. This categorical priority is reflected in the fact that what Christ asks of us is not what we readily want to do and not something in which we recognize our vision of our humanity: "He bids us come and die."[68]

The same ambiguity of possible interpretations rides along as the interpreters move to the Tegel prison letters. For the "logological" slant, the "suffering of God in the world" centers about the drama or the trauma, or the intellectual scandal, of the condescendence of becoming human or "secular." Then "secular interpretation," a "this-worldly" understanding of transcendence, constitutes itself the divine humiliation: "To this-worldliness corresponds the suffering of God in the world."[69] Yet there shimmers through just a hint of the other option, what Bonhoeffer calls "being caught up ... into the Messianic event."[70]

Trial Balance

At most, this walk through the commonest sources, with one leading question in hand, may have sharpened our vision of the issue. Bonhoeffer neither began nor ended with a vision of discipleship cognate with that of the Anabaptists. He came closest, in *Discipleship* and *Life Together*, to the "legal" and the "mystical" aspects. As his Christological preoccupations were more dogmatic than exegetical or historical, he was not driven either to concreteness about the pre-passion Jesus nor to any abiding challenge to the axioms of Constantinian political ethics.[71] Such a concretization would have been eminently compatible with the "nonreligious interpretation of biblical concepts" (for what could have been

68. Ibid., 100.

69. Müller, *Von der Kirche zur Welt*, 375, quoted in Phillips, *Christ for Us*, 195–96.

70. Phillips, *Christ for Us*, 100, 102, 104, on the prison letters; Bonhoeffer, *Letters and Papers*, 361–62: "Being caught up in the way of Christ" refers here to persons in the Gospel accounts for whom following Christ was costly; not to the cost of Jesus as model but others sharing sacrificially in his movement.

71. With the one near exception just noted.

less cultic or otherworldly than Jesus's social style?), but it did not occur to Bonhoeffer then. It would have put "God's suffering in the world" into the form of a politically relevant, "non-religious," "secular" paraphrase; but instead those slogans were left to the Bultmannians, who somehow think that "existential interpretation" is non-religious, and to Hanfried Müller, who assumes that socialist promises for party-led history are the same as "*Mündigkeit.*"

In closing let me state synthetically what has become clear analytically. The difference between a discipleship of implicit obedience (*The Cost of Discipleship*) and a discipleship of conformity with Jesus (Zwingli, Grebel, Sattler) is manifold:

a. Formally, the former centers on the quality of the disciple's devotion, i.e., in anthropology, in a new equivalent of pietism's and mysticism's concern for authenticity, while the latter centers on the shape of the Master's obedience, i.e., on history;

b. Substantially, the former centers on the Master's words, or on the creed's words about him, the latter on his life, his decisions, and his fate;

c. Behaviorally, the former cannot, and the latter can, accept exclusion from secular sovereignty as the cost of conformity;

d. Systematically, the former sees in the *concept* of incarnation a nexus between two worlds whereby what people already are and are doing is ratified, the secular made God's instrument; the latter sees incarnation as an *event*, whereby we are commanded to see in the whole man Jesus, including his suffering at the hands of "what men are and are doing," the whole counsel of God, whose suffering in the world is precisely that he lets men push him to its edge.

The elements in the earlier *Discipleship* that kept Bonhoeffer from the latter kind of conclusion include:

a. the pietistic conception of the cross as the breaking of inner resistances in the acknowledgement of one's sinfulness;

b. the location of the meaning of atonement in the metaphysical transaction of incarnation more than in the creation of the church.

Of both of these elements it can be said that they are inherently "religious." They are the kind of material which the Tegel letters tend to challenge.

In this sense, then, the later Bonhoeffer was still moving beyond the "obedience" kind of discipleship and toward the "conformity" kind; what kept him from the latter was the kind of tradition he was progressively dismantling. What hides this continuing movement from many interpreters is their assumption that they must take the double-agent activity of the early 1940s as a prime paradigm of the ethics of the Tegel letters. These interpreters make of Bonhoeffer's complicity in plotting for a projected tyrannicide an ethical paradigm and see the later writings as Bonhoeffer's apology for that involvement. Since tyrannicide is not what the Sermon on the Mount commands, the interpretation goes, of course *Nachfolge* had to be left behind.

If the conspiracy were to be taken as a prime paradigm, then truly there would have to be a "shift" somewhere. Bonhoeffer would then have to be seen as turning away from the reality of the visible church even though the Tegel letters testify to the contrary.[72] He must be seen as forsaking the continuity of the faith, even though the "non-religious interpretation of biblical concepts" had the announced precise intent of reaffirming that continuity in a changing world. The—unsuccessful—plotting on Hitler's life must be seen as the crowning work of his life even though he was not at its center[73] and it did more harm than good.[74]

But Bonhoeffer did not say that *Nachfolge* had to be left behind. He roundly affirms his continuing satisfaction with its main thrust, and what he "would say differently now" has to do with its churchly tone, not with its moral content. The Tegel letters are as a matter of fact strikingly devoid of any self-justifying effort to use his own political

72. Note his use of the *Losungen* and hymns, his reference to *Arkandisziplin*, and his speculations about the shape of the disestablished church in another generation.

73. The plot was well underway before Bonhoeffer became responsibly involved. He became a participant, not of his own initiative, but because through his brother-in-law he could hardly be kept from knowing about it. His services were not within its policy making or planning but as a kind of "minister for foreign church relations."

74. There is a peculiar twist in the reasoning commonly used in the argument for Christian participation in the responsible use of violence. The inefficacy of non-violent means, which is presupposed, is cited to justify violence. Yet the inefficacy of violent means is somehow never fed back into the system. That someone died for a cause seems to disqualify any testing of the pragmatic case for resort to force.

involvement as a model for the renewed possibility of Christian secular moral discourse that he seeks.[75] Ethical deliberation about the duty of tyrannicide is not used to exemplify God's suffering in the world. Nor is the Christian's struggle with hard and dirty decisions so used. The "acceptance of involvement in guilt" (*Schuldübernahme*) that is necessary in all human ethical commitment is not derived from the sinfulness of any particular act, as if the Canaris conspirators were "responsibly accepting guilt" any more than someone else. Guilt is not thus linked to specific wrongful acts. Jesus Christ's exemplary "assumption of guilt" occurred without any misdeed at all. The concern for "secular interpretation" can in none of its occurrences fairly be seen as a cover for the retraction of what Bonhoeffer in *Discipleship* had previously affirmed Christ to be and to have said.

The hypothesis therefore remains a live one—I do not claim for it more than that it may aid further interpretation by challenging some yet untested taken-for-grantednesses—that the conspiracy activity was in Dietrich Bonhoeffer's own mind a necessary and justified exception, a detour, rather than a prime paradigm, to the direction his ethical thought was taking. That direction was still unfocused[76] and still in flux. It had not yet taken him to a reassessment of the remaining "religious" axioms keeping him from a more "conformity" oriented discipleship; but to the end, that was the way his thought was moving.

The explanation for the absence of a more "Jesulogical" or "conformity" element is probably far simpler. It probably never came to his mind. Nothing in his education or his experiences would have raised it. Or if such thoughts arose they were probably swept aside lest his originality, already quite risky in his own estimation, be written off as a renewed liberalism (optimism about finding the Jesus of history, or the use of Jesus's humanity to weaken the affirmation of his deity) or as enthusiasm (optimism about our really doing God's will).

More challenging than the historical question, *why* Bonhoeffer's Christology did not lead him to a "Jesulogical" type of discipleship, is the systematic question, whether it could have or now could. If our

---

75. To make his own choices and achievements a model for others was very clearly not Bonhoeffer's style, though it is a besetting temptation of hagiographers.

76. Formally the main flaw in the argument of those who find in the *Letters* a finished system for justifying tyrannicide is the contradiction with his own clear witness to the exploratory character of his new formulations.

historical hypothesis, that Dietrich Bonhoeffer never saw and rejected such a view, but rather that he never got around to it, can be supported, then the systematic hypothesis may be hazarded that the culmination of "non-religious" rephrasing of Christology would consistently drive us progressively to substitute preoccupation with "Jesulogical" substance (who was Jesus and what did he want?) for "logological" concern for form (how can you say a man was God?). This would be more genuinely what Bonhoeffer talked about than the non-biblical neo-religiousness of the existentialists or the new Constantinianism of Hanfried Müller's claim that Marxism is to replace the West as the "form of Christ in the world."

To move in this direction would not be to despise the "logological" questions, but only to subordinate speculation about incarnation to the fact of incarnation. It could well be argued, as I have been hinting all along, that only this interpretation of the incorporation of the pre-passion Jesus into the Christological foundation of ethics can fulfill the true purpose of the Chalcedonian affirmation that He who is confessed as *vere Deus* had to be first seen as *vere homo*.[77]

Then the whole Jesus, from his desert temptation and Nazareth platform sermon, through his moral teaching and founding of an evangelization movement, to the cross and resurrection, is our model of worldly manhood. It is of his whole career that we would then say, "One looks in Christology upon the *whole* historical man Jesus and says of him: this is God."[78]

Slightly corrected draft of August 1987

---

77. The Christologies of Logos and preexistence in the New Testament (Colossians 1, Hebrews 1, John 1) were not developed out of a speculative concern about two natures. Their concern was just the opposite. In the face of the Gnostic dualism, which set up another kind of insight beside the historicity of Jesus, the affirmation of these earliest high Christologies was intended precisely to safeguard the normativeness of Jesu [... The note breaks off at this point in Yoder's manuscript. Presumably he is referring to the normativeness of Jesus's historical life—Eds.].

78. Phillips, *Christ for Us*, 82; cf. Bonhoeffer, *GS* 3:233.

8

Following-After and Becoming Human
A Study of Bonhoeffer and Kierkegaard

Brian Gregor

ACCORDING TO JÜRGEN MOLTMANN, THE NOTION OF DISCIPLESHIP is "a Cinderella of Protestantism." For a long time it was a lowly and despised stepsister. In the established churches it was considered an excess of the pietist fringe, that is, "the 'voluntary' groups on the left wing of the Reformation—the people who were notoriously slandered as 'enthusiasts', 'fanatics', 'do-gooders' or 'radicals.'"[1] At the same time, it also threatened to contaminate the gospel with the works-righteousness of the medieval *imitatio Christi*. One of Dietrich Bonhoeffer's many achievements, Moltmann proposes, was to make it possible to mention discipleship in polite society.[2] Bonhoeffer gave the theme of discipleship a degree of respectability and credibility that it had rarely been afforded in these theological and ecclesial circles.

What is missing from Moltmann's story, however, is recognition of Søren Kierkegaard's importance in rehabilitating the theme of discipleship from a Protestant perspective as well as of his significant influence on Bonhoeffer's treatment of the theme in *Discipleship*. For Kierkegaard and Bonhoeffer alike, the theme of discipleship arose in response to a persistent, troubling question. As Kierkegaard articulates it in a journal entry from 1852: What sort of ethics should one adopt, if one dares to call oneself a Christian? Given the reality of Christ's atonement, what sort of existential manifestation does this event take "year after year"?[3]

---

1. Moltmann, "Consequences of Discipleship," 79.
2. Ibid.
3. Hong and Hong, *Søren Kierkegaard's Journals and Papers*, 355 (entry 1912) (cita-

This question also troubled Bonhoeffer.[4] It is the question of ethical concreteness, and Kierkegaard and Bonhoeffer both offer the same answer: The concrete manifestation of faith must take the form of *following after* Christ and being conformed to his image. The Danish term Kierkegaard uses is *Efterfølgelse*, while Bonhoeffer's German term is *Nachfolge*, and these cognates translate the Greek *akolouthein*, which means to go after or behind someone.[5] Faith is not a merely cognitive relation of assent to correct doctrine but is rather a whole-person response to the call of Christ. Faith is inseparable from the obedient response of following after Christ in concrete, everyday existence.

Kierkegaard's influence on Bonhoeffer's concept of discipleship has been well documented,[6] so the present essay will not focus primarily on tracing this influence. Instead, I will bring these two thinkers into dialogue on the theme of following-after and its role in becoming human. This dialogue will address several points: Kierkegaard's and Bonhoeffer's shared critique of the idealist account of subjectivity and their emphasis on the finitude and concreteness of existence; their efforts to retrieve the biblical category of following after Christ as a corrective to the cheap grace that came to characterize Lutheran Christendom; their dialectical understanding of the relation between faith and obedience, as well as the relation between passivity and activity; and finally, the role of the imagination in following after Christ.

What It Is to Be a Human Being

For Kierkegaard and his pseudonyms, *becoming human* is fundamentally a matter of *becoming subjective*. In the *Concluding Unscientific Postscript*, the pseudonym Johannes Climacus argues that every human being has the task of becoming subjective. This is related to his infamous claim that "truth is subjectivity." This is not, *nota bene*, a plea for subjectiv*ism* but rather recognition that being in the truth is not merely a matter of having the right cognitive content. It concerns my

tions from *Søren Kierkegaard's Journals and Papers* are cited hereafter as *JP*, followed by entry number).

4. On ethical concreteness as a question arising from Bonhoeffer's reading of Barth, see Bethge, *Bonhoeffer: A Biography*, 182–86.

5. Barth, *Church Dogmatics*, 534.

6. For more on Kierkegaard's influence on Bonhoeffer in this regard, see Kelly, "Kierkegaard as 'Antidote.'"

first-person relation to that content—in other words, the way I live the truth. Objective thinking focuses exclusively on the content of thought,[7] but it forgets that the thinker is also a concrete, existing human being. The task of becoming subjective is therefore a matter of passionately appropriating the truth; it is a matter of making decisions and acting on them in the real world, rather than in the world of abstract possibilities. Thus another pseudonym, Anti-Climacus, writes that truth is not a matter of knowing but of being, such that one's life becomes an expression of the truth.[8] This is not to exclude the cognitive aspect of one's relation to the truth, but rather to say that knowing cannot be separated from the existential *how* of one's standing in the truth.

In the *Postscript* Climacus goes on to argue that becoming subjective is the *highest* task of every human being.[9] Yet according to Climacus, every human being also has an impulse to go beyond this task and become something more than subjective, and thus more than human.[10] Humans tend to take subjectivity as a "matter of course," as a launching pad to bigger and better things. This is what Climacus discerns in Hegel's system—namely, the philosopher's delusion that one can abstract from one's concrete existence and become absolute, achieving a God-like view that comprehends reality as a systematic whole. On this point Kierkegaard is an important influence on Bonhoeffer's critique of philosophy. In *Act and Being* Bonhoeffer approvingly cites Kierkegaard's remark that this sort of philosophizing forgets that the thinker exists.[11] But in reality the thinker cannot abstract himself out of his immersion in being. The thinker always exists *in medias res*. Following Kant, Bonhoeffer argues that the human being is suspended between two limit points, as a sort of *being-between* the thing-in-itself and transcendental apperception.[12] In other words, the thinking subject can know neither the reality of the world, nor the thinking subject itself, as they are in themselves; these are limits that resist thinking and its

---

7. Kierkegaard, *Concluding Unscientific Postscript*, 202.
8. Kierkegaard, *Practice in Christianity*, 205.
9. Kierkegaard, *Concluding Unscientific Postscript*, 133.
10. Ibid., 130.
11. *DBWE* 2:39.
12. Ibid., 35.

impulse to become a closed system. As a consequence, thinking cannot transcend these limits and achieve a systematic totality of thought.

Bonhoeffer takes up Heidegger's use of the term *Dasein* to designate the distinctly human mode of being, and while his terminology evokes Heidegger's description of Dasein's existential thrownness (*Geworfenheit*), his account of being-between more closely resembles Kierkegaard's understanding of concrete existence as "interestedness," that is, inter-*esse*.[13] For Kierkegaard, the task of becoming authentically human requires that the existing subject "receive its own finitude," which means being pulled away from its drive for closure and instead "exposed" to the fundamental openness and passivity in which subjectivity originates.[14] In Bonhoeffer's terms, this means being broken out of the incurvature of the *cor curvum in se* (the heart turned in on itself) and recognizing that the thinking I is not its own alpha and omega, nor the point in which thought and reality are reconciled as a systematic totality.

Philosophical thinking does not typically aspire to become subjective. It wants to be *absolute*. Climacus tries to call the thinker away from philosophical pretensions to divinity, back to the task of becoming a concrete, existing human being. On the one hand, this is a plea for modesty: "Let us be human beings," he writes.[15] Let us be honest about our finitude. But, on the other hand, to exist as a human being is no modest endeavor. What the systematic philosopher takes to be the simplest of things is really the most difficult task of all.[16] Ironically, when the philosopher tries to become something *more* than subjective, he ends up becoming something *less*. By operating at the level of abstract thought, he fails to take up the task that is distinctly human.

---

13. Bonhoeffer's commitment to limits and the impossibility of thinking reaching totality are more akin to Kierkegaard (and Levinas) than to Heidegger, which is evident in Bonhoeffer's critique of Heidegger's ontology for its failure to remain genuinely open. Despite Heidegger's emphasis on finitude, he ends up offering a picture of Dasein's self-understanding as a self-enclosed finitude—a totality that cannot be genuinely open for the transcendence of revelation (*DBWE* 2:72–73).

14. See Kangas, *Kierkegaard's Instant*, 156–57.

15. Kierkegaard, *Concluding Unscientific Postscript*, 114.

16. Ibid., 308.

❖ ❖ ❖

A central feature of Climacus's position is his claim that "[i]t is really the God-relationship that makes a human being a human being."[17] The relation to God is what distinguishes authentic human being from the sort of sham-existence that proceeds by imitating others. Climacus gives the example of a congenial partygoer, who is by all outward estimations a successful human being. His success lies in his ability to mimic the manners and actions appropriate to his social circumstances. Yet he is like a "puppet character," a "satire" on human existence. This is not because he is merely unoriginal, but for the more fundamental reason that the God-relation is lacking: "It is really the God-relation that makes a human being a human being, but this is what he would lack." True human being is existing before God (*coram Deo*). This God-relation is not merely a matter of making the right theological assertions, or making the right religious observances. As Climacus never tires of reminding us, we do not come to be in the truth simply by learning objective truths by rote. Religious truth—the "*essential truth*" about the concrete, existing human being in relation to God—lies in the existential *how* of subjectivity.

The human being tries to find its way to true humanity by mimicking "the others," and ends up living a sham existence. However, it is also important to recognize that when Kierkegaard argues that the true God-relation occurs in Christian faith, this God-relation does involve a mimetic, imitative relation. Christ is the example, the prototype (*Forbillede*) who shows us what it is to be human. As Anti-Climacus writes in *The Sickness unto Death*, "Out of love, God becomes man. He says: Here you see what it is to be a human being . . . Look this way, he says, and know for certain what it is to be a human being."[18] In the incarnate Christ we encounter the true God as well as true humanity. Becoming a Christian, and becoming truly human, requires that we follow after Christ. But according to Kierkegaard this basic Christian insight had been obscured by Protestant Christendom, and so it was in need of retrieval. It is on this point that Kierkegaard's influence on Bonhoeffer is most apparent.

17. Ibid., 244.
18. Kierkegaard, *Sickness unto Death*, 127–28.

Retrieving the Practice of Discipleship

In §66 of his *Church Dogmatics*, where he examines the call to follow after Jesus in discipleship, Karl Barth writes that Bonhoeffer's *Discipleship* is "easily the best" that has been written on the subject. In Barth's judgment the depth and precision of the opening sections are such that he admits he is "almost tempted simply to reproduce them in an extended quotation."[19] One wonders if Bonhoeffer might have made a similar admission regarding Kierkegaard's journals, since the discussion in the opening sections of *Discipleship* draws so much from them. In addition to deriving the book's title from Kierkegaard,[20] Bonhoeffer makes frequent and heavy use of Kierkegaard's journals in unpacking the meaning of discipleship, such that it is possible to trace the influence of these journals almost point for point through the early chapters of Bonhoeffer's book. While I will not conduct such a comparison here,[21] some further remarks on Kierkegaard's and Bonhoeffer's respective attempts to retrieve the category of following-after are in order.

Against Cheap Grace

Kierkegaard and Bonhoeffer both decidedly oppose the model of the order of salvation (*ordo salutis*) that construes faith and obedience as separable realities. Such a separation implies that faith is the crux of Christian existence, while obedience is only a secondary consequence of faith. The danger of this separation is the implication that since one is not saved by works, the life of following after Christ in obedience is a laudable but nonessential feature of Christian existence. Kierkegaard and Bonhoeffer both critique this distorted understanding of faith out of the conviction that while grace cannot be earned, it can be cheapened. In order to avoid a gospel of cheap grace, then, it is necessary to insist on the biblical understanding of following after Christ.

---

19. Barth, *Church Dogmatics*, 533.

20. Daphne Hampson reports the account of Franz Hildebrandt, one of Bonhoeffer's friends, who was with him when he found the term in an encyclopedia article on Kierkegaard. See her *Christian Contradictions*, 267.

21. Geffrey B. Kelly's footnotes in the *DBWE* edition of *Discipleship* are very helpful for cross-referencing Bonhoeffer's text with pertinent passages in Kierkegaard's journals.

According to Kierkegaard, *Efterfølgelse* is the defining mark of genuine Christian faith. But Kierkegaard was convinced that the biblical theme of following after Christ had been discarded by the cultural Protestantism of his day. What characterizes faith in the Gospels is the obedient following of Christ, but Kierkegaard claims this was nowhere to be seen in his social, political, and religious context. If there is any warrant for the claim that following-after is an essential feature of Christian faith, Kierkegaard did not find it by observing it among his contemporaries. Instead, he discovered this theme by revisiting the New Testament, and he wanted his contemporaries to admit honestly that they (Kierkegaard included) did not live up to the ideal requirement of Christianity as it appears in the New Testament.

In a journal entry from 1850, Kierkegaard offers a brief genealogy of the category and practice of imitation. Imitation originated during the time of Christ's ministry; to be a disciple of Christ meant to follow after (*følge efter*) him, since he is the "prototype" (*Forbillede*) of Christian existence.[22] While the Gospels reflect this understanding, Paul's epistles shift the focus to the theme of atonement, and with the Pauline emphasis on Christ as the redeemer, the category of Christ as the prototype receded.[23] The category of following came back into focus during the Middle Ages, but during that period Christians acquired the mistaken idea that it was possible to succeed in resembling Christ. Kierkegaard identifies three main distortions that resulted from medieval asceticism. First, it mistakenly assumed that the *imitatio Christi* was a matter of *copying* Christ, of replicating his actions and perhaps even going beyond them.[24] As a result, the medieval mindset posited ascetic activity as an absolute *telos*, so that poverty and suffering became ends in themselves rather than consequences of a life lived in witness to the truth.[25] Second, it created the mistaken impression that imitation is

---

22. *JP* 1877.

23. "To be sure, it is precisely the apostle who had not been a witness to Christ's life, had not lived with him, the later apostle, Paul, who most strongly stresses the Atonement and almost overlooks imitation" (*JP* 1911). Cf. *JP* 1920: "If there is any question of a difference between the 'gospels' and the 'epistles,' it must be that in the 'epistles' there is stress on Christ as the Redeemer, on his reconciling death, on grace; in the gospels Christ is more the prototype."

24. *JP* 1917.

25. *JP* 1866, 1893.

the task of extraordinary individuals, thus obscuring the fact that following after Christ is required of all Christians.[26] Third, the medieval concept of imitation was bound to notions of works-righteousness, that is, the view that imitation can accrue as merit before God. Kierkegaard blames this error on the fact that imitation had become a category of the extraordinary: "how in the world could meritoriousness otherwise have arisen if imitation [*Efterfølgelsen*] had been clearly maintained simply as the requirement"? Following or imitating Christ comes to characterize an upper tier of religious devotion, a claim to merit before God, and a basis for boasting. By treating following-after as a category of the extraordinary, it opens the door for "meritoriousness" to enter in, "and after that all the blasphemous lunacy associated with it."[27] The flip side of this coin is that those who were not living in monasteries or following ascetic programs were thereby excused from the requirement of following Christ.

During the Middle Ages, then, the practice of following "was in full motion," but it was also "off course." Luther rightly attacked the idea that copying Christ in ascetic and monastic practice could earn merit before God. But the outcome of Luther's corrective was not a redefined and relocated concept of following; instead, the Lutheran legacy was that following was abolished altogether. Grace could be had on the cheap, since there was no longer any emphasis on Christ as the prototype. To be sure, this was not Luther's intent—something Kierkegaard recognizes and laments: "O, Luther, who more than you has been used by adherents [*Tilhængere*] for the very opposite of what he intended?"[28] But according to Kierkegaard, Luther presented an irresistible opportunity for a certain secular mindset that wanted to be able to call itself Christian, yet at the cheapest price possible. Hearing Luther once, then listening again (just to be sure, since this proclamation seemed too good to be true!), this mindset said to itself: "'Excellent! This is something for us. Luther says: It depends on faith alone. He himself does not say that his life expresses works, and since he is now dead it is no longer an actuality. So we take his words, his doctrine—and we are free from all

---

26. *JP* 1914.
27. Ibid. (Cf. *DWBE* 4:47).
28. *JP* 1923.

works—long live Luther!'"[29] Luther's mistake was in failing to anticipate the opportunism of the secular mindset that simply wanted to be done with the rigorousness of Christian faith: "O, you honest man, why did you not suspect how sly we human beings are! Why did you not have eyes in the back of your head so you could have prevented what was going on behind your back!"[30] Luther's mistake, Kierkegaard suggests, came from a lack of suspicion regarding human motives.

Given the common view that Luther's view of human nature is overly pessimistic, there is a certain irony in Kierkegaard's description of Luther as having been too optimistic in his estimation of how people would respond to the gospel of grace.[31] In any case, Kierkegaard faults Luther for not sufficiently stressing the fact that the New Testament (the gospels in particular) presents the category of following as an essential requirement of Christian existence.[32] Luther may have taken this for granted; after all, his breakthrough to the Pauline view of justification by grace through faith came as a conclusion after twenty years as an Augustinian monk. But Luther's followers did not have this presupposition, and so they assumed grace and forgiveness as their starting point. Yet there is a crucial difference between grace as a conclusion and grace as a presupposition. Kierkegaard argues that "there is an enormous difference if someone at the peak of all scholarly achievement suddenly stops and says: No, it does not depend on science and scholarship—and if a bricklayer's apprentice leaps up and says the same thing." In a situation like this, Kierkegaard argues, the difference between the presupposition and the conclusion is clear: "But why, then, do we not want to understand that there is this kind of difference when someone (Luther, for example), after having fasted and disciplined his flesh for twenty years and consequently conscious of being able to do this and able at any time to do this if necessary, says: No, it does not depend on this—and when we say the same thing, we who have not even tried. Are there no grounds for being suspicious about oneself if one has not tried at all?"[33]

29. Kierkegaard, *For Self-Examination*, 16.

30. *JP* 1904.

31. Cf. Alberto Gallas on Kierkegaard's critique of "Luther's insufficient and overoptimistic knowledge of human nature" ("Carnivalization of Christendom," 19).

32. *JP* 1922.

33. *JP* 2542; cf. *JP* 2543: "And just as I, if I were an innkeeper who could neither read nor write, just as I then—because I would be aware of not having the presuppositions

This distinction between the presupposition and the conclusion becomes a central insight in Bonhoeffer's *Discipleship*. Bonhoeffer reformulates Kierkegaard's point with the example of Faust: "When Faust says at the end of his life of seeking knowledge, 'I see that we can know nothing,' then it is a conclusion, a result. It is something entirely different than when a student repeats this statement in the first semester to justify his laziness. Used as a conclusion, the sentence is true; as a presupposition, it is self-deception."[34] Against this gospel of cheap, or even *stolen*,[35] grace, Kierkegaard and Bonhoeffer both attempt to retrieve and rehabilitate the category of following after Christ. In order to preclude misinterpretation, however, they both find it necessary to work out a properly dialectical treatment of the relation between faith and obedience.

The Dialectic of Faith and Obedience

The medieval error was to assume that the ascetic practice of the *imitatio Christi* could provide a method of earning merit. The Lutheran error, by contrast, was to steal grace and use it as a license for a secularized existence. This corresponds to an objectified understanding of Christianity as a system of doctrine requiring nothing more than intellectual assent.[36] Much to the contrary, Kierkegaard contends that "Christianity is a *believing* and a very particular kind of existing [*Existeren*] corresponding to it—*following after* [*Efterfølgelse*]."[37] It is a fundamental existential reorientation. Kierkegaard repeatedly uses the image of an existential *collision* to describe the consequences of actively following Christ.[38] Human beings are inclined to minimize this require-

---

that scholar had, presuppositions which gave him the right to say 'It is not scholarship that matters'—would not dare to take it as a result and repeat it, just so would I far less (for the matter is far more important) take the Lutheran principle as a result, since I am convinced that I am completely inexperienced in that which may be called the presupposition which can make the Lutheran principle truth in me."

34. *DBWE* 4:51.
35. *JP* 1917.
36. *JP* 1902.
37. *JP* 1880 (translation altered).
38. "By acting your life will come into collision with all existence [*Tilværelsen*]" (*JP* 1902). Cf. *JP* 1859, 1868, 1869, 1880, 1882, 1925; also cf. Kierkegaard's *Judge for Yourself!* (Kierkegaard, *For Self-Examination*, 169–70, 191).

ment because genuine obedience leads the faithful self on a collision course with the world; it means witnessing for the truth and against untruth. This inevitably results in suffering,[39] which is unavoidable in authentic Christian existence. Such is the path of taking up one's cross and following after Christ. As Bonhoeffer observes, when Christ calls us, his call leads us to death. He calls us to follow him to the cross, and this is a path of suffering because his call summons us to break from the world and die to ourselves—to our attachments, wishes, and desires.[40]

Given Kierkegaard's and Bonhoeffer's attempts to retrieve the category of following-after, we are faced with a question of priority. Which has priority: faith or following? In order to understand Kierkegaard we need to recognize that he sees these two categories in a dialectical relation, such that we cannot posit one without implying the other. On the one hand, we can locate faith prior to following "inasmuch as it is necessary for me to have in faith that which I am to imitate." On the other hand, we can locate following prior to faith "inasmuch as it is necessary that I, by some action which is marked in some measure by conformity to the Christian ethic (the unconditioned), collide with the world in such a way that I am brought into the situation and the situational tension in which there can first be any real question of becoming a believer."[41] Faith and following are interdependent, and any attempt to separate them results in an abstraction. Considered in this dialectical manner, it is impossible to understand Christian existence properly without both of these elements.

In order to answer the question of priority, everything depends on what kind of priority is at stake. If it is a matter of justification before God, Kierkegaard is clear that we are only justified by grace, through faith. Soteriologically, faith has priority over imitation. Here Kierkegaard is in full agreement with Luther.[42] But we need to distinguish this soteriological order from temporal or chronological order.

39. *JP* 1905.
40. *DBWE* 4:87–88.
41. *JP* 1880.
42. "The error from which Luther turned was an exaggeration with regards to works. And he was right; he did not make a mistake—a person is justified solely and only by faith" (Kierkegaard, *For Self-Examination*, 193). A few pages later, Kierkegaard also notes his anxiety over the way Christianity's "high requirement" can so easily turn into a doctrine of meritoriousness and that this is what he fears "most of all" (197).

On this point Bonhoeffer is particularly instructive, as *Discipleship* presents a somewhat clearer articulation of Kierkegaard's dialectic. Bonhoeffer frames the dialectic in terms of faith and obedience, arguing that it is correct to recognize that faith has priority in the sense that we are justified on the basis of faith alone rather than by obedient works. But it is another thing to suggest that faith is *chronologically* prior to obedience, that is, that faith is a first point followed at a later point by obedience. Conversely, it is also misleading to suggest that obedience simply precedes faith chronologically. Either way, "faith and obedience are torn apart."[43] Faith and obedience are contemporaneous, existing in an "indissoluble unity." The two are not reduced to a simple identity, but neither can they be separated from each other. On the one hand, "faith is the precondition of obedience," such that only believers obey. On the other hand, "obedience is the precondition of faith," such that only the obedient believe: "A concrete commandment has to be obeyed in order to come to believe.... Faith is possible only in this new state of existence created by obedience."[44]

Bonhoeffer also develops Kierkegaard's insights by explicitly thematizing the role of the *call* in initiating the situation in which faith becomes possible. He illustrates this through a reading of Mark 1:16–18, which recounts Christ's call and Peter's response. According to Bonhoeffer's reading of the text, the call of Christ creates an entirely new situation. The notion of the "situation" recalls Kierkegaard, who describes the need for a "decisive act" by which one enters the situation (*Bestedelse*) in which faith is possible.[45] But what Bonhoeffer adds to this description is closer attention to how the call of Christ creates this situation. This call "creates existence anew."[46] Disciples are "called away and are supposed to 'step out' of their previous existence, they are supposed to 'exist' in the strict sense of the word."[47] This is a call that issues from beyond the scope of their own human possibilities and initiative. For this reason, Bonhoeffer argues that the call itself is grace.[48]

---

43. *DBWE* 4:63.
44. Ibid., 64.
45. Kierkegaard, *For Self-Examination*, 191.
46. *DBWE* 4:62.
47. Ibid., 58.
48. Ibid., 66.

At the same time, Bonhoeffer is careful to emphasize the need for a free response to this call. The call is radically other; it comes from beyond the self and creates a situation that the self cannot initiate or create itself. Peter does not seek out Christ, nor does he respond on his own terms. Peter has no power to convert himself. Yet there is one thing he can do: he can leave his nets.[49] The call creates the new situation, but this situation still requires an active response. Similarly, when Christ calls Peter to step out of the boat and come to him on the water, Peter needs to take this step. To be sure, this "first step of obedience is itself an act of faith in Christ's word. But it would completely misrepresent the essence of faith to conclude that the step is no longer necessary, because in that step there had already been faith."[50] Such an interpretation would tear apart the essential unity of faith and obedience.

Bonhoeffer organizes his description of obedience around this image of the *first step*, which is the active response of the disciple. The disciple continues to be a human agent. The call creates the situation in which faith can be possible, but only by responding with the first step can one enter "the situation of being able to believe . . . Those called must get out of their situations, in which they cannot believe, into a situation in which faith can begin."[51] The call of Christ requires that one take this first step into actuality; otherwise the appeal to "faith" is in danger of being "cheap grace" and "pious self-deception."

Bonhoeffer's account of this dialectic of faith and obedience is very Kierkegaardian, and it is important to keep this dialectic in mind when considering Kierkegaard's insistence on the indispensable role of "the voluntary" in following after Christ. Kierkegaard argues that we should not treat voluntary following so much as a consequence of faith but as "a matter of coming into the situation where I can become a Christian." Only via the step of obedience does it become possible to have faith. Luther was correct, as far as he went, in ordering things as follows: "Christ is the gift—to which faith corresponds. Then he is the prototype [*Forbilledet*]—to which imitation corresponds." At times Kierkegaard formulates things this way himself: "Imitation or discipleship does not come first, but 'grace'; then imitation follows as a fruit of

---

49. Ibid., 64.
50. Ibid., 66.
51. Ibid., 62.

gratitude, as well as one is able."[52] However, Kierkegaard also complains that Luther was insufficiently dialectical, since he failed to preserve the other point—that Christ is also the prototype who requires that we follow after him. Only with following-after as our presupposition can we understand Christ as the gift of grace. In order to correct this one-sidedness, then, Kierkegaard contends that it is more accurate to put it as follows: "(1) imitation in the direction of decisive action whereby the situation for becoming a Christian comes into existence; (2) Christ as gift—faith; (3) imitation as the fruit of faith."[53] Given the state of affairs that Kierkegaard discerned in Christendom, this emphasis on decisive, voluntary action may have been a necessary corrective, but it also needs to be handled with care lest it imply that the initial movements of following-after (step 1) are self-initiated. As Bonhoeffer shows, this activity is already initiated by the prior grace of Christ's call. The disciple's response to this initiating call is then one of faith and obedient following, and it is crucial that we grasp the dialectical relation between these two, since neither one can subsist without the other.[54]

Activity and Passivity in Christian Existence

Like Kierkegaard's emphasis on active striving, Bonhoeffer's account of *Nachfolge* insists that we need to take the first step and follow Christ into the situation in which Christian existence becomes possible. For both thinkers this emphasis on activity is dialectically calibrated to correct the distortions of Lutheran Christendom and its presupposition of cheap grace. But a critic might object that this supposed dialectical

52. JP 1886.
53. JP 1908.
54. This is why Kierkegaard cautions himself about the dangers of staring "one-sidedly" at Christ the prototype and thereby going astray: "It is the dialectical element connected with Christ as the gift, as that which is given to us (to call to mind Luther's standard classification). But dialectical as my nature is, in the passion of the dialectical it always seems as if the contrasting thought were not present at all—and so the one side comes first of all and most strongly" (JP 1852). In another journal entry from 1849, we see a similar point regarding the importance of understanding Christ dialectically—as *prototype* as well as *gift*, the object of following as well as faith. Dialectically, Luther was correct to stress Christ as gift, as grace; but this insight was "taken completely in vain, so that the 'imitator' [*Efterfølgeren*] in no way resembles the prototype but is absolutely undifferentiated, and then grace is merely slipped in" (JP 1862). Thus Kierkegaard emphasizes Protestantism's need for a corrective in the other direction.

unity of faith and obedience is ultimately a contradiction. How can we reconcile this emphasis on the disciple's active response with the point that there is a fundamental passivity at the origin of faith (and likewise at the origin of human being)?

Bonhoeffer is aware of this tension, and he became more conscious of it in his later writings, such as in one well-known letter to Eberhard Bethge. During his period of study in America, Bonhoeffer had become friends with the French pacifist Jean Lasserre, and in one conversation they considered what they wanted to do with their lives. Lasserre confessed a desire to become a saint, and Bonhoeffer writes that this is probably what happened. But despite his admiration for Lasserre, Bonhoeffer disagreed and said that he would like to "learn to have faith." Bonhoeffer admits that it was some time before he recognized the "depth of this contrast" between sainthood and faith. He had considered it possible to acquire faith by striving after an ideal of a holy life and admits that *Discipleship* marks the culmination of his thinking in that direction. Thus Bonhoeffer admits that while he stands by that earlier book, he also recognizes its dangers.[55]

Bonhoeffer elaborates that "the dangers of that book" lie in the "attempt to make something of oneself." This is the danger in striving to embody any ideal, whether it be "saint," "converted sinner," "churchman," "righteous" or "unrighteous," "sick" or "healthy." Christian *metanoia* is a transformation of one's vision of the world, but this does not simply consist in adopting a new existential ideal after which one strives. The difference is between ethical striving after an ideal and ontological participation in the being of Christ. The latter means living "completely" and "unreservedly" in this world, with all of its responsibilities, joys, and difficulties: "In so doing we throw ourselves completely into the arms of God, taking seriously, not our own sufferings, but those of God in the world—watching with Christ in Gethsemane."[56] Christian existence is not only *following after* Christ, but *being in* Christ. Indeed, we will see below that the latter is a necessary condition for the former.

It is worth noting, however, that while Bonhoeffer discerns certain dangers in his early account of discipleship, the text of *Discipleship* does try to guard against interpreting Christian existence as an ethical or

---

55. Bonhoeffer, *Letters and Papers*, 369.
56. Ibid., 370.

religious project of self-making. In the final chapter of the text he argues that we are called to be like Christ (*kathos Christos*) only because we are already in Christ: "Only because we bear Christ's image already can Christ be the 'example' whom we follow."[57] Christ (and, indeed, the whole Trinity) indwells the Christian.[58] Christ is in us, and conversely we are in Christ, and this participation brings us into our true humanity.[59] Moreover, this participation is the reality from which our active obedience and conformation originates. Prior to our active striving, we are *already* in Christ; we are called to bear the image and likeness of Christ because we have already been shaped into this image and already bear this likeness.[60]

This insight is in keeping with Bonhoeffer's *Act and Being*, where he argues that "the existence of human beings is always already 'being-in.'"[61] The human being finds herself already immersed in being, prior to her conscious activity. This is true of our fallen being-in-Adam as well as our later being-in-Christ. Bonhoeffer derives this point from Luther, who argues that, in faith, being is prior to acting, and, even more fundamental still, is being acted-upon.[62] As Bonhoeffer puts it, the order of priority is passivity (*pati*)—being (*esse*)—acting (*agere*).[63]

This order of priorities is also important for understanding the first step of obedience. While it is true that the "first step" of obedience is an act of taking a position, it is not an autonomous self-positing. Instead, it is a response to a prior call from Christ, and this call is what initiates the being of the disciple. The call is a necessary condition of discipleship, because the disciple does not posit herself as disciple. The disciple must be called into being. This call itself is grace, and Bonhoeffer even

57. *DBWE* 4:287.
58. Ibid., 286–87.
59. Ibid., 285.
60. Ibid., 287.
61. *DBWE* 2:108.
62. Ibid., 116 n. 48.

63. Ibid., 121; As we saw in the first section, this Lutheran ranking of priorities also appears in Kierkegaard. Against the idealist view, for Kierkegaard subjectivity does not come into being in a self-positing act. Subjectivity is inextricably intertwined in existence. Prior to its activity, it is already inter-*esse*, and at the very origin of subjectivity is a fundamental passivity, such that coming into being is a matter of receiving a gift rather than an act of self-positing. It is a further task for Kierkegaard scholarship to determine the relation between this inter-*esse* and the voluntary act of following-after.

claims that this grace is in a certain sense *irresistible*.[64] The call is not an abstract universal possibility to be contemplated and decided upon by a naked, arbitrating will. The call is an election.

The call to follow after Christ undermines two key features of the idealist view of human subjectivity (expressed most pointedly by Fichte's *Wissenschaftslehre*): (1) the claim that subjectivity originates in a self-positing act, and (2) moral autonomy. Both of these features aim to establish the thinking *Ich* as its own alpha and omega, but Bonhoeffer's description of the call shows that the human person comes into being through the address of another, not through a word that it speaks to itself. In his inaugural lecture, "The Anthropological Question in Contemporary Philosophy and Theology," Bonhoeffer argues that human self-understanding requires a point of unity (*Einheitspunkt*) from which one is genuinely addressed. Idealism depicts a subject who addresses itself autonomously[65] and has the immanent potential to determine its own existence as good because it already has autonomous rational access to the universal moral law. The subject is therefore self-positing as well as self-mediating. But Bonhoeffer diagnoses this drive for autonomy as a symptom of the *cor curvum in se* that characterizes the old Adamic humanity. By contrast, the new humanity of Christ overcomes this insistence on autonomous self-activity by giving the new humanity of Christ as a gift, as a grace that can only be received in faith.[66]

The Image of Christ and Human Imagination

In Bonhoeffer's critique of the autonomous, incurved *Ich*, human rationality is a primary point of contention. There are good reasons to focus on the status of rationality: the *imago Dei* is often identified with reason, and humanity's attempt to be "like God" (*sicut Deus*) so often

---

64. *DBWE* 4:60.

65. *DBWE* 10:389–90.

66. Contrast this with Kant's Christology, which seeks to preserve the rational autonomy of morality. Christ can therefore not introduce a new law heteronomously but must confirm the universal moral law. Christ, the "founder" of Christianity, "speaks not as a commander who requires obedience to *his will*, but as a friend of mankind who places in the hearts of his fellow men their own well-understood wills, i.e., the will in accord with which they would themselves freely act" ("The End of All Things," 102).

fixates on its rational capacities.[67] The modern human being in particular cites self-critical reason as evidence of its potential to be genuinely autonomous and self-sufficient. The status of reason is pivotal in our understanding of who we are and what it is to be human, which is one reason why Bonhoeffer discerns an implicit yet inextricable link between epistemology and anthropology. As he observes in the introduction to *Act and Being*, "the meaning of epistemology [*Erkenntnistheorie*] is anthropology." Consequently, when the human capacity to know is in question, so is the very being of the human.[68]

It is entirely appropriate that Bonhoeffer's anthropological reflections seek to clarify the status of reason, but no investigation of the epistemological-anthropological question can be complete without an examination of the human *imagination*. Yet the theme of the imagination is underrepresented in Bonhoeffer's thought, which is surprising since it plays a vital role in the epistemology of Kant as well as post-Kantian idealism and romanticism. Given the importance of this milieu for Bonhoeffer's intellectual formation, one would expect him to engage its account of the imagination. In this regard Bonhoeffer can benefit from further dialogue with Kierkegaard, who recognized the importance of the imagination in his engagement with post-Kantian thought. Even more importantly, given our present topic, Kierkegaard articulates the role of the imagination in following after Christ.[69] In light of Bonhoeffer's discussion of the image of Christ (*das Bild Christi*) as having a transformative potency in the being of the disciple, it is only fitting that we make a few brief observations about the role of the imagination in the relation of discipleship.

While Bonhoeffer does not articulate a proper account of the imagination (*Einbildungskraft*), near the end of *Discipleship* he makes an observation that does recognize the ontological significance of the image (*das Bild*). He observes that

> every human being bears an image. As a human being we are not merely word, thought, or will. Rather, before and in all of these we are a human being, a form, an image, a brother or sister.

---

67. For Bonhoeffer's contrast between Adam created in the image of God and fallen Adam becoming "like God," see *DBWE* 3:113.

68. *DBWE* 2:30.

69. For a more detailed discussion of Kierkegaard on imagination and following-after, see my essay "Thinking through Kierkegaard's Anti-Climacus."

A human being thus develops not only a new way of thinking, willing, and doing things, but a new image, a new form. In Jesus Christ, God's own image has come into our midst in the form of our lost human life, in the likeness of sinful flesh. God's own image becomes revealed in Jesus' teaching and in his deeds, in his life and in his death. In him God has created anew the divine image on earth.[70]

In creating the *imago Dei* anew, Christ also becomes the image of the new humanity, so that by participating in Christ we are "given our true humanity."[71] We are "drawn into Christ's image" and "changed into the likeness of Christ's form,"[72] and in this transformation we become truly human.

According to Bonhoeffer, image is ontologically constitutive; it is the fundamental shape, the *how*, of one's being. He uses the German *Bild* to translate the Greek *morphē*, or form. Bonhoeffer makes a similar point in *Ethics* with the term *Gestalt*, when writing of conformation to the *Gestalt Christi*. Conformation is a "metamorphosis, a complete inner change of the existing form, a 'renewal' of the mind ... This 'metamorphosis' of human beings can only mean overcoming the form of the fallen human being, Adam, as con-formation [*Gleichgestaltung*]."[73] Bonhoeffer also describes this transformation as "*Umgestaltung*, 'reshaping.'"[74] Like *Discipleship*, *Ethics* describes conformation as a matter of being transformed *by* the *Gestalt Christi*. One is not simply transformed *into* this *Gestalt*, but is transformed *by* this *Gestalt*: "The form of Jesus Christ takes form in human beings. They do not take on their own self-determined forms. What gives them form and holds them in this new form is always only the form of Jesus Christ."[75] Here Bonhoeffer's humanism comes even more fully into view, as he writes that the forms of human being "are not imitations or repetitions of Christ's form, but the form of Christ that takes form in human beings. Again, human beings are not transformed into an alien form, the form of God, but into the form that belongs to them, that is essentially their own." One of the

70. *DBWE* 4:283–84.
71. Ibid., 285.
72. Ibid., 286.
73. *DWBE* 6:322.
74. Ibid., n. 81.
75. Ibid., 95–96.

most significant consequences of Christ's incarnation is that it is the condition for true humanity: "Human beings become human because God became human."[76] Human beings are not made divine. To be human is to be conformed to the one who became human, was crucified, and was resurrected.[77]

Since Bonhoeffer uses *Bild* to translate the Greek *morphē*, and later replaces *Bild* with *Gestalt*, it might seem that we are making an illicit inference by moving from image (*Bild*) to imagination (*Einbildungskraft*). One might object that Bonhoeffer is describing a metaphysical rather than epistemological concept of form—in other words, that he is describing the structure of human being rather than the act of human knowing. In response to this objection we should recall *Act and Being*, where Bonhoeffer argues that an epistemology appropriate for Christian revelation must maintain the conjunction between act *and* being, epistemology *and* ontology. He therefore argues that act is always *in reference to* being, and being *is* in reference to act.[78] This means that while the image of Christ has a real ontological efficacy of its own, this transformative reality is at the same time given in and through the noetic acts of the believer. This point is relevant to our earlier discussion of activity and passivity in the life of faith, since Bonhoeffer recognizes that there is both passivity and activity involved in the encounter with revelation (in this case, the image of Christ).

Although Bonhoeffer's description here is strongly Kantian, he does not examine one of the central elements of Kant's transcendental deduction, namely, the imagination. As a result, Bonhoeffer leaves a certain ambiguity regarding the interplay of activity and passivity. According to Kant's transcendental deduction, the imagination is the locus of this interplay; the imagination mediates between the spontaneity of the understanding and the receptivity of sensibility, so that intuition can conform to the categories of the understanding.[79] Thus imagination is not merely reproductive, not a mere association of ideas; instead, it is genuinely *productive*. It is important to recognize, though, that while Kant argues that the role of the imagination is productive, it

---

76. Ibid., 96.
77. Ibid., 94–95.
78. *DBWE* 2:120–22.
79. See B151–52 in Kant, *Critique of Pure Reason*, 164–65.

does not *project* a reality of its own creation. This point has important implications for an epistemology of revelation, insofar as the imagination can act as the locus of revelation[80] without being its source or point of origin. Otherwise, theology would confirm Feuerbach's suspicion that theological discourse is an imaginative projection of anthropological insights. Unfortunately, though, in *Discipleship* the Feuerbachian account of imagination is the only one Bonhoeffer explicitly addresses, writing that the "prototype from which the human form takes its shape is either the imaginative form of God based on human projection, or it is the true and living form of God which molds the human form into the image of God."[81] This disjunction seems to suggest that the imagination can only hinder the genuine encounter with God. But what if the imagination is the locus of this encounter? What if the true and living form of God, which we encounter in the image of Christ, in fact addresses us and transforms us in and through the imagination?

Some of Bonhoeffer's other remarks in *Discipleship* are primed for just this insight. For example, consider his claim that the image of Christ "will transform those who look at it": "Those who behold Christ are being drawn into Christ's image, changed into the likeness of Christ's form."[82] But we need to ask how this beholding occurs: Not as a purely rational contemplation, but also *in the imagination.* Christian *metanoia*, the transformation of our minds (the metamorphosis of our *nous*) that Paul describes in Romans 12:2, is only partial if it does not affect our entire noetic process. Thus it cannot apply exclusively to reason but must include the imagination as well. *Metanoia* entails that we begin to imagine differently. In the imagination, we are addressed by the power of new, eschatological possibilities. As Paul Ricoeur has argued, "it is in the *imagination* that the new being is first formed in me." Prior to reason and prior to the will is the imagination,[83] and it is through the imagination that the image of Christ calls us into being as disciples, summoning us and drawing us forward in the new existence of following after Christ.

---

80. Green, *Imagining God*, 43.
81. DBWE 4:283.
82. Ibid., 286.
83. Ricoeur, "Philosophical and Theological Hermeneutics," 33.

As we behold the image of Christ, we are drawn out and transformed into his likeness. Here Bonhoeffer agrees with Kierkegaard, who can enrich Bonhoeffer's description because of his closer attention to the role of the imagination in "being drawn" by the image of Christ. In *The Sickness unto Death*, Anti-Climacus argues that imagination "is the capacity *instar omnium*"—the capacity for all capacities; thus "whatever of feeling, knowing, and willing a person has depends upon what imagination he has."[84] Likewise in *Practice in Christianity*, Anti-Climacus argues that the power of the imagination "is the first condition for what becomes of a person."[85] In and through the imagination, the self is addressed by the power of the possible.[86]

The image of Christ is not, however, simply an example or ideal possibility that we need to actualize through our own self-directed powers. The image has a power of its own that draws us forward, incorporating us into the being of Christ and conforming us to his likeness. Anti-Climacus offers a rich description of the way God uses the imagination to draw us out into the life of faith. He illustrates this process with a scenario in which a young man is drawn out by the image of Christ, such that he desires to resemble this image. The image "exercises its power over him, the power of love, which is indeed capable of everything, above all of making alike; his whole deepest inner being is transformed little by little, and he seems to be beginning to resemble,

---

84. Kierkegaard, *Sickness unto Death*, 30–31.

85. Kierkegaard, *Practice in Christianity*, 186.

86. In a journal entry from 1854, Kierkegaard writes: "Imagination is what providence uses to take men captive in actuality, in existence, in order to get them far enough out, or within, or down into actuality. And when imagination has helped them get as far out as they should be—then actuality genuinely begins" (*JP* 1832). At the same time, Anti-Climacus also offers a sharp critique of imagination insofar as it can leave the self to linger in the realm of possibility. Then imagination [*Phantasie*] can give way to the fantastic [*Phantastiske*], such that the self becomes lost in reverie, envisioning abstract possibilities rather than engaging in concrete existence. It is easy to take Christ as the object of poetic admiration, to warm oneself with sentimental religious daydreams, and to fancy oneself a good Christian; but this is qualitatively different from actually following Christ. Consequently, if imagination is the first condition for what becomes of a person, the second condition is the will. The self must venture forth from possibility into actuality, taking that first step into existence. Thus the image of Christ should not become a fantastic figure to which we relate from afar, because Christ requires that we follow after him. Christ is the prototype (*Forbillede*) and "you must conform to his life" (*Practice in Christianity*, 100; *JP* 1864).

however imperfectly, this image."[87] The image (*Billede*) of Christ, the prototype (*Forbillede*), draws the young man out and sustains him through the ongoing process of becoming a Christian.

What is intriguing about Anti-Climacus's description is that the image of Christ exerts a transformative potency over the young man, such that he is gradually conformed to this image. This parallels Bonhoeffer's point that the image of Christ exerts its transformative power in us. Our conformation is possible because Christ indwells us, such that the image of Christ takes shape within us and conforms us to himself.[88] The image itself has a transformative potency.[89] Christ enacts this conformation in us, so that the self is conformed *to* the likeness of Christ *by* the form of Christ. There is therefore a prior passivity that enables our active following. We can imitate Christ truly only insofar as we are already in him. And this provides the context for interpreting Ephesians 5:1, with which Bonhoeffer concludes *Discipleship*: As one who bears the image of Christ, the follower (*Nachfolger*) of Jesus is called to be an imitator (*Nachahmer*) of God.[90]

◆ ◆ ◆

We have seen that there are significant similarities between Bonhoeffer and Kierkegaard, particularly in their common desire to combat the cheap grace of Lutheran Christendom by retrieving the biblical category of following after, in their dialectical understanding of the relation between faith and obedience, as well as in their conviction that following after Christ is the path of becoming truly human. Their positions are not identical, and in another context it would be worth contrasting their understanding of such themes as the church community and the worldliness of faith. For now, though, I have pointed to differences of emphasis regarding two main points: First, the status of the call as a grace that initiates the relation of discipleship, and, second, the role of the imagination in this relation. The strength of Bonhoeffer's account is that he highlights the way the image of Christ transforms us; but he does not examine the power of the imagination as a human capacity,

---

87. Kierkegaard, *Practice in Christianity*, 193.
88. *DBWE* 4:285.
89. Ibid., 281.
90. Ibid., 288.

nor its role in the human being's conformation to the image of Christ. Kierkegaard, by contrast, offers a somewhat more general philosophical-anthropological account of imagination and its role in the structure of subjectivity. Further consideration of this point requires attention to the relation between the image of Christ and other types of images (somewhat parallel to the relation between the divine word and the human word), but on the basis of this broader description of imagination, Kierkegaard highlights its vital role in following after and being conformed to the image of Christ. With this description Kierkegaard can enrich Bonhoeffer's account of discipleship. The call to follow after Christ addresses us with a new, eschatological possibility, and the call does this in and through the imagination.

9

Con-Formation with Jesus Christ

Bonhoeffer, Social Location, and Embodiment

Lisa E. Dahill

WHAT DO WE LEARN FROM DIETRICH BONHOEFFER ABOUT BEING AND becoming human? That question animating this volume of essays pushes deep into Christian anthropology, ecclesiology, social analysis, and Christology—that is to say, it invites us into the territory of the *body*. To assert that the questions at the heart of Bonhoeffer's thinking and witness are inherently matters of reflective Christian *embodiment* in the world may seem so clear as not to warrant comment; obviously humans are constituted as bodies, and anything we might say about our humanity and life together in the world must take account of that fact. Yet despite the centrality of the body in human life—and in Bonhoeffer's own theology, on many levels—few scholars have devoted extended attention to the significance of human embodiment for Bonhoeffer.[1] That fact inspired my initial desire to explore this territory for the present volume. I thought that linking the topic of embodiment to Bonhoeffer's insights on conformation (*Gleichgestaltung*) with Christ would be a fruitful way in, opening provocative questions about how persons in various social locations—with very different "forms" of embodiment, giving rise to

---

1. In fact, as note 2 below makes clear, until recently few scholars have devoted attention to human embodiment as an explicit focus of Christian theological reflection at all. In the case of Bonhoeffer, the most developed survey of this material, though limited to the material in *Ethics* and the chapter on the "Body of Christ" in *Discipleship*, is Vosloo, "Body and Health." In the chapter "Song of Songs" in *Earth Community*, Larry Rasmussen develops the significance of Bonhoeffer's theology of the body within his broader incarnational vision; cf. especially 307–13.

very different experiences of being human—are *con*-formed to Jesus Christ. I began working on this essay on this basis.

Then this past November (2009) the film *Precious* (based on *Push: A Novel* by Sapphire, 1996) was released and came to my local movie theater; I saw it the weekend it opened here. This film, directed by Lee Daniels and starring Gabourey Sidibe in the title role of Claireece Precious Jones, explodes off the screen in opening the heart and life of an impoverished African-American 16-year-old in 1980s Harlem. Precious Jones, obese and friendless, has been a victim of rape by her father and of multiple layers of abuse by her mother apparently all her life. She is now pregnant for the second time by her father; the first child, a three-year-old with Down's syndrome, is being raised by Precious's grandmother, while Precious's mother is supporting herself and Precious on welfare. Overwhelmed with the pain of her daily life, shamed further by the assumptions of promiscuity her pregnancies evoke, Precious is illiterate and failing in seventh grade until she is referred to an alternative school. There for the first time she experiences herself seen and loved as she is, and she slowly begins to stand up for herself and, soon, her newborn son: a fragile hope and humanity emerging that makes the subsequent discovery that the years of rape have also infected her with her father's HIV-positive status all the more shattering.

The film shook me in inviting its viewers so frankly into this level of pain and in the ways Precious's story pushes questions of embodiment in relation to the experience of being human. Her bodily experience is far indeed from that of Bonhoeffer, at least in his pre-war life. Raped, tormented, pregnant, impoverished, HIV-positive, and belonging to an oppressed racial minority whose members' bodies bear centuries of such torture—Precious is everything Dietrich as a privileged Aryan male body is not. Yet she too is human, and the film's greatest power comes not in its scenes of torture, shocking as those are, but in so profoundly evoking this humanity. In the process the film pulled open the questions of this essay even further.

And so I will trace these themes of embodiment in Bonhoeffer's writings and see how they illumine the story opened in the film *Precious*—and how the character depicted there in turn sheds new light on the concerns of this essay and volume. Along the way, I will also note—as originally planned, but with a new resonance—how

Bonhoeffer's categories of "con-formation with Christ" give further language to the experience of being and becoming human.

First, then, Bonhoeffer and embodiment. The topic of embodiment itself is of course endlessly complex, perhaps the most complex of any theological locus, since for Christians the uniting of the fullness of human and divine reality in the flesh of Jesus Christ means that consideration of the body opens out into very nearly every other topic imaginable.[2] And Bonhoeffer himself treats many of these connections (in addition to bearing in his own body the marks of both privilege *and* of captivity, suffering, and death under the terror of the Nazi regime[3]), which means that even the apparently more manageable topic of "Bonhoeffer and embodiment" also quickly becomes almost impossibly complex. From all that could be said on this topic, worthy of a full-length monograph, I will therefore sketch five key features of Bonhoeffer's view of the human body: its essential goodness, its rights to life and joy, its role as "limit" to one another, its centrality in Christian community, and its indwelling by God.

In his 1933 lectures on Genesis, published as *Creation and Fall*, Bonhoeffer takes up the creation of human bodies from the good earth God has made. Commenting on Genesis 2:7 ("The Human Being as Earth and Spirit"), he notes: "It is God's earth out of which humankind

---

2. The complexity of this subject means that its literature is correspondingly vast, though in many ways still systematically thin. For centuries, despite their incarnational religion, Christian theologians with few exceptions tended to ignore or sideline questions of human embodiment and its theological significance; beginning in the 1970s with feminist and liberation perspectives of various kinds, however, the body is coming into focus as a primary locus of Christian reflection. Often these treatments engage other disciplines from a variety of perspectives: from post-modern psychoanalytic theory to the philosophy of food or the connections between spirituality and sexuality, from the coercive power of media portrayals of normative body images to the intersections of race and gender, and from the implications of our biological immersion in creation to the economic and political complexity of the Body of Christ—and any number of other topics in between, from reproduction to disability to aesthetics and the senses, from play and sports to technology and virtuality, from death to our species' future on earth. Recent theological works spanning many of these complexities include Isherwood and Stuart, *Introducing Body Theology*; Copeland, *Enfleshing Freedom*; Prokes, *Toward a Theology of the Body*; Creamer, *Disability and Christian Theology*; Bieler and Schottroff, *The Eucharist*; Prosser MacDonald, *Transgressive Corporeality*; and McFague, *Body of God*.

3. On interconnections of power, control, embodiment, and discipline—with interesting resonances for Bonhoeffer's own situation—see Foucault, *Discipline and Punish*.

is taken. From it human beings have their *bodies*. The body belongs to a person's essence. The body is not the prison, the shell, the exterior, of a human being; instead a human being is a human body. A human being does not 'have' a body—or 'have' a soul; instead a human being 'is' body and soul. The human being in the beginning really is the body."[4] Larry Rasmussen has developed the ecological significance of Bonhoeffer's clear rooting of human embodiment—and therefore our life itself—in the earth.[5] Among other gifts, this connection with earth and the broader creaturely and animal life of all things establishes within human existence a biological and emotional thickness of inherent relationality with other creatures, including other human beings. Attention to this biological level of existence—one's own or that of others—thus matters as much as do the emotional and spiritual realms: as Bonhoeffer goes on to assert, "[t]o live *as a human being* means to live as a body in the spirit. Flight from the body is as much flight from being human as is flight from the spirit. The body is the form in which the spirit exists, as the spirit is the form in which the body exists."[6] Indeed, in his *Ethics* Bonhoeffer will insist that we care for others' physical needs as the proper and indispensable means of "preparing the way" for them to hear and receive the Word of grace.[7] For it is in the body that the human needs for the essential means of life, for protection from assault and violence, and for joy and freedom are met—or not. Bonhoeffer's development of these inherently physical rights (particularly the right to bodily joy) represents a notable contribution of his unfinished *Ethics*.[8] For Bonhoeffer, body and soul are one reality: both are part of the goodness of God's creation, and both are equally essential aspects of human life and of the particular human being.

---

4. *DBWE* 3:76–77. Editorial note 9, at the word "essence," quotes Emil Brunner on this point; editorial note 10, at the end of the penultimate sentence of the above quote, cites Wilhelm Vischer and Ernst Georg Wendel.

5. See Rasmussen, "Song of Songs." Rasmussen includes treatment of this topic as well in the forthcoming volume edited by Peter Frick, *Interpreting Bonhoeffer*.

6. *DBWE* 3:78.

7. *DBWE* 6:146–70, esp. 163.

8. Ibid., 185–217. See also *DBWE* 16:377–78, Bonhoeffer's final circular letter prior to his imprisonment (I/212), on joy that embraces the body too, including Jesus's body wounded and risen. Finally, see *DBWE* 8:393–95, on the polyphony of life in which earthly and erotic joys and loves have their own good place, and the further citations provided in note 32 at the end of this essay.

For it is precisely in our physical particularity—our bodies—that we function as "limit" for one another. In describing Adam's encounter with newly created Eve, Bonhoeffer picks up the language he had developed in *Sanctorum Communio* of the other as *Grenze* or *Schranke* ("boundary/limit" or "barrier"). There, and throughout his life, he insists that it is in our encounter with the barrier or limit created by some "other" that *persons*—mature and responsible agents, selves, "I"s before God—are formed.[9] His theology of the formative role of such an encounter, in which the other mediates the ultimate alterity of God working to create and re-create persons, remains in place here in *Creation and Fall*; but now this "other" is an actual person with a name: Eve. She functions as an "other" for Adam precisely in her embodiment, her having a human body mirroring his own: the flesh of another reveals to Adam simultaneously the reality and goodness of his own human nature, shared with Eve (which he had been unable to see mirrored in the animals), and his individuality in distinction from her. Thus her existence specifically—or concretely—as body creates a person-forming limit to his original loneliness and dominance, and they love each other.[10]

By the time he wrote *Discipleship*, Bonhoeffer's understanding of the limit created by the person—and specifically the body—of the other had deepened; here he articulates fully for the first time the insight made real for him in his conversion that the intimate and ultimate Other encountered in another's body and being—the One encountering and forming us as persons—is Jesus Christ. In *Discipleship* Bonhoeffer insists on the necessarily bodily nature of our life with Jesus in discipleship—in our bodies and in his Body[11]—and in *Life Together* he explores the essentially physical nature of Christian community:[12] for, again, it is

---

9. Clifford Green wrote the first sustained study of these motifs in *Bonhoeffer: A Theology of Sociality*. See also Ford, "Polyphonic Living"; and Bongmba, "The Priority of the Other."

10. In the original creation, for Bonhoeffer, the partnership of this woman and man derives from the balancing of limit and love in the body of the other: "The helper who is a partner had to be at once the embodiment of Adam's limit and the object of Adam's love" (*DBWE* 3:98).

11. *DBWE* 4:213–17.

12. *DBWE* 5:29: "The physical presence of other Christians is a source of incomparable joy and strength to the believer . . . The believer need not feel any shame when yearning for the physical presence of other Christians, as if one were still living too much in the flesh. A human being is created as a body; the Son of God appeared on

precisely in our physical life together that we are forced to confront not only others' weaknesses but our own at their most painful depth and to be drawn together into the redeeming love that will re-create us as fully human beings in the Body of Christ. It is no accident that *Life Together* begins with the priority of physical community of human beings and ends in the sacrament of the Lord's Body: for the entire life of Christian discipleship for Bonhoeffer is an embodied one, with an embodied Lord whose Body encompasses many bodies indeed.[13]

For Bonhoeffer's deeply Lutheran appreciation of the Incarnation and thus the essential materiality, earthiness, and bodiliness of Christian faith permeates all his writings and gives him language to articulate how the flesh of Jesus Christ bears both the very fullness of divine life and grace *and* the fullness of human pain, sin, brokenness, and death—all of it (and all of us) held together in him in love. Hear his extended reflection on the gift of the Incarnation:

> "Human nature"—that is the nature, the essence, the flesh of all people, thus also my nature, my flesh . . . Perhaps we moderns would put it most clearly that in the birth of Jesus Christ God took on humanity, not just a single human being. But this taking on occurred—and this is the unique miracle of the Incarnation—physically. The body of Jesus Christ—that is our flesh. He bears our flesh . . . Thus the Christmas testimony for all people is that you are accepted; God has not rejected you but bears physically all your flesh and blood. Look at the manger! In the body of the child, in the Son of God made flesh, is your flesh; all your need, worry, distress, even all your sin is borne, forgiven, and sanctified.[14]

Thus by the mystery of Jesus's becoming flesh all humanity, indeed specifically all human bodies (not only those of Christians), are physically united to God in him, their pain and sin borne in love. We hear these familiar phrases of Jesus "assuming" all humanity or "bearing our

---

earth in the body for our sake and was raised in the body. In the sacrament the believer receives the Lord Christ in the body, and the resurrection of the dead will bring about the perfected community of God's spiritual-physical creatures. Therefore, the believer praises God . . . for the bodily presence of the other Christian."

13. I have commented elsewhere on how Bonhoeffer's emphasis on the physicality of Christian communal life provides a helpful corrective to contemporary fascination with "virtuality." See Dahill, "Dietrich Bonhoeffer," particularly 337–38.

14. *DBW* 15:540 (my translation).

sins" on the cross and may tend to skim over them; but to understand Bonhoeffer we must hear them as radically incarnationally as he intends: *in his body* Jesus bears our bodies and all the world's bodies, Christian or not. The church as the place of sacramental union with Christ is not the sole or privileged place of such physical communion but rather the community of those who realize—who make real—explicitly and visibly for the world the physical reality of mercy and love in which all the world is already held, borne, and saved.[15] Bonhoeffer thus writes in his *Ethics*:

> In the body of Jesus Christ, God is united with humankind, all humanity is accepted by God, and the world is reconciled to God. In the body of Jesus Christ, God took on the sin of all the world and bore it. There is no part of the world, no matter how lost, no matter how godless, that has not been accepted by God in Jesus Christ and reconciled to God. Whoever perceives the body of Jesus Christ in faith can no longer speak of the world as if it were lost, as if it were separated from God ... [T]he church-community of believers is to make this known to the world by word and life. This means not being separated from the world, but calling the world into the community [*Gemeinschaft*] of the body of Christ to which the world in truth already belongs.[16]

To live in Christ is to see in the bodies of all human beings—no matter how tortured or apparently far from grace—their embrace in this love and to treat them accordingly: to live in such a way that the physical embrace of all human and creaturely bodies in the love of God is experienced as true *for them*.

Thus far the primary contours of Bonhoeffer's theology of human embodiment. What insight might this embodied perspective provide into the experience opened by the film *Precious*? And how, if at all, might the perspective of the character Precious herself nuance Bonhoeffer or push him further? I wonder this since I am interested in Bonhoeffer's theology and spirituality not only in themselves (in the abstract, as it were), but in their potentially illuminating power for real human lives today; and the life of Precious Jones represents a provocative conversation partner with his theology, a test of its scope. In fact, M. Shawn Copeland has suggested in her recent book, *Enfleshing Freedom: Body,*

15. See *DBWE* 6:47–68, especially 54–55, 58–60, 62–67. See also ibid., 84–85.
16. *DBWE* 6:67.

Race, and Being, that black female bodies represent the paradigmatic test case for *all* theology produced in a racist and sexist context bent on the subjugation, torture, silencing, and even outright destruction of bodies that differ so egregiously from the sanctioned white male norm.[17]

In framing this broad question I am aware that it—like that of embodiment in Bonhoeffer—is bigger than a short essay can adequately contain. I wish here simply to point to some fruitful places where I see Bonhoeffer's theology of the body engaging the story of Precious Jones. First, I note the subversive potential implicit in Bonhoeffer's assertion of Eve's (female) body as *limit* to Adam. That is, I am intrigued by the possibility of developing more fully what Bonhoeffer simply notes: that Eve (precisely in her physicality, the fullness of her embodied personhood) is the one whose "otherness" forms Adam for the first time as a truly human person. The fact that it is a woman whose embodied alterity deepens the humanity of a man is a point Bonhoeffer does not remark on; but it is a pivotal insight nevertheless. Bonhoeffer's notion of the body of the other as person-creating "limit," *illustrated paradigmatically in this story of Eve vis-à-vis Adam*, holds the potential to recast all theologies of patriarchal dominance (including key elements of Bonhoeffer's own). In distinction from implicit or explicit theologies of female degradation vis-à-vis the male throughout Christian history, that is, Bonhoeffer implicitly counters any notion of female human beings as mere "object" of the male's rage, lust, or other infantile projections.[18]

---

17. Copeland, *Enfleshing Freedom*; Copeland frames her theology explicitly within the United States' cultural, political, and intellectual permeation by century after century of slavery. While the German context in which Bonhoeffer came of age and primarily functioned was not stamped by slavery, Willie Jennings of Duke University has recently argued that Germany's competitive drive in the late nineteenth century to arrive on the international scene as a colonial power produced a "hyper-masculinity" of racist belligerence which, following the Versailles humiliation and stripping of its colonies, merged with centuries of Christian anti-Judaism to produce the vicious anti-Semitism of Nazism (Jennings, "In the Form of the Aryan"). Thus Bonhoeffer's theology—like that of U.S. theologians—emerges within a context of profound racist and sexist violence and must similarly be evaluated by its power to challenge these anti-Christian ideologies.

18. In noting that it is the female Eve who paradigmatically encounters and forms the personhood of the male Adam, I am in no way attempting to comment on or draw Bonhoeffer into contemporary discussions of the proper Christian definition of marriage. Rather, as I hope is clear, I am interested in how (within heterosexual relations, but much more within the church and society at large) Bonhoeffer's naming of the female as agent of formation—indeed, *in persona Christi*—undermines theologies of

To take this further with regard to the story of Precious Jones, Bonhoeffer's theology of the body of another as *limit* invites viewers to see in Precious—specifically as an African-American female body—precisely this limit forming *us* more deeply as human beings in encounter with her. If indeed it is black women's bodies in particular who are most pervasively violated, marginalized, and "invisible-ized" in a racist, sexist society, then to view Precious—like Eve—as person-forming *limit* to those of us in positions of relative social dominance in relation to her becomes an instance of precisely that "privileging [of] the black woman's body" that Copeland asserts must recast completely what being human means.[19] Such an assertion echoes Bonhoeffer's own recognition prior to his imprisonment and death of the supreme hermeneutical power of the view from below: "[I]t remains an experience of incomparable value that we have for once learned to see the great events of world history from below, from the perspective of the outcasts, the suspects, the maltreated, the powerless, the oppressed and reviled, in short from the perspective of the suffering."[20] Bonhoeffer himself remained unable to grasp the full implications of his own insight—specifically with regard to women's humanity and the challenge this presents to his implicit and explicit assertions of male privilege. But his articulation of the person-forming (and thus politically transforming) power of female embodiment for the full development of human life remains an important resource, especially when specified even further in those—like Precious—who are the most invisible and degraded of human bodies.

Second, when Bonhoeffer's insight on the person-forming power of the embodied "other" connects fully with the Christological core of his faith in his later works, we see the even more radical implication emerging that it is Eve, the "other," who bears the image and power of *Jesus Christ* in accomplishing this person-forming power. Taken again a step further with reference to Precious, we glimpse in this excruciatingly violated girl the fullest image and form of Jesus Christ himself—not simply as his suffering is visible in hers, a connection perhaps easier

---

male dominance. I do not know any treatment of Bonhoeffer with relation to questions of same-sex marriage; any such analysis would need to be far more complex than simply lifting Bonhoeffer's treatment of Adam and Eve out of context.

19. Copeland, *Enfleshing Freedom*, 2.

20. From "After Ten Years," written in late 1942 and published as the Prologue to *Letters and Papers* (*DBWE* 8:52).

to glimpse, but precisely in the ways her alterity challenges our social structures, functions as limit to our unconscious notions of what being human means, and thus mediates Jesus's own power to re-form and shape every viewer of the film precisely in our otherness from Precious on a fundamental level into his own form and image. In this view, it is not political correctness but theological truth that insists on imaging Jesus as black and female within a slavery-grounded nation, a radically woman- and girl-silencing world.[21]

This language of Jesus "forming" us into his own "form" begins for Bonhoeffer already in *Sanctorum Communio* as he speaks of the "person-forming" power of the other; but it comes to fullest development in the chapter of his *Ethics* titled "Ethics as Formation."[22] Here he explores the ways in which, by the power of the Holy Spirit, "[t]he form of Jesus Christ takes form in human beings"[23]—developing this through the three-fold pattern of the Incarnate One (or "the one who has become human"[24]), the Crucified One, and the Risen One. To take seriously Precious Jones as an image of Jesus Christ precisely in her body's divergence from U.S. cultural norms of privilege—her blackness, her femaleness, her obesity, her poverty, her vulnerability to abuse— would indeed have the power to form, re-form, or transform her viewers into a vastly more human society, with a radically more expansive vision of humanity in the image and form of Jesus Christ. But what does it mean, not merely for us who observe her, for whom she may have a transforming, even iconic role, but *for Precious herself*, to speak of being "formed" into this form of Christ? Is this a liberating word for one who is already living on the underside?

In my book, *Reading from the Underside of Selfhood: Bonhoeffer and Spiritual Formation*, I examine Bonhoeffer's vision of Christian spiritual formation as it emerges from his own social location and context in Hitler's Germany. It is a vision with relevance to many contemporary Christians, particularly those of us living in contexts of unjust privilege and/or in places of necessary resistance to entrenched

---

21. On this see, e.g., Johnson, "Feminist Theology"; Hopkins, *Being Human*; Douglas, *What's Faith Got to Do With It?*; and Young, *Dogged Strength*.

22. See the chapter titled "The Christian Concept of Person and Concepts of Social Basic-Relation" in *DBWE* 1:34–57; and *DBWE* 6:76–102.

23. *DBWE* 6:95.

24. Ibid., 94.

political structures. But, I argue, for all its beauty and convincing power, his is not a universal perspective (nor, given his lifelong repudiation of reliance on general principles, would he desire us to see it thus). In the ways he writes as a member of his society's elite—assuming his readers have similar mobility, freedom, power, and the means of life at their disposal—his words may not always ring true with redemption for those in situations of captivity, abuse, desperate poverty, or immediate danger. In particular, I assert, he does not recognize the ways pervasive violence and silencing (including, though not only, that operative in traditional female socialization) create selves whose needs on their own terms are radically different from his. For instance, his lifelong and almost always unqualified insistence on the necessity of turning away from one's own needs toward those of others provided a means of grace and life for him, as a privileged male socialized into psychic isolation from others.[25] This insistence on selflessness, so liberating for Bonhoeffer, does not however provide the means or incentive for Precious Jones—in a completely different social and psychic context—to recognize that she has needs in the first place, let alone to step toward her own reality and away from the poisonous words and actions of her viciously abusive parents. What for Bonhoeffer was transforming—to turn from one's own needs toward others—is how Precious has survived at all for 16 years; it is not the way into a new life of hope or freedom for her. This survival necessity of instinctively turning from self to other—to meet the other's demands before s/he attacks me again—is in fact the shape of the sin in her life, the pervasive violation of her self by others. Instead of continuing in "selfless" orientation to these others, Precious somehow has to learn to stand up for herself against her parents and risk losing the only

---

25. This broad assertion obviously requires complex unpacking, a task I undertake across the chapters of my *Reading from the Underside of Selfhood*. In particular, see chapter two on Bonhoeffer's own formation as a "separative" self, chapter four on the very different socialization of those who experience trauma or abuse, and chapter five, in which I place these perspectives in mutually illuminating conversation with one another. See also the studies by Jones (*Trauma and Grace*), Coakley (*Powers and Submissions*), and Park and Nelson (*Other Side of Sin*) for further perspectives on the interrelations of trauma, power, feminism/gender, and sin in Christian spirituality. In *Men and Masculinities in Christianity and Judaism*, editor Björn Krondorfer has gathered a wealth of material exploring many of these topics from a distinctively masculine perspective; I look forward to engaging this material as well in the future.

home she has ever known; this requires a previously unthinkable level of orientation *toward* her own needs and away from theirs.[26]

Can Bonhoeffer's theology of con-formation with Christ provide resources for such a shift? He begins his development of this material auspiciously, with a grasp that the incarnation of God in Jesus Christ spells good news for all human beings, all human bodies—indeed, the embrace of every human person precisely in their created reality. We might expand his insight to say that gender, race, culture, class, genetic make-up, sexual orientation, personality, family patterns, individual flaws and gifts: all are part of the real humanity—*my* humanity—embraced in Christ. As he insists in *Life Together,* so here in *Ethics* as well Bonhoeffer repudiates any attempt to set up an ideal humanity, an ideal community, an ideal self, from which the real inevitably suffers in comparison: "God becomes a real human being. While we exert ourselves to grow beyond our humanity, to leave the human behind us, God becomes human; and we must recognize that God wills that we be human, real human beings ... God loves real people without distinction."[27] I hear Bonhoeffer's invitation to conformation with the human One, the Incarnate One, to be helpful for all persons; all of us, rich or poor, Dietrich and Precious, live with layers of internalized distortion of reality that obstruct any attempt to live a fully human life. To glimpse and learn to accept who we really are, in all humility and grace, as created by God, is the work of a lifetime.

When he moves to consideration of the form of the Crucified and Risen One, however, the material in *Ethics* needs further expansion; surely we sense here as much as anywhere the effects of Bonhoeffer's own location in the nightmare of Nazism. For in *Ethics* he is able to describe conformation with Jesus crucified as including only the experience of divine judgment of our sin and complicity with evil.[28] And his discussion of conformation with the Risen One reveals at best a hid-

---

26. In my book I trace many important ways Bonhoeffer's writings and witness do open resources for just such self-awareness, self-assertion, self-defense, and self-offering in the world; see especially 195–222, where I outline how Bonhoeffer read through this social-location lens provides crucial means of psychic and spiritual empowerment for those on the "underside of selfhood," including the ultimate gift of invitation into the life of Jesus himself.

27. *DBWE* 6:84, see also 94; and *DBWE* 4:284–85. On the priority of the real over the ideal in Christian community and life, see *DBWE* 5:35–38.

28. *DBWE* 6:88ff, 94–95, and *DBWE* 4:285–86.

den participation in new life, with only a "glimmer" visible "here and there" of anything changed.[29] By 1942, when his own involvement in the conspiracy and personal vulnerability to the powers of evil—as well as that of nations and the Jewish people—has accelerated considerably, he is able to articulate an implicit con-formation with the Crucified One precisely in the extraordinary "view from below" cited earlier, experiencing the continuing crucifixion of all the exploited and marginalized "brothers and sisters" of Jesus; and in his prison writings he will be drawn ever more fully "into the arms of God" in the sufferings of the world.[30] Such *embodied* conformation to the Crucified One—with its astonishing glimpse of the Beloved in the very flesh of those most hated and tormented on earth—carries revelatory power in helping orient Christians toward the actual lives and needs of people like Precious; even more important, however, it can help Precious herself and all who suffer see *in their own flesh* and wounds the presence of One who is not far from them but as close as their very bodies.

And in prison—even more, surely, as a fruit of his engagement[31]— he begins to articulate as well the contours of love, blessing, bodily and even erotic life, and gratitude, all woven into a polyphony of trust; here I sense him exploring further, though without much explicit language in this direction, what it might mean to speak of con-formation with the Risen One.[32] Brought into an astonishing new hope by the gift of falling in love with Maria, he is invited—precisely in the unexpected and embodied encounter with this other, the exhilaration of an embodied future together—into a fuller conception than he could have imagined in *Ethics* of what the life of resurrection might and did mean.

29. *DBWE* 6:95, 91–92, and *DBWE* 4:286.

30. Bonhoeffer, *Letters and Papers*, 370 (*DBWE* 8:486).

31. An in-depth analysis of the ways Bonhoeffer's relationship with Maria von Wedemeyer shaped his writing and spirituality in prison has not yet appeared. For reference to the powerful impact on Bonhoeffer of falling in love in 1942–43, see my essay, "Bonhoeffer's Late Spirituality."

32. A primary place where Bonhoeffer articulates his understanding of the resurrection for Christians come of age is in *Letters and Papers*, 336-37 (*DBWE* 8:447–48; letter to Eberhard Bethge, dated June 27, 1944). On polyphony, cf. also ibid., 303 (*DBWE* 8:393–94); on blessing, ibid., 374 (*DBWE* 8:491–93); on gratitude, ibid., 370, 383–84 (*DBWE* 8:486, 505). For more on Bonhoeffer's views regarding divine and human love, eroticism, and desire, see Zimmerling, "Gottesliebe und irdische Liebe," 35–47. And for a marvelous discussion of this opening into fullness of life in the prison letters, see Wüstenberg, *Theology of Life*.

For surely conformation with the Risen One is not meant to be experienced *only* as "glimmers ... here and there" in our life in the body, together and alone and in the world. Surely "the Lord is risen indeed!"— the unbelievable believed Word of hope that's received as true *for me*— does change hearts and lives and even bodies in real life. What does this Word mean for a particular person—for Precious Jones or anyone else? In its particularities I don't know, for with Bonhoeffer I trust that the call into deeper, fuller life in following Christ must be discerned anew each day, in each new context on its own terms.[33] But I do know that being invited into this risen life of Jesus Christ—in the flesh, not only in the soul and heart and mind—matters profoundly, and that those who glimpse this reality "here and there" are obliged *for the sake of their witness to others* to cultivate this resurrection life in their own flesh and soul and heart and mind as assiduously as possible. Precious's choice to take account of her own needs, to turn away from her abusers and let the Risen One inhabit her—whether or not she has access to Christian language or community for this process—matters profoundly, for herself and for her children and for all those with whom her life is connected. She needs to hear God's judgment on her sin, her own enmeshment in the abuse that is suffocating her; but equally (and initially, much more) she needs to experience God's presence with her in her pain and God's astonishing power to lift her free of it, in the body, in real life. To be invited into con-formation not only with the Incarnate One who loves her precisely as she is, and with the Crucified One who bears her own pain and abuse in his body, but also with the Risen One who bears her out of hell and into a new life—still impoverished, still HIV-positive, still dealt a very difficult hand in life, yet *alive* to herself and the world and the One who loves her—is the very means of redemption itself.

Ultimately the form of Christ takes many forms, many bodies, in an endless formation of love. And ultimately the form of scholarly writ-

---

33. Bonhoeffer did not live to complete a fully developed theology of discernment, but the topic emerges organically from his lifelong insistence on concrete reality over abstract generalizations and his years of attentive listening for the Word of God in his own prayerful spiritual practice. In the conspiracy he moves toward explicit focus on discernment of the will of God within this situation of extraordinary complexity. See in particular *DBWE* 6:320–36; his entire *Ethics* (as reconstructed by Eberhard Bethge) in fact begins with the fundamental question: "What is the will of God?" (*DBWE* 6:47). For a full development of the place of discernment in Bonhoeffer's spirituality and theology, see Dahill, *Underside of Selfhood*, 55–59, 205–7, 217–21, and especially 87–92.

ing too gives way to a new form: hymn form, sung form, poetic form, embodied form. Bonhoeffer himself moved into poetry as his death approached, and at the end he spoke with only his body's language: the ultimate release into the arms of God, his ashes dispersed through the incinerator into the wind with those of countless millions. In the course of his body's journey Bonhoeffer was himself borne into the risen life of the One killed outside the city, whose body is glimpsed, here and there, still in the lives of those who love. Such life is precious indeed. May we live it too.

10

Responding to Human Reality

Responsibility and Responsiveness in Bonhoeffer's Ethics[1]

Ulrik Becker Nissen

A central motif in the ethics of the Danish theologian and philosopher K. E. Løgstrup is the mutual trust between persons encountering each other, giving rise to an ethical demand that is universal. Løgstrup has a phenomenological starting point, describing an ontological structure according to which human beings are delivered over into each other's hands, thereby raising an ethical demand. In every encounter with another human being there is an ethical demand requiring care for the other.[2] For Løgstrup this is a universal demand and therefore not something unique to the Christian tradition. Therefore, Løgstrup also argues that there is no Christian ethics, as the ethical demand in itself is known to all human beings.[3]

When we compare Løgstrup's position with that of Bonhoeffer, it is interesting to note that Bonhoeffer, in the short text from the summer of 1932, "Gibt es eine christliche Ethik?," also raises the question whether there is a Christian ethics.[4] Unfortunately, the text is based on notes from Bonhoeffer's lecture, and these notes are so fragmentary that

---

1. This essay is part of a larger research project on Lutheran social ethics titled "Social Ethics between Universality and Specificity: A Study on the Identity of Christian Social Ethics with Particular Emphasis on Dietrich Bonhoeffer's Ethics." The project is financed by the Carlsberg Foundation and the Danish Research Council for the Humanities.

2. Løgstrup, *Ethical Demand*, 17ff.

3. Ibid., 105ff.

4. *DBW* 11:303–13.

it is not possible to reconstruct his reflections or arguments.[5] However, in his earlier Barcelona lecture, "Grundfragen einer christlichen Ethik,"[6] Bonhoeffer appears, based on a line of thought that holds resemblances to Løgstrup, to dismiss the notion of a "Christian" ethics. As Løgstrup emphasizes the encounter with the other as the place where the ethical demand arises, Bonhoeffer argues similarly that there are no Christian norms and principles,[7] and it is in the concrete moment that one discerns how one should respond to the other.[8] But even if Bonhoeffer appears to share some ideas with Løgstrup, it is quite clear in his posthumously published *Ethics* that he maintains the idea of a Christian ethics—even one with a specifically Christological approach. Consequently, it has almost become a commonplace to state that Bonhoeffer's ethics is fundamentally a Christological ethics.[9] Nevertheless, even if Bonhoeffer clearly does have a Christian ethics, this does not mean that he disregards those features of life that are common to all human beings. Indeed, this is one of Bonhoeffer's significant contributions—that he is able to maintain the universal and the specific dimensions of Christian ethics at the same time. This is also seen in Bonhoeffer's understanding of responsibility.

In Bonhoeffer's *Ethics* there is an underlying Christological mode of thought penetrating the whole work. This is a Christology with classical Chalcedonian traits—which becomes quite clear when we view it in the light of his Christology lectures, which are the most detailed exposition of his Christology.[10] This Chalcedonian position may be used

5. See the notes by the editors in both ibid., 303 n. 1, and *GS* 5:275–77 on the fragmentary character of this text. See also Feil, *Theologie Dietrich Bonhoeffers*, 37 n. 36.

6. *DBW* 10:323–45.

7. Ibid., 323.

8. Ibid., 329.

9. See, e.g., Clifford Green's introduction to the recent translation of the German original of *Ethics* (*DBWE* 6:6ff.). The centrality of Jesus Christ in Bonhoeffer's ethics is also demonstrated in, e.g., Burtness, *Shaping the Future*, 30ff. Burtness shows how this is a central theme in both classical commentators on Bonhoeffer and in Bonhoeffer's own texts.

10. *DBW* 12:327ff.; "Das Chalcedonense ist eine sachliche, alle Denkformen sprengende, lebendige Aussage des Christus. In klarste, aber paradoxe Lebendigkeiten ist alles hineingezogen" (ibid., 328). See ibid., 279–348, for Bonhoeffer's lectures on Christology. These lectures have also been translated into English as *Christ the Center*, and more recently appeared in *DBWE* 12:299–360. I will not go into further details here on Bonhoeffer's Chalcedonian Christology but instead refer the reader to Abromeit,

to affirm the universal and the specific dimensions of Christian ethics at the same time.[11] Bonhoeffer uses the expression that there is a polemic unity between these two dimensions. There is a constant unity and difference between these two dimensions of Christian ethics—much like the two natures of Christ. In that way the underlying Chalcedonian Christology paves the way for an understanding of Christian ethics in which Bonhoeffer would be able to follow Løgstrup in the endorsement of the universal character of Christian ethics and still maintain the idea of a specific Christian ethics.[12] This is the thesis of the present essay, i.e., that the Christological foundation of Bonhoeffer's ethics makes it possible for him to maintain the universal and specific dimensions of Christian ethics at the same time, and that this is exemplified in his understanding of responsibility.

The focus of the essay will be on Bonhoeffer's *Ethics*. Bonhoeffer talks about this work as his "*Lebensaufgabe*," thereby indicating its importance.[13] Furthermore, commentators have pointed to Bonhoeffer's own understanding of this work as the culmination of his theology.[14] This work is therefore taken as the hermeneutical starting point, and other works of Bonhoeffer are included in the light of this work. Methodologically, the essay is primarily analytical. It is my primary intention to analyze Bonhoeffer's understanding of responsibility in the light of the mentioned thesis, though I will also touch on select contemporary positions in order to shed light on Bonhoeffer's view. In the first part of this essay, the focus will be on the universal dimension of Bonhoeffer's understanding of the concrete encounter with the other.

Das Geheimnis Christi, and Nissen, "The Christological Ontology of Reason." For a general overview of central themes in Bonhoeffer's Christology, see Pangritz, "Who is Jesus Christ, for Us, Today?"

11. See, e.g., Sherman, "Vital Center," where Bonhoeffer's ethic plays a central role in an outline of a Chalcedonian social ethic.

12. When I refer to the Chalcedonian Christology as a means of affirming the universal and specific dimensions of Christian ethics at the same time, I am not using this Christological symbol in a strict dogmatic sense in its original, historical context. I am using it in a more general and analogical sense, where it may be understood as a figure explaining the relation between the reality of God and the reality of the world. In this analogical sense it comes close to the understanding of the real presence, which I comment on later in the essay.

13. Cf. Bethge, *Dietrich Bonhoeffer*, 804–5; see *DBW* 8:237.

14. Green, *Theology of Sociality*, 327; see also *DBW* 8:577.

I will argue that this view implies an affirmation of the universality of Christian ethics. The second part of the essay will then explain the Christological foundation in more detail. This section will demonstrate the more specific Christological implications of Bonhoeffer's understanding of responsibility, focusing on the motifs of vicarious representation, willingness to bear guilt, and willingness to suffer for the other. The third—and last—part of the essay then argues that the universal and specific dimensions in Bonhoeffer's understanding of responsibility appear in his understanding of the mandates. The mandates bring together the universal and specific dimensions of responsibility in a concrete responsibility for the other.

The Universal Dimension—The Concrete Encounter with the Other

On several occasions Bonhoeffer's ethics has been brought into dialogue with various representatives of an ethics of proximity. In particular, the ethics of Martin Buber and of Emmanuel Levinas are often brought into a discussion with Bonhoeffer.[15] There are good reasons for this, because as early as his dissertation, *Sanctorum Communio*, Bonhoeffer establishes an understanding of the person as a relational being.[16] Using terminology that holds remarkable resemblance to Buber's work *Ich und Du*, published only four years prior to Bonhoeffer's dissertation,[17] Bonhoeffer immediately links responsibility and the encounter with the other in establishing a Christian understanding of the person. While Bonhoeffer and Buber both argue that responsibility arises in the encounter with the other,[18] Bonhoeffer takes the argument a step further by integrating an understanding of God as creator into his understanding of the You, the other as a

---

15. See, e.g., Arnett, *Dialogic Confession*; Bongmba, "The Priority of the Other"; Green, "Human Sociality"; Gregor, "Bonhoeffer's 'Christian Social Philosophy'"; Root, "Practical Theology"; Weinrich, *Der Wirklichkeit begegnen*. Apart from Wyller, *Glaube und autonome Welt*, I am not aware of any study that compares the ethics of the Danish theologian and philosopher K. E. Løgstrup with Bonhoeffer. This could be a study well worth undertaking.

16. *DBW* 1:19ff.

17. See also Green, "Human Sociality," 114ff., for a discussion of this resemblance.

18. *DBW* 1:32.

real, concrete You:[19] "One human being cannot of its own accord make another into an I, an ethical person conscious of responsibility. *God or the Holy Spirit joins the concrete You; only through God's active working does the other become a You to me from whom my I arises. In other words, every human You is an image of the divine You.*"[20] However, even if Bonhoeffer has a different emphasis, one should not ignore that he does speak about human reality as the place where responsibility arises in the immediate encounter with the other.

In Bonhoeffer's *Ethics*, the understanding of responsibility as arising from human reality follows from the Christological foundation. The Christological core of Bonhoeffer's ethics also implies an affirmation of the whole of human reality. This is clear already in the opening section of his *Ethics*, where he emphatically argues that there is only one reality—i.e., the Christ-reality that rejects any attempt to divide human reality into separate spheres.[21] As there is only one Christ-reality, Bonhoeffer can speak affirmatively of human reality without seeing this in conflict with the lordship of Christ. One of the passages where Bonhoeffer makes the link between being human and being responsible for the other is in the first version of the section entitled "History and Good" in his *Ethics*.[22] There Bonhoeffer argues against the idea of the individual as an isolated being who has an absolute criterion by which to determine good and evil. This is fundamentally a fiction and a reduction of the ethical dimension of the human condition.[23] Parallel to this is the temptation to pull back from the ethical responsibilities of historical existence in a safeguarding of oneself by some general principles that are applied to any situation regardless of the consequences. Both of these isolations of the individual are a negation of the historicity of human existence.[24]

In response to these approaches, Bonhoeffer argues in favor of an understanding of the human being as being in the immediate encounter with the other. Responsibility for the other arises out of this immediate

19. Ibid., 33.
20. *DBWE* 1:54–55.
21. *DBWE* 6:54ff.
22. Ibid., 219–45.
23. Ibid., 219–20.
24. Ibid., 220.

encounter. Further, this is not just a responsibility for the individual but a responsibility for entire communities and groups of communities: "a human being necessarily lives in encounter with other human beings and . . . this encounter entails being charged, in ever so many ways, with responsibility [*Verantwortung*] for the other human being. History arises out of accepting this responsibility for other human beings or for entire communities or groups of communities."[25] As is clear from these passages, Bonhoeffer sees the individual as fundamentally interrelated with other human beings and with groups and communities of other human beings. The individual is not isolated but always in relation to the other. In this sense, Clifford Green is correct when he speaks of Bonhoeffer's theology as a "theology of sociality."[26]

This is made even clearer in the following passage, where Bonhoeffer speaks of the ethical situation as arising in the moment a person accepts responsibility for the other. The ethical dimension is not something that exists as a static norm. Rather, the ethical dimension is given in the concrete encounter with the other and in the acceptance of responsibility for this other human being: "The moment a person accepts responsibility for other people—and only in so doing does the person live in reality—the genuine ethical situation arises. This is really something different from the abstract way in which people usually seek to come to terms with the ethical problem. The subject is no longer the isolated individual, but the one who is responsible for other people. The action's norm is not a universal principle, but the concrete neighbour, as given to me by God."[27] For Bonhoeffer this means that the concrete encounter with the other is the ethical situation in which responsibility arises. The ethical individual acts in freedom in this concrete situation. As there is no universal principle that defines the ethical situation beforehand, and no norm that guides the ethical discernment independently of the immediate encounter, the ethical individual acts freely. The individual is left to judge the situation on her or his own and

---

25. Ibid.

26. This is the central thesis in Green, *Theology of Sociality*, 392. Green shows how the concept of sociality may be seen already in the early phase of Bonhoeffer's thought and how this can be followed throughout his life and in his writings at the different phases of his thought.

27. *DBWE* 6:221.

answer for the consequences of the action without any support from other people or principles.[28]

At the same time, however, the individual is also bound by the situation. The concrete encounter with the other carries with it a given necessity or commandment,[29] which it is one's task to discern. The individual is thrown into the twilight where ethical discernment is challenged by relativity, knowing that one must not only determine the good, but also obey the ethical demand arising in this encounter and in faith risk the choice between good and evil. In many situations the difference between good and evil will not be clear. The responsible individual will not have a choice between good and evil, but is left to choose between right and right, wrong and wrong.[30] Therefore, since he argues that responsibility and freedom are mutually dependent concepts,[31] Bonhoeffer maintains that one cannot escape the uncertainty. In this situation the responsible individual is bound to God and the neighbor, is left in ignorance of the good, and must surrender to the necessities of the concrete situation: "As responsible action, the good takes place without knowing, by surrendering to God the deed that has become necessary and is nevertheless (or because of it!) free."[32]

Here we find—once again—this double-sidedness that is so characteristic of Bonhoeffer's thought. It is in this uncertainty, this unawareness of the will of God, that we find the will of God. It is in the mystery of history—just as Bonhoeffer would speak of the mystery of reality—that the will of God is present in the situation where it is not known: "Precisely those who act in the freedom of their very own responsibility see their activity flowing into God's guidance. Free action recognizes itself ultimately as being God's action, decision as God's guidance, the venture as divine necessity. In freely surrendering the knowledge of our own goodness, the good of God occurs. On this ultimate perspective can we speak about the good in historical action."[33] This also implies for Bonhoeffer that it is in the uncertainty given within historical existence

---

28. Ibid.
29. Ibid.
30. Ibid., 284.
31. Ibid., 283.
32. Ibid., 284.
33. Ibid., 284–85.

that the responsible individual is also called to be obedient to the will of God. There is nothing peculiar about the concrete situation in which the individual meets the will of God. It is given in everyday life and can be known by everyone.[34] However, even if responsibility presumes freedom and thereby the uncertainty of good and evil, Bonhoeffer still maintains obedience as part of responsibility. For Bonhoeffer both freedom and obedience are realized in responsibility.[35]

This realization is also the point where Bonhoeffer moves beyond what we could call the universal dimension of responsibility. Throughout this section I have demonstrated the universality of responsibility. I have argued that it is in the concrete encounter with one's neighbor that responsibility arises. As such there is nothing unique or particular about this encounter and the responsibility arising from it. However, for Bonhoeffer it is the Christological presuppositions of his ethics that make it possible for him to argue for both this universal dimension and the more specific—i.e., more explicitly Christological—dimension at the same time. This Christological foundation becomes apparent in his deliberations on the relation between freedom and obedience. In Christ, freedom and obedience come together. Without the two being united, freedom would lead to arbitrariness, and obedience would lead to slavery. In Christ both are affirmed and held together. As Bonhoeffer writes:

> Jesus stands before God as the obedient one and as the free one. As the obedient one, he does the will of the Father by blindly following the law he has been commanded. As the free one, he affirms God's will out of his very own insight, with open eyes and a joyful heart; it is as if he re-creates it anew out of himself. Obedience without freedom is slavery, freedom without obedience is arbitrariness. Obedience binds freedom, freedom ennobles obedience . . . Obedience knows what is good and does it. Freedom dares to act and leaves the judgment about good and evil up to God . . . Obedience has tied hands, freedom is creative. In rendering obedience, human beings observe God's Decalogue, in exercising freedom, they create new decalogues (Luther).[36]

---

34. Ibid., 286.
35. Ibid., 288.
36. Ibid., 287–88.

The Christological Qualification—Being Christ for the Other

The link between the universal dimension of Bonhoeffer's notion of responsibility and the more specific aspect is derived from his understanding of the one Christ-reality. In the opening section of his *Ethics* he immediately makes the point that anyone who wishes to deal with the issues of a Christian ethics is forced to give up the question about how one can do good. Instead, he argues, a Christian ethics must be concerned with the question of what the will of God is.[37] This has to do with the very nature of reality. Rather than seeing oneself and the world as ultimate realities, one should recognize these realities as embedded "in a wholly other ultimate reality, namely, the reality of God the Creator, Reconciler, and Redeemer."[38] The main concern of Christian ethics then becomes the question about how the reality of God can everywhere show itself to be the ultimate reality. Everything is an abstraction as long as God is not known in faith to be the ultimate reality.[39] However, for Bonhoeffer it is important that this is not meant to disdain the actual world. Rather, this should be seen as an affirmation of the world as it is known in the revelation of God in Jesus Christ. Therefore, "[t]he source of a Christian ethic is not the reality of one's own self, not the reality of the world, nor is it the reality of norms and values. It is the reality of God that is revealed in Jesus Christ."[40]

This Christological understanding of reality is also found when Bonhoeffer addresses the question of responsibility. For Bonhoeffer responsibility is concordant with the notion of reality: "Responsible people are not called to impose a foreign law on reality. On the contrary, their action is in the true sense '*in accord with reality.*'"[41] However, this should not be understood as servility to the "facts of reality." According to Bonhoeffer, such servility can lead to irresponsibility, as it tends to give priority to the expedient rather than the good. At the same time, the principled protest *against* reality also loses accordance with reality. For Bonhoeffer it is important that reality is both affirmed and negated

---

37. Ibid., 47.
38. Ibid., 48.
39. Ibid.
40. Ibid., 49.
41. Ibid., 261.

at the same time. This double-sidedness is closely related to Bonhoeffer's underlying Chalcedonian Christology.[42] In this Christologically shaped understanding of the "Yes" and "No" to reality, reality finds its true foundation and source of responsibility. As this notion is central for the topic of this essay, a longer quotation from Bonhoeffer on the topic seems justified:

> In any action that is truly in accord with reality, acknowledgment of the status quo and protest against the status quo are inextricably connected. The reason for this is that *reality* [*die Wirklichkeit*] is first and last not something impersonal [*Neutrum*], but *the Real One* [*der Wirkliche*], namely, the God who became human. Everything that actually exists receives from *the* Real One, whose name is Jesus Christ, both its ultimate foundation and ultimate negation, its justification and its ultimate contradiction, its ultimate Yes and its ultimate No. *Trying to understand reality without the Real One means living in an abstraction, which those who live responsibly must always avoid* [my italics]; it means living detached from reality and vacillating endlessly between the extremes of a servile attitude toward the status quo and rebellion against it.[43]

This simultaneous affirmation and negation of reality is closely linked to Bonhoeffer's understanding of life itself—in its entirety—as a response to the word of God addressed to us in Jesus Christ.[44] This "responsive" life is what Bonhoeffer calls "responsibility": "This life, lived in answer to the life of Jesus Christ (as the Yes and No to our life), we call 'responsibility' [*Verantwortung*]. This concept of responsibility denotes the complete wholeness and unity of the answer to the reality that is given to us in Jesus Christ."[45] Larry Rasmussen is therefore also correct when he states that responsibility is a person's basic answering to life itself. Responsibility arises from this answering to reality as it is constituted in various relationships: "Responsibility in the first instance, then, is the basic answering (*Verantwortung*) of a person to life itself, the fundamental response of one's own life as constituted in and by relationships.

---

42. For a more detailed analysis of the Chalcedonian Christology implied in Bonhoeffer's notion of reality, see Nissen, "Letting Reality Become Real."

43. *DBWE* 6:261–62.

44. Ibid., 254.

45. Ibid.

Responsibility is an overall life-orientation affecting all particular actions and specific responsibilities."[46]

This also means that the notion of responsibility is given an ontological plenitude that implies that the fullness of responsibility is derived from its Christological foundation.[47] The biblical sense of responsibility fundamentally means taking responsibility for Jesus Christ. The Christian is called to answer for and take responsibility for what has happened through Jesus Christ.[48] In this responsibility the Christian represents Christ before human beings, but at the same time she represents human beings before Christ, as she takes responsibility for human beings before Christ. The Christian is thereby held responsible before God and before human beings at the same time:

> [B]y being responsible for Christ, who is life, before human beings, and only thus, I simultaneously take responsibility for human beings before Christ. I *simultaneously* represent Christ before human beings, and represent human beings before Christ. My answering [*Verantwortung*] for Christ before human ears simultaneously reaches the ears of Christ as my answering for human beings. Being accountable [*Verantwortung*] *for* Jesus Christ before human beings at the same time means being accountable for human beings before Christ; only thus can I take responsibility for myself before God and before human beings.[49]

For Bonhoeffer, the understanding of responsibility as grounded in the Christ-reality as a whole also implies that responsibility carries with it certain Christological traits. We will look at three of these traits: vicarious representation, willingness to bear guilt, and willingness to suffer for the other. In each of these traits responsibility has a specifically

---

46. Rasmussen, "Ethics of Responsible Action," 219. The same point is also made in McKenny, "Responsibility," when he differentiates between imputability, accountability, and liability in the notion of responsibility. It is in connection with the concept of accountability that McKenny elaborates on the Latin *respondeo* and the German *Verantwortung* as the "root sense of responsibility" (246ff.). On this issue of the relation between responsibility and responsiveness, see also Dabrock, "Responding to 'Wirklichkeit,'" 49–80.

47. On Bonhoeffer's ethic as an ethics of plenitude, see Nissen, "Dietrich Bonhoeffer and the Ethics of Plenitude."

48. *DBWE* 6:255.

49. Ibid., 256.

Christological character, even while it remains grounded in reality as a universal actuality for all human beings.

First of all, there is the notion of *vicarious representation*. For Bonhoeffer the very notion of responsibility is intrinsically related to the concept of vicarious representation.[50] Responsibility is a concept that in its very foundation is derived from the vicarious representation of Jesus Christ. True human responsibility is rooted in God's becoming human and in the manner in which this brought about the vicarious representation of Jesus Christ on behalf of all human beings. For Bonhoeffer it is only possible to speak of true responsibility on the basis of this source and from this origin:

> Jesus Christ is the very embodiment of the person who lives responsibly . . . [H]e lives only as the one who in himself has taken on and bears the selves of all human beings. His entire life, action, and suffering is vicarious representative action . . . In this real vicarious representative action in which his human existence consists, he is the responsible human being par excellence. *All human responsibility is rooted in the real vicarious representative action of Jesus Christ on behalf of all human beings. Responsible action is vicarious representative action* [my italics]. Vicarious representative action is not presumptuous and overbearing only insofar as it is grounded in God's becoming human, which brought about the real vicarious representative action of Jesus Christ on behalf of all human beings. It is only on this ground that there is genuine vicarious representative action and thus responsible action.[51]

This motif of vicarious representation holds several implications for Bonhoeffer. First, he points to the relation between love and freedom. In the vicarious action of Jesus Christ we do not find an abstract proclamation of ethical ideology but rather a concrete enactment of God's love. In the same way the human being is not called to a realization of ethical ideals but into a life lived in God's love. Just as the vicarious action of Jesus Christ fulfilled the commandments of God's righteousness in concrete action for all human beings, the Christian is called to a loving surrender of self in the concrete reality of other

---

50. Ibid., 231–32, 257–58.
51. Ibid., 231–32.

human beings.[52] This leads Bonhoeffer to his notion of the mandates—even if he does not mention them right here—, as he uses the examples of the father or the statesman to exemplify this concreteness of vicarious representative action.[53] Bonhoeffer can, therefore, equate vicarious representative action with responsibility: "Nobody can altogether escape responsibility, which means vicarious representative action. Even those who are alone live as vicarious representatives. Indeed, they do so in an especially significant sense, since their lives are lived in a vicarious representative way for human beings as such, for humanity as a whole."[54] Bonhoeffer argues that responsibility for oneself is only meaningful if it is understand as responsibility for oneself as a human being, i.e., for humanity. This is exemplified in Jesus Christ. Even if Jesus lived alone, this did not exempt him from responsibility. Rather, his responsibility had the character of vicarious representative action for all human beings. Therefore, the vicarious representative action of Jesus Christ is the foundation and source of responsibility. Through Jesus Christ all of life is marked by this vicarious representation: "Jesus—the life, our life—the Son of God who became human, lived as our vicarious representative. Through him, therefore, all human life is in its essence vicarious representation . . . All that human beings were supposed to live, do, and suffer was fulfilled in him. In this real vicarious representative action, in which his human existence consists, he is the responsible human being par excellence. Since he is life, all of life through him is destined to be vicarious representative action."[55]

Another motif is *the willingness to bear guilt*. Bonhoeffer illustrates this with the classical example of Kantian ethics, which argues that if one is hiding a friend being pursued by a murderer and is confronted by the murderer, one should answer honestly and affirmatively about the person one is hiding. Against this conclusion Bonhoeffer argues that in this case the responsibility bound to Christ will lead one into responsibly accepting the culpability of telling a lie. As responsibility is grounded in reality as a whole it carries with it Christological traits,

---

52. Ibid., 232.
53. Ibid., 257–58.
54. Ibid., 258.
55. Ibid., 258–59.

such as the willingness to bear guilt.[56] The willingness to bear guilt and become guilty for the other is a central notion in Bonhoeffer's Christological understanding of responsibility: "[T]he structure of responsible action involves . . . *willingness to become guilty* [*Bereitschaft zur Schuldübernahme*]."[57] Bonhoeffer links this closely to Jesus Christ as the origin of responsibility and uses Jesus's life as the role model for the willingness of the Christian to bear guilt. Jesus was not concerned with the proclamation of new ethical ideas and his own goodness. He did not seek his own perfection at the expense of human beings. Rather, as the one who acts responsibly within historical existence he becomes guilty—driven by his love. It is out of his sinlessness, his selfless love, that he becomes guilty.[58] It is in this unselfish and sinless willingness to bear the guilt of others that all responsibility has its origin, according to Bonhoeffer. It is in the willingness of Jesus Christ to bear guilt that the responsible person finds the origins of true responsibility—a responsibility that carries with it the willingness to bear guilt:

> [I]n this sinless-guilty [*sündlos-schuldig*] Jesus Christ all vicarious representative responsible action [*stellvertretend verantwortliches Handeln*] has its origin. Precisely because and when it is responsible, because and when it is exclusively concerned about the other human being, because and when it springs from the selfless love for the real human brother or sister—it cannot seek to withdraw from the community of human guilt. Because Jesus took the guilt of all human beings upon himself, everyone who acts responsibly becomes guilty.[59]

Bonhoeffer even goes as far as to say that those who seek to avoid becoming guilty divorce themselves from the ultimate reality of human existence and thereby also from divine justification.[60]

In the willingness to bear guilt, discipleship is taken on as a further dimension of responsibility. Even if the point can be made that Bonhoeffer's notion of responsibility signals a development of his views in his earlier *Discipleship*, where he argues more in favor of obedience,[61]

56. Ibid., 280.
57. Ibid., 275.
58. Ibid.
59. Ibid.
60. Ibid., 276.
61. *DBW* 4:69, 152.

it would be wrong to read his *Ethics* as departing from this earlier work. In the well-known passage from his *Letters and Papers from Prison* he states that even if he now sees the dangers of this work, he still stands by what he wrote.[62] This is also apparent in his reflections on responsibility. Just as obedience leads the disciple into following the crucified one and carrying the cross of Jesus Christ, the responsible Christian is also led to bear guilt, suffering, and persecution.

Here responsibility carries with it a third Christological trait, namely, *the willingness to suffer for the other*. Bonhoeffer explicitly links the willingness to suffer and the notion of responsibility in his reflections on the relation between the church and the world.[63] Bonhoeffer sets out by reflecting on various concepts that had become homeless during the "years of trial,"[64] such as reason, culture, humanity, tolerance, and autonomy. These concepts had often been turned against the church and Christianity, but now they sought refuge in the shadow of the church.[65] This is a return to the origin of these concepts in Jesus Christ. In a concise passage Bonhoeffer states the centrality of Jesus Christ in the following way: "Only that which participates in Christ can endure and overcome. Christ is the center and power of the Bible, of the church, of theology, but also of humanity, reason, justice, and culture. To Christ everything must return; only under Christ's protection can it live."[66] This leads Bonhoeffer to reflect on the tension between the words "Whoever is not against us is for us" (Mark 9:40) and "Whoever is not for me is against me" (Matt 12:30). He argues that these words belong necessarily together as the exclusive and all-encompassing claim of Jesus Christ.[67] That the lordship of Christ is a concrete reality is a central point for Bonhoeffer. The lordship of Christ is made manifest in the concreteness of lawlessness, persecution, and suffering. This is also where Bonhoeffer makes the explicit link to the notion of responsibility. For Bonhoeffer the church discovers the breadth of its responsibility in

62. *DBW* 8:542.
63. *DBWE* 6:339–51.
64. Bonhoeffer is alluding to the situation in Germany in the 1930s and 40s during the rise of National Socialism. But due to the necessary caution with which he had to proceed, the allusions are only made implicitly.
65. *DBWE* 6:341.
66. Ibid.
67. Ibid., 344.

persecution and suffering. The church sees its true responsibility in the light of fellowship with the suffering one:

> [I]t is the concrete suffering of lawlessness, organized lies, of hostility to humankind and acts of violence; it is the persecution of justice, truth, humanity, and freedom that drove people, to whom these values were precious, under the protection of Jesus Christ and thus under his claim; and this experience caused the church-community of Jesus Christ to discover the breadth of its *responsibility* [my italics] . . . [T]he crucified Christ has become the refuge, justification, protection, and claim for these higher values and their defenders who have been made to suffer. It is with the Christ, persecuted and suffering together with his church-community, that justice, truth, humanity, and freedom seek refuge. It is the Christ who is unable to find shelter in the world, the Christ of the manger and the cross who is cast out of the world, who is the shelter to whom one flees for protection; only thus is the full breadth of Christ's power revealed. The cross of Christ makes both sayings true: "whoever is not for me is against me" and "whoever is not against us is for us."[68]

In this understanding there is a remarkable parallel between Bonhoeffer and the terminology of John Howard Yoder when speaking of "discipleship as political responsibility." Yoder's main concern in *Discipleship as Political Responsibility* is to demonstrate some of the main lines in the New Testament view of the state and see what this implies for the Christian as a follower of Christ. In one of the last sections of this short book,[69] Yoder outlines how the cross of Christ is an ordinary part of the Christian life and the church. It is not something peculiar, but rather something to be expected. Yet at the same time it is not to be conceived of in legalistic terms. It is a following of Jesus as partaking in the very being of Christ. It is as a person already participating in Christ that the Christian is called to follow Jesus. Following Jesus is the form of the Christian's freedom: "[F]ollowing Jesus really means basing our action on our participation in Christ's very being . . .

68. Ibid., 345–46; Bonhoeffer also elaborates on the willingness to suffer with reference to the Beatitudes. See, e.g., *DBWE* 4:108–9; and *DBWE* 6:346–47. For Bonhoeffer it is important that this is not just a willingness to suffer for the sake of a confession of Christ. Rather, Bonhoeffer is speaking about the willingness to suffer and to carry responsibility for a just cause. It may so happen that in this concrete moment of suffering and responsibility one may find oneself calling upon Christ and belonging to Christ.

69. Yoder, *Discipleship*, 58–61.

This is not about some legalistic approach to copying Jesus, but rather about participating in Christ. We are already part of his body; we do not become so through following him. Following Jesus is the result, not the means, of our fellowship with Christ. It is the form of Christian freedom and not a new law."[70]

Bonhoeffer could have said the same thing. Therefore, it is also a misreading of Bonhoeffer to see his *Discipleship* as reflecting a different Bonhoeffer than the one we meet in *Ethics*. Rather, the two works mark different accents in one and the same theology, one and the same theologian. However, even if they are not fundamentally different, they still mark different emphases. Whereas the call to discipleship is stronger in *Discipleship*, the understanding of the one Christ-reality and the Christian living and partaking in Christ in this reality is made clearer in his *Ethics*. In *Discipleship* the call to bear the cross of Christ is stronger. Bonhoeffer has a whole section dedicated to this.[71] Here Bonhoeffer makes the call to bear the cross explicit and argues that the disciple is called to suffering and being rejected, just as Christ was the suffering and rejected one: "Just as Christ is only Christ as one who suffers and is rejected, so a disciple is a disciple only in suffering and being rejected, thereby participating in crucifixion. Discipleship as allegiance to the person of Jesus Christ places the follower under the law of Christ, that is, under the cross."[72] Bonhoeffer does not give up the call to bear the cross in his *Ethics*, as is clear from previously quoted passages, but he does turn it in a new direction. This new direction is marked by his concern to find a *via media* between the radical call to discipleship and an accommodation to given worldly norms and ideals. Whereas Bonhoeffer in his *Discipleship* is occupied with the radical call to follow Christ, his aim in *Ethics* is rather to argue for a position between radicalism and compromise.[73] It is important here to remember that he does not give up on the radical nature of the call to discipleship. But he does balance it with the notion of freedom and this leads him to the concept of responsibility.

70. Ibid., 61.
71. *DBW* 4:77–85.
72. *DBWE* 4:85.
73. *DBW* 6:144ff.

The Universal and the Specific—On the Mandates as a Concrete Response to Reality

In the two preceding sections we have seen that Bonhoeffer understands responsibility as both a Christologically universal and a more specific concept. These two aspects can be seen as derived from the underlying Chalcedonian Christology of Bonhoeffer's ethics. Just as the person of Jesus Christ is perceived "in two natures, without confusion and without change . . . without separation and without division," the universal and specific dimensions of responsibility are different and yet one in the Christ-reality. However, since Bonhoeffer continuously emphasizes the concrete—indeed, the understanding of the link between responsibility and the concrete encounter with the other is a reflection of this—we will now turn to some of the concrete implications of this understanding of responsibility.[74] In this last part of this essay, we will turn to the more social ethical implications of Bonhoeffer's notion of responsibility. I will argue that the universal and specific dimensions of responsibility come together in Bonhoeffer's understanding of the mandates.[75]

From the very outset of his discussion of the mandates, Bonhoeffer establishes a clear link between his understanding of creation and Christology. In the opening section on the Christ-reality, Bonhoeffer argues that all of creation has been created through Christ and toward Christ and has its existence only in Christ. The world therefore has its being in relation to Christ, and this relation becomes concrete in the divine mandates. In the context of the present essay, this may be seen as an endorsement of the universal and specific dimensions of the mandates:

> The world stands in relationship to Christ whether the world knows it or not. This relation of the world to Christ becomes

---

74. See also Prüller-Jagenteufel, *Befreit zur Verantwortung*, for possibly the most recent extensive analysis of Bonhoeffer's ethics (with particular emphasis on the concept of responsibility); see 236–436 for an analysis of how Bonhoeffer's understanding of justification is made concrete in his ethics.

75. In order to understand Bonhoeffer's notion of the mandates, it is important to keep the historical and theological background in which it was formulated in mind. The editors of Bonhoeffer's *Ethics* have provided the reader with a good background (*DBWE* 6:68 n. 75). See also, e.g., Rasmussen, "Ethics of Responsible Action," 206–25, and Green, *Theology of Sociality*, 323–25, for short overviews of Bonhoeffer's understanding of the mandates.

concrete in certain *mandates of God* in the world. The scripture names four such mandates: *work, marriage, government, and church*. We speak of divine mandates rather than divine orders, because thereby their character as divinely imposed tasks [*Auftrag*], as opposed to determinate forms of being, becomes clearer. In the world God wills work, marriage, government, and church, and God wills all these, each in its own way, through Christ, toward Christ, and in Christ.[76]

Therefore, Bonhoeffer also argues that one cannot separate the "worldly" from the "spiritual" in the understanding of the mandates. It makes no sense to speak of some of the mandates as more "worldly" than others. Rather, they are all to be seen as divine mandates in the world: "It is a matter of '*divine*' mandates in the midst of the world, whether they concern work, marriage, government, or church."[77] As such they are "divine" mandates within the world. In this sense the mandates hold a double meaning that resembles the double-sidedness of the concept of responsibility. In the worldly sense the mandates are universal—the world stands in this relationship to Christ whether it knows it or not—, whereas the specific dimension is derived from their origin in God's will and fulfillment in Christ. Therefore, Bonhoeffer also makes it clear that the mandates do not possess this divine character in and of themselves. The "divinity" of the mandates is derived from their origin, existence, and destination in Christ. Since Bonhoeffer wanted to emphasize the continuous relation of the mandates to God—in a critique of a static understanding—he emphasizes that God's will is present in the mandates. God wills each of the mandates and seeks their fulfillment in Christ: "These mandates are divine, however, only because of their original and final relation to Christ. Detached from this relation, 'in themselves,' they are not divine, just as the world 'in itself' is not divine."[78] Bonhoeffer is careful not to ascribe a divinity to the mandates in their givenness. Rather, it is because of the mandates' origin in God's commandment, for Christ's sake, that the mandates have a divine character.[79]

76. *DBWE* 6:68–69.
77. Ibid., 69.
78. Ibid.
79. It is interesting to note here the parallel with Luther's understanding of the divine character of the three estates. As is the case with Bonhoeffer, Luther also argues that the estates are divine, but that this is not given with the estates per se—rather, the divine character is derived from the will of God as the source. See, e.g., Nissen, "Between Unity and Differentiation."

This underlying double-sidedness of the mandates is also endorsed in the last section of his *Ethics*, "The Concrete Commandment and the Divine Mandates."[80] Here Bonhoeffer makes the grounding in the revelation of Christ the determining criterion. The commandment of God as it is revealed in Jesus Christ meets all human beings as an expression of divine love in the form of the mandates. As such the mandates continuously reveal the will of God. Again Bonhoeffer makes use of the notion of vicarious representation, as the bearer of the mandate acts as a stand-in for the one issuing the commission.[81] And again Bonhoeffer emphasizes the dynamic aspect of the mandates as well as their divine character and their foundation in the commandment of God.[82] However, for Bonhoeffer it is equally important that the mandates are seen as an affirmation of worldly life. First of all, the mandates are fundamentally intertwined, as they are "with-one-another [*Miteinander*], for-one-another [*Füreinander*], and over-against-one-another [*Gegeneinander*]."[83] In this formulation Bonhoeffer comes close to a traditional formulation of the Lutheran understanding of the "real presence" in the communion. As Luther argued—based on the Latin rendering *hoc est* of the gospels' account of the institution of the Lord's Supper—that the bread and wine *is* the body of Jesus Christ in, with, and under the bread and wine,[84] Bonhoeffer's use of this formulation is made to argue for the worldly as well as the divine character of the mandates. Even though Bonhoeffer was only able to write on the mandate of the church in the section on "The Commandment of God in the Church"[85]—since his arrest in April 1943 prevented him from completing the manuscript—this section leaves us with a clear argument for both the worldly and the divine character with regard to this specific mandate.

It is particularly in the passage where Bonhoeffer reflects on the cross that we find the understanding of the affirmation of the world in

---

80. *DBWE* 6:388ff.

81. Ibid., 389.

82. Ibid., 390.

83. Ibid., 393.

84. Cf., e.g., Matt 26:26–30 in *Biblia Sacra: Iuxta Vulgatam Versionem* (1994). The parallel with Luther's understanding of the real presence of Christ in Bonhoeffer's understanding of the mandates is also noted by the editors of Bonhoeffer's *Ethics*: see *DBW* 6:404 n. 42 and *DBWE* 6:401 n. 44.

85. *DBWE* 6:394ff.

Christ. For Bonhoeffer the worldliness of the world is given its identifying mark in the cross. The cross is the sign of the godlessness of the world in its rejection of Christ. However, the cross is also the reconciliation of the godless world with God. Therefore, the cross of Christ sets the world free to live in genuine worldliness before God. This also implies—a point that is central for the argument in this essay—that the cross of Christ overcomes "the divisions, tensions, and conflicts between the 'Christian' and the 'worldly,' and calls us to single-minded action and life in faith in the already accomplished reconciliation of the world with God."[86] In the cross of Christ true worldliness is made possible, as it proclaims the lordship of Christ over all of creation: "A life of genuine worldliness is possible only through the proclamation of the crucified Christ. Thus it is not possible in contradiction to the proclamation, and also not beside it in some kind of autonomy of the worldly; but it is precisely 'in, with, and under' the proclamation of Christ that a genuinely worldly life is possible and real."[87] For Bonhoeffer it is important to maintain this foundation in the cross of Christ. The world will always strive toward its own deification, an absolutizing of its worldliness in separation from the cross of Christ. In this situation it will fall under its own spell, setting itself in the place of God. In so doing the world ceases to be world in its striving to be something else than what it is. It becomes a pseudo-worldliness ultimately negating what it really is. Rather, Bonhoeffer argues for a "full-blown worldliness," where the world has the freedom and the courage to be "a world that in its godlessness is reconciled with God."[88] In this formulation, the important point for Bonhoeffer is *that there is a genuine worldliness only and precisely because of the proclamation of the cross of Jesus Christ.*[89]

With regard to the remaining three mandates—family, culture, and government—we can only presume that Bonhoeffer would have established much the same kind of argument. This is further supported by his reflections on the implications of the lordship of Jesus Christ.[90] For Bonhoeffer it is important that this is not conditioned by any earthly

---

86. Ibid., 400.
87. Ibid., 400–401.
88. Ibid., 401.
89. Ibid.
90. Ibid., 401–2.

limitations. It is a lordship over all of creation: "It is the lordship of the one through whom and toward whom all created being exists, indeed the one in whom alone all created being finds its origin, essence, and goal."[91] This is an affirmation both of the worldliness and of the lordship of Jesus Christ.

The lordship of Jesus Christ leads us back to Bonhoeffer's notion of responsibility. In the section "The Place of Responsibility" he takes his starting point in the German concept "*Beruf*"—vocation. It is part of this concept that there is somebody calling one to a specific task or form of life. Accordingly, Bonhoeffer also points to the biblical meaning of this concept and argues that it is in the "encounter with Jesus Christ, [that] a person experiences God's call [*Ruf*], and in it the calling [*Berufung*] to a life in community with Jesus Christ."[92] This calling is immediately linked both to the incarnation of Christ and to the notion of responsibility. It is a call of grace that meets and claims the human being exactly in the worldly conditions as they are. The human being is called to live in the world and to live justified before God in whatever state he or she lives. In this Christological foundation of the call, where the world is affirmed as it is, we again see a distinctly Chalcedonian character. And this is closely linked to responsibility. As Bonhoeffer says, "From Christ's perspective this life is now my vocation; from my own perspective it is my responsibility."[93] In the following sections Bonhoeffer distances himself from two misunderstandings—cultural Protestantism and monasticism. Whereas the former tends to equate the faithful performing of one's obligations with vocation, the latter is in danger of escaping from the world. Bonhoeffer wants to emphasize both the call that transcends earthly obligations and the worldly character of these obligations.[94] It is only in this double-sided understanding of the call of Jesus Christ to live responsibly within the world that the call maintains at once both its worldly realization and Christological foundation: "The question of the place and the limit of responsibility has led us to the concept of vocation. However, this answer is valid only where vocation is understood simultaneously in all its dimensions. The call of Jesus Christ is the call

---

91. Ibid., 402.
92. Ibid., 290.
93. Ibid.
94. Ibid., 290–91.

to belong to Christ completely; it is Christ's address and claim at the place at which this call encounters me ... Vocation is responsibility, and responsibility is the whole response of the whole person to reality as a whole ... Responsibility in a vocation follows the call of Christ alone."[95]

In this call of Christ the different strands of thought in the present essay come together. Throughout this essay the question has been whether we can find a Chalcedonian theme in Bonhoeffer's understanding of responsibility, and what this implies for the universal and specific dimensions of Christian ethics. With the example of responsibility, we have seen how Bonhoeffer's understanding of this concept implies an affirmation of the worldly and specifically Christian aspects at the same time. This parallels the understanding of the two natures of Christ as it is formulated in Chalcedonian Christology. In the first section we looked at the universal dimension of responsibility in Bonhoeffer's understanding of responsibility. There, we saw how Bonhoeffer argues for the concrete encounter with the other as the source of responsibility. Secondly, we turned to the more specific Christological qualification of responsibility. In this part of the essay we demonstrated that the universal dimension of responsibility is never separate from its more specific Christological implications. Therefore, Christologically central notions such as vicarious representation, willingness to bear guilt, and the willingness to suffer for the other are central to Bonhoeffer's understanding of responsibility. In the last section we turned to the place where this responsibility becomes concrete. There we demonstrated that the universal and specific dimensions of Bonhoeffer's understanding of responsibility come together in his notion of the mandates as the concrete place of responsibility.

---

95. Ibid., 292–93.

Bibliography

Abraham, Martin. "Wort und Sakrament, oder: Wovon die Kirche lebt." In *Bonhoeffer und Luther: Zentrale Themen ihrer Theologie*, edited by Klaus Grünwaldt, Christiane Tietz, and Udo Hahn, 123–54. Hannover: VELKD, 2007.

Abromeit, Hans-Jürgen. *Das Geheimnis Christi: Dietrich Bonhoeffers erfahrungsbezogene Christologie*. Neukirchener Beiträge zur systematischen Theologie 8. Neukirchen-Vluyn: Neukirchener Verlag, 1991.

Aquinas, Thomas. *The Summa Theologica*. Translated by Fathers of the English Dominican Province. Vol. 2. Chicago: Encyclopedia Britannica, 1988.

Aristotle. *Poetics*. In *The Basic Works of Aristotle*, edited by Richard McKeon, 1455–87. New York: Random House, 1941.

Arnett, Ronald C. *Dialogic Confession: Bonhoeffer's Rhetoric of Responsibility*. Carbondale: Southern Illinois University Press, 2005.

Athanasius. *On the Incarnation: The Treatise De Incarnatione Verbi Dei*. Translated and edited by A Religious of C.S.M.V. Yonkers, NY: St. Vladimir's Seminary Press, 1996.

Augustine. *The City of God against the Pagans*. Edited and translated by R. W. Dyson. New York: Cambridge University Press, 1998.

Bainton, Roland H. *Erasmus of Christendom*. London: Collins, 1969.

Balthasar, Hans Urs von. *Herrlichkeit: Eine theologische Ästhetik*. Bd. III/2: 2. Teil: *Neuer Bund*. Freiburg: Johannes Verlag Einsiedeln, 1969.

———. *Theo-Drama: Theological Dramatic Theory*. Vol. 3, *The Dramatis Personae: The Person in Christ*. Translated by Graham Harrison. San Francisco: Ignatius Press, 1992.

———. *A Theology of History*. San Francisco: Ignatius, 1994.

Barth, Karl. *Church Dogmatics*. Vol. 4. Part 2. Edited by Geoffrey W. Bromiley and T. F. Torrance. Translated by Geoffrey W. Bromiley. Edinburgh: T. & T. Clark, 1958.

———. *The Humanity of God*. Translated by John Newton Thomas and Thomas Wieder. London: Collins, 1961.

Bauckham, Richard. *God Crucified: Monotheism and Christology in the New Testament*. Grand Rapids: Eerdmans, 1999.

Bauman, Zygmunt. *Postmodern Ethics*. Cambridge: Blackwell, 1993.

Bender, Harold S. "The Anabaptist Vision." *Mennonite Quarterly Review* 18.2 (1944) 67–88.

Bethge, Eberhard. *Dietrich Bonhoeffer: A Biography*. Revised and edited by Victoria J. Barnett. Minneapolis: Fortress, 2000.

———. *Dietrich Bonhoeffer: Theologe—Christ—Zeitgenosse: Eine Biographie*. 8. korrigierte Auflage. Gütersloh: Gütersloher Verlagshaus, 2004.

———. "The Nonreligious Scientist and the Confessing Theologian: The Influence of Karl-Friedrich Bonhoeffer on His Younger Brother." In de Gruchy, ed., *Bonhoeffer for a New Day*, 39–56.

———. "Self-Interpretation and Uncertain Reception in the Church Struggle." In *The German Church Struggle and the Holocaust*, edited by Franklin H. Littell and Hubert G. Locke, 167–84. Detroit: Wayne State University Press, 1974.

Biblia Sacra: Iuxta Vulgatam Versionem. 4. verbesserte Auflage. Stuttgart: Deutsche Bibelgesellschaft, 1994.

Bieler, Andrea, and Luise Schottroff. *The Eucharist: Bodies, Bread, and Resurrection*. Minneapolis: Fortress, 2007.

Billings, Todd. *Calvin, Participation, and the Gift: The Activity of Believers in Union with Christ*. Oxford: Oxford University Press, 2008.

Boff, Leonardo. *Jesus Christ Liberator: A Critical Christology for Our Time*. Translated by Patrick Hughes. Maryknoll, NY: Orbis, 1972.

Bongmba, Elias Kifon. "The Priority of the Other: Ethics in Africa—Perspectives from Bonhoeffer and Levinas." In de Gruchy, *Bonhoeffer for a New Day*, 190–208.

Bonhoeffer, Dietrich. *Christ the Center*. Translated by Edwin Robertson. New York: Harper & Row, 1978.

———. *The Cost of Discipleship*. Translated by R. H. Fuller. London: SCM, 1959.

———. *Dietrich Bonhoeffer Werke*. Edited by Eberhard Bethge et al. 17 Bände und 2 Ergänzungsbände. Gütersloh: Gütersloher Verlagshaus, 1986–1999.

———. *Dietrich Bonhoeffer Works*. Victoria J. Barnett, Wayne Whitson Floyd Jr., and Barbara Wojhoski, general editors. 16 vols. Minneapolis: Fortress, 1996–.

———. *Ethics*. Edited by Eberhard Bethge. Translated by Neville Horton Smith. New York: Macmillan, 1955/1965.

———. *Gesammelte Schriften*. Edited by Eberhard Bethge. 6 vols. Munich: Kaiser, 1958–74.

———. *Letters and Papers from Prison*. Translated by Reginald Fuller et al. New greatly enlarged ed. New York: Simon & Schuster, 1971/1997.

———. *Nachfolge*. Munich: Kaiser, 1958.

———. *No Rusty Swords: Letters, Lectures and Notes 1928–1936, from the Collected Works of Dietrich Bonhoeffer, Vol. 1*. Edited by Edwin H. Robertson. Translated by Edwin H. Robertson and John Bowden. London: Collins, 1965.

———. *A Testament to Freedom: The Essential Writing of Dietrich Bonhoeffer*. Edited by Geffrey B. Kelly and F. Burton Nelson. San Francisco: HarperSanFrancisco, 1995.

Boyarin, Daniel. *A Radical Jew: Paul and the Politics of Identity*. Berkeley: University of California Press, 1994.

Brandt, Sigrid. "'Christus als Gemeinde existierend'? Überlegungen zur ekklesiologischen Rede von 'Kollektiv' im Anschluss an und in Auseinandersetzung mit Dietrich Bonhoeffer." In *Resonanzen: Theologische Beiträge. Festschrift für Michael Welker*, edited by Sigrid Brandt and Bernd Oberdorfer, 161–80. Wuppertal: Foedus, 1997.

Brunner, Emil. *The Divine Imperative*. Translated by Olive Wyon. Philadelphia: Westminster, 1947.

Buber, Martin. *Reden über das Judentum*. Berlin: Schocken, 1932.

Buck, August. *Humanismus: Seine europäische Entwicklung in Dokumenten und Darstellungen*. Freiburg: Alber, 1987.
Buckley, James J. "A Field of Living Fire: Karl Barth on the Spirit and the Church." *Modern Theology* 10.1 (1994) 81–102.
Burtness, James H. *Shaping the Future: The Ethics of Dietrich Bonhoeffer*. Philadelphia: Fortress, 1985.
Carter, J. Kameron. *Race: A Theological Account*. New York: Oxford University Press, 2008.
Certeau, Michel de. *The Practice of Everyday Life*. Translated by Steven Rendall. Berkeley: University of California Press, 1984.
Class, Gottfried. *Der verzweifelte Zugriff auf das Leben: Dietrich Bonhoeffers Sündenverständnis in* Schöpfung und Fall. Neukirchener Beiträge zur systematischen Theologie 15. Neukirchen-Vluyn: Neukirchener Verlag, 1994.
Clement of Alexandria. "Exhortation to the Heathen." In Roberts and Donaldson, *Ante-Nicene Fathers*, 171–206.
———. "Stromata, Or Miscellanies." In Roberts and Donaldson, *Ante-Nicene Fathers*, 347–401.
Coakley, Sarah. *Powers and Submissions: Spirituality, Philosophy, and Gender*. Oxford: Blackwell, 2002.
Copeland, M. Shawn. *Enfleshing Freedom: Body, Race, and Being*. Minneapolis: Fortress, 2010.
Creamer, Deborah Beth. *Disability and Christian Theology: Embodied Limits and Constructive Possibilities*. Oxford: Oxford University Press, 2009.
Dabrock, Peter. "Responding to 'Wirklichkeit': Reclaiming Bonhoeffer's Approach to Theological Ethics between Mystery and the Formation of the World." In *Mysteries in the Theology of Dietrich Bonhoeffer: A Copenhagen Bonhoeffer Symposium*, edited by Kirsten Busch Nielsen, Ulrik Nissen, and Christiane Tietz, 49-80. Göttingen: Vandenhoeck & Ruprecht, 2007.
Dahill, Lisa E. "Bonhoeffer's Late Spirituality: Challenge, Limit, and Treasure." *Journal of Lutheran Ethics* (December 2006). http://www.elca.org/What-We-Believe/Social-Issues/Journal-of-Lutheran-Ethics/Issues/December-2006/Bonhoeffers-Late-Spirituality-Challenge-Limit-and-Treasure.aspx.
———. "Dietrich Bonhoeffer (1906–45), *Life Together*." In *Christian Spirituality: The Classics*, edited by Arthur Holder, 329-40. London: Routledge, 2010.
———. *Reading from the Underside of Selfhood: Bonhoeffer and Spiritual Formation*. Princeton Theological Monograph Series 95. Eugene, OR: Pickwick, 2009.
de Gruchy, John W., editor. *Bonhoeffer for a New Day: Theology in a Time of Transition: Papers Presented at the Seventh International Bonhoeffer Congress, Cape Town, 1996*. Grand Rapids: Eerdmans, 1998.
———, editor. *The Cambridge Companion to Dietrich Bonhoeffer*. Cambridge: Cambridge University Press, 1999.
———. "Christian Humanism: Reclaiming a Tradition; Affirming an Identity." *CTI Reflections*. Vol. 8. Center of Theological Inquiry. Princeton, NJ. 19 Apr 2009. http://www.ctinquiry.org/publications/reflections_volume_8/degruchy.htm.
———. *Christianity, Art, and Transformation*. Cambridge: Cambridge University Press, 2001.
———. *Confessions of a Christian Humanist*. Minneapolis: Fortress, 2006.

de Gruchy, John W., Stephen Plant, and Christiane Tietz, editors. *Dietrich Bonhoeffer's Theology Today: A Way between Fundamentalism and Secularism?/Dietrich Bonhoeffers Theologie Heute: Ein Weg zwischen Fundamentalismus und Säkularismus?* Gütersloh: Gütersloher Verlagshaus, 2009.

Dilschneider, Otto. *Die evangelische Tat: Grundlagen und Grundzüge der evangelischen Ethik.* Gütersloh: Bertelsmann, 1940.

Douglas, Kelly Brown. *What's Faith Got to Do With It? Black Bodies/Christian Souls.* Maryknoll, NY: Orbis, 2005.

Eagleton, Terry. *Reason, Faith, and Revolution: Reflections on the God Debate.* New Haven: Yale University Press, 2009.

Farner, Oskar. *Huldrych Zwingli. Band 2: Seine Entwicklung zum Reformator (1506–1520).* Zurich: Zwingli, 1946.

Feil, Ernst. *Die Theologie Dietrich Bonhoeffers: Hermeneutik, Christologie, Weltverständnis.* 5. Auflage. Studien zur systematischen Theologie und Ethik 45. Berlin: LIT Verlag, 2005.

———. *The Theology of Dietrich Bonhoeffer.* Translated by Martin Rumscheidt. Philadelphia: Fortress, 1985.

Fellmann, Walter, editor. *Hans Denck: Schriften, Teil 2.* Gütersloh: Bertelsmann, 1956.

Ferry, Luc. *Man Made God: The Meaning of Life.* Translated by David Pellauer. Chicago: University of Chicago Press, 2002.

Flogaus, Reinhard. *Theosis bei Palamas und Luther: Ein Beitrag zum ökumenischen Gespräch.* Göttingen: Vandenhoeck & Ruprecht, 1997.

Ford, David F. "Polyphonic Living: Dietrich Bonhoeffer." In *Self and Salvation: Being Transformed,* 241–65. Cambridge Studies in Christian Doctrine. Cambridge: Cambridge University Press, 1999.

Foucault, Michel. *Discipline and Punish: The Birth of the Prison.* Translated by Alan Sheridan. 2nd ed. New York: Vintage, 1995.

Frick, Peter. "Dietrich Bonhoeffer's Theological Anthropology: The Case of Racism." In *Creed and Conscience: Essays in Honour of A. James Reimer,* edited by Karl Koop, Paul Doerksen, and Jeremy Bergen, 135–51. Kitchener, ON: Pandora, 2007.

———, editor. *Interpreting Bonhoeffer: Essays on Method and Approaches.* International Bonhoeffer Interpretation Series. Berlin: Lang, forthcoming.

Gadamer, Hans-Georg. *Truth and Method.* Translated by J. Weinsheimer and D. G. Marshall. 2nd rev. ed. New York: Crossroad, 1989.

Gallas, Alberto. "Carnivalization of Christendom." *Kierkegaardiana* 24 (2007) 9–45.

Gay, Peter. *The Enlightenment: An Interpretation,* Vol. 1, *The Rise of Modern Paganism.* London: Wildwood, 1973.

Gerlach, Gernot. *"Bekenntnis und Bekennen der Kirche" bei Dietrich Bonhoeffer: Entscheidungen für sein Leitbild von Kirche in den Jahren 1935–36.* Münster: LIT Verlag, 2003.

Godsey, John D. *Preface to Bonhoeffer.* Philadelphia: Fortress, 1965.

———. *The Theology of Dietrich Bonhoeffer.* London: SCM, 1960.

Green, Clifford J. *Bonhoeffer: A Theology of Sociality.* Rev. ed. Grand Rapids: Eerdmans, 1999.

———. "Bonhoeffer in the Context of Erikson's Luther Study." In *Psychohistory and Religion: The Case of Young Man Luther*, edited by Roger A. Johnson, 162–96. Philadelphia: Fortress, 1977.

———. "Bonhoeffer, Modernity and Liberation Theology." In *Theology and the Practice of Responsibility: Essays on Dietrich Bonhoeffer*, edited by Wayne Whitson Floyd Jr. and Charles Marsh, 117–31. Valley Forge, PA: Trinity, 1994.

———. "Bonhoeffer's Quest for Authentic Christianity: Beyond Fundamentalism, Nationalism, Religion, and Secularism." In de Gruchy, Plant, and Tietz, *Dietrich Bonhoeffer's Theology*, 335–53.

———. "Human Sociality and Christian Community." In de Gruchy, *Cambridge Companion*, 113–33.

———. "Pacifism and Tyrannicide: Bonhoeffer's Christian Peace Ethic." *Studies in Christian Ethics* 18.3 (2005) 31–47.

Green, Clifford J., Kirsten Busch Nielsen, Hans Pfeifer, and Christiane Tietz, editors. *Dietrich Bonhoeffer Jahrbuch/Yearbook* 3 (2007/2008). Gütersloh: Gütersloher Verlagshaus, 2008.

Green, Garrett. *Imagining God: Theology and the Religious Imagination*. Grand Rapids: Eerdmans, 1989/1998.

Gregor, Brian. "Bonhoeffer's 'Christian Social Philosophy': Conscience, Alterity, and the Moment of Ethical Responsibility." In Gregor and Zimmermann, *Bonhoeffer and Continental Thought*, 201–25.

———. "Thinking through Kierkegaard's Anti-Climacus: Art, Imagination, and Imitation." *The Heythrop Journal* 50 (2009) 448–65.

Gregor, Brian, and Jens Zimmermann, editors. *Bonhoeffer and Continental Thought: Cruciform Philosophy*. Bloomington: Indiana University Press, 2009.

Grosshans, Hans-Peter, editor. *One Holy, Catholic and Apostolic Church: Some Lutheran and Ecumenical Perspectives*. Geneva: LWF Studies, 2009.

Gutiérrez, Gustavo. "The Limitations of Modern Theology: On a Letter of Dietrich Bonhoeffer." In Gutiérrez, *Power of the Poor*, 222–34.

———. *The Power of the Poor in History*. Translated by Robert R. Barr. Maryknoll, NY: Orbis, 1983.

———. "Theology from the Underside of History." In Gutiérrez, *Power of the Poor*, 169–221.

———. *A Theology of Liberation: History, Politics, and Salvation*. Translated and edited by Sister Caridad Inda and John Eagleson. Rev. ed. Maryknoll, NY: Orbis, 1988.

Gutter, Ruth. *Innerste Konzentration für den Dienst nach Aussen: Grundlinien der mittleren und späteren Ekklesiologie Bonhoeffers in ihrer systematischen Bedeutung für die ökumenische Bewegung heute*. Europäische Hochschulschriften 23/703. Frankfurt: Lang, 2000.

Hampson, Daphne. *Christian Contradictions: The Structures of Lutheran and Catholic Thought*. Cambridge: Cambridge University Press, 2001.

Harvey, Barry. "Life in Exile, Life in the Middle of the Village: A Contribution of Dietrich Bonhoeffer to a Post-Christendom Ecclesiology." In de Gruchy, Plant, and Tietz, eds., *Dietrich Bonhoeffer's Theology*, 229–43.

Hecker, Konrad. "Humanism." In *Encyclopedia of Theology: A Concise Sacramentum Mundi*, edited by Karl Rahner, 665–70. London: Burns & Oates, 1975.

Hegel, Georg Wilhelm Friedrich. *Lectures on the Philosophy of Religion: The Lectures of 1827.* 1 vol. ed. Edited by Peter C. Hodgson. Oxford: Clarendon, 2006.

Hegstad, Harald. *Den virkelige kirke: Bidrag til ekklesiologien* [The Real Church: Contributions to Ecclesiology]. Oslo: Tapir Akademisk Forlag, 2009.

Heither, Theresia. "Theologische Voraussetzungen." In *Commentarii in epistulam ad Romanos: Römerbriefkommentar*, by Origen, translated by Theresia Heither. Erstes und Zweites Buch. Freiburg: Herder, 1990.

Hildebrandt, Franz. "Barmen: What to Learn and What Not to Learn." In *The Barmen Confession: Papers from the Seattle Assembly*, edited by Hubert G. Locke, 285–302. Toronto Studies in Theology 26. Lewiston, NY: Mellen, 1986.

———. "The Gospel and Humanitarianism." PhD diss., Cambridge University, 1941.

———. "The Interpretation of Luther at the Present Time." In *"And Other Pastors of Thy Flock": A German Tribute to the Bishop of Chichester*, edited by Franz Hildebrandt, 135–46. Cambridge: Cambridge University Press, 1942.

Hodes, Aubrey. *Encounter with Martin Buber.* London: Lane, 1972.

Hong, Howard V., and Edna H. Hong, editors and translators. *Søren Kierkegaard's Journals and Papers.* Vol. 2. Bloomington: Indiana University Press, 1970.

Hopkins, Dwight N. *Being Human: Race, Culture, and Religion.* Minneapolis: Fortress, 2005.

Horkheimer, Max. *Critical Theory: Selected Essays.* Translated by Matthew J. O'Connell et al. New York: Herder & Herder, 1972.

Hunsinger, George. Review of *The Sociality of Christ and Humanity: Dietrich Bonhoeffer's Early Theology, 1927–1933*, by Clifford Green. *Newsletter*, International Bonhoeffer Society for Archive and Research, no. 18 (January 1980) 2–6.

Irenaeus. "Irenaeus Against Heresies." In *The Ante-Nicene Fathers. Vol. 1: The Apostolic Fathers, Justin Martyr, Irenaeus*, edited by Alexander Roberts and James Donaldson, 315–567. *The Ante-Nicene Fathers: The Writings of the Fathers down to A.D. 325.* 1885. Revised by A. Cleveland Coxe. 10 vols. Grand Rapids: Eerdmans, 2004.

Isherwood, Lisa, and Elizabeth Stuart. *Introducing Body Theology.* Cleveland: Pilgrim, 2000.

Janicaud, Dominique. *On the Human Condition.* Translated by Eileen Brennan. Thinking in Action Series. London: Routledge, 2005.

Jasper, Ronald C. D. *George Bell, Bishop of Chichester.* London: Oxford University Press, 1967.

Jennings, Willie J. "In the Form of the Aryan: Bonhoeffer and the Dilemmas of Global Imperial Masculinity." Paper presented in the Bonhoeffer: Theology and Social Analysis Group of the American Academy of Religion, Montréal, QC, November 2009.

Johnson, Elizabeth A. "Feminist Theology and Critical Discourse about God." In *She Who Is: The Mystery of God in Feminist Theological Discourse*, 33–41. New York: Crossroad, 1992.

Jones, Serene. *Trauma and Grace: Theology in a Ruptured World.* Louisville: Westminster John Knox, 2009.

Jüngel, Eberhard. *Entsprechungen: Gott-Wahrheit-Mensch: Theologische Erörterungen II.* Tübingen: Mohr/Siebeck, 2002.

---. *Das Evangelium von der Rechtfertigung des Gottlosen als Zentrum des christlichen Glaubens: Eine theologische Studie in ökumenischer Absicht*. Tübingen: Mohr/Siebeck, 2006.

Kangas, David J. *Kierkegaard's Instant: On Beginnings*. Bloomington: Indiana University Press, 2007.

Kant, Immanuel. *Critique of Pure Reason*. Translated by Norman Kemp Smith. New York: St. Martin's Press, 1929.

---. "The End of All Things." In *Perpetual Peace and Other Essays*, translated by Ted Humphrey, 93–105. Indianapolis: Hackett, 1983.

---. *Religion Within the Boundaries of Mere Reason*. Edited by Allen Wood and George di Giovanni. New York: Cambridge University Press, 1998.

Kaunda, Kenneth D. *A Humanist in Africa: Letters to Collin M. Morris*. London: Longmans, 1966.

Kelly, Geffrey B. "Kierkegaard as 'Antidote' and as Impact on Dietrich Bonhoeffer's Concept of Christian Discipleship." In *Bonhoeffer's Intellectual Formation*, edited by Peter Frick, 145–65. Tübingen: Mohr/Siebeck, 2008.

Kierkegaard, Søren. *Concluding Unscientific Postscript* to Philosophical Fragments. Vol. 1. Edited and translated by Howard V. Hong and Edna H. Hong. Princeton: Princeton University Press, 1992.

---. *For Self-Examination/Judge For Yourself!* Edited and translated by Howard V. Hong and Edna H. Hong. Princeton: Princeton University Press, 1990.

---. *Practice in Christianity*. Edited and translated by Howard V. Hong and Edna H. Hong. Princeton: Princeton University Press, 1991.

---. *The Sickness unto Death*. Edited and translated by Howard V. Hong and Edna H. Hong. Princeton: Princeton University Press, 1980.

Klein, Naomi. *The Shock Doctrine: The Rise of Disaster Capitalism*. Toronto: Knopf Canada, 2008.

Koop, Karl, editor. *Confessions of Faith in the Anabaptist Tradition 1527–1660*. Kitchener, ON: Pandora, 2006.

Krebs, Manfred, and Hans-Georg Rott. *Quellen zur Geschichte der Täufer. Band VII, Elsass I, No. 70*. Gütersloh: Gerd Mohn, 1959.

Krondorfer, Björn, editor. *Men and Masculinities in Christianity and Judaism: A Critical Reader*. London: SCM, 2009.

Lange, Frits de. "A Particular Europe, a Universal Faith: The Christian Humanism of Bonhoeffer's Ethics in Its Context." In *Bonhoeffer's Ethics: Old Europe and New Frontiers*, edited by Guy Carter, René van Eyden, Hans-Dirk van Hoogstraten, and Jurjen Wiersma, 81–96. Kampen: Kok Pharos, 1991.

Levinas, Emmanuel, and Jill Robbins. *Is It Righteous to Be?: Interviews with Emmanuel Levinas*. Stanford: Stanford University Press, 2001.

Lindbeck, George. "What Is the Future? A Christian Response." In *Christianity in Jewish Terms*, edited by Tikva Frymer-Kensky, David Novak, Peter Ochs, David Fox Sandmel, and Michael A. Signer, 357–66. Boulder, CO: Westview, 2000.

Løgstrup, Knud Ejler. *The Ethical Demand*. Notre Dame, IN: University of Notre Dame Press, 1997.

Lubac, Henri de. *Catholicism: Christ and the Common Destiny of Man*. Translated by Lancelot C. Sheppard and Elizabeth Englund. San Francisco: Ignatius, 1988.

---. *Catholicisme: les aspects sociaux du dogme*. Paris: Cerf, 1983.

Lupáč, Martin. *Probacio preceptorum minorum.* Edited by Amadeo Molnar. *Communio Viatorum* 9.1–2 (1966) 55–62.
Luther, Martin. *Lectures on Romans, 1515–1516. Luther's Works*, vol. 25. Edited by Hilton C. Oswald. Saint Louis: Concordia, 1972.
MacIntyre, Alasdair. "Epistemological Crises, Dramatic Narrative, and the Philosophy of Science." In *Why Narrative?*, edited by Stanley Hauerwas and L. Gregory Jones, 38–157. Grand Rapids: Eerdmans, 1989.
Maritain, Jacques. *True Humanism.* Translated by M. R. Adamson. London: Bles, 1938.
Marty, Martin, editor. *The Place of Bonhoeffer: Problems and Possibilities in His Thought.* New York: Association, 1962.
McCabe, Herbert. *God Matters.* London: Chapman, 1987.
McFague, Sallie. *The Body of God: An Ecological Theology.* Minneapolis: Fortress, 1993.
McKenny, Gerald P. "Responsibility." In *The Oxford Handbook of Theological Ethics*, edited by Gilbert C. Meilaender and William Werpehowski, 237–53. Oxford: Oxford University Press, 2005.
Mennonite Encyclopedia. 4 vols. Edited by Harold S. Bender et al. Scottdale, PA: Mennonite Publishing House, 1959.
Milbank, John. *Theology and Social Theory: Beyond Secular Reason.* 2nd ed. Malden, MA: Blackwell, 2006.
Moltmann, Jürgen. "The Consequences of Discipleship." In *The Power of the Powerless*, translated by Margaret Kohl, 79–87. San Francisco: Harper & Row, 1983.
Moyo, Dambisa. *Dead Aid: Why Aid Is Not Working and How There Is a Better Way for Africa.* New York: Farrar, Straus & Giroux, 2009.
Müller, Hanfried. *Von der Kirche zur Welt.* Leipzig: Köhler & Amelang, 1961.
Nielsen, Kirsten Busch. "Critique of Church and Critique of Religion in Bonhoeffer's Late Writings." In de Gruchy, Plant, and Tietz, eds., *Dietrich Bonhoeffer's Theology*, 319–34.
———. *Syndens brudte magt: En undersøgelse af Dietrich Bonhoeffers syndsforståelse* [The Broken Power of Sin: An Investigation into Dietrich Bonhoeffer's Understanding of Sin]. Copenhagen: University of Copenhagen, 2008. Forthcoming in German: *Die gebrochene Macht der Sünde: Der Beitrag Bonhoeffers zur Hamartiologie* (2010).
Nietzsche, Friedrich Wilhelm. *The Birth of Tragedy, and The Case of Wagner.* Translated by Walter Kaufmann. New York: Vintage, 1967.
———. "On the Afterworldly." In *Thus Spake Zarathustra*, in *The Portable Nietzsche*, edited by Walter Kaufmann, 142–45. New York: Penguin, 1976.
Nissen, Ulrik Becker. "Between Unity and Differentiation: On the Identity of Lutheran Social Ethics." In *The Sources of Public Morality: On the Ethics and Religion Debate*, edited by Ulrik Nissen, Svend Andersen, and Lars Reuter, 152–71. Münster: LIT Verlag, 2003.
———. "The Christological Ontology of Reason." *Neue Zeitschrift für systematische Theologie und Religionsphilosophie* 48 (2006) 460–78.
———. "Dietrich Bonhoeffer and the Ethics of Plenitude." *Journal of the Society of Christian Ethics* 26.1 (2006) 97–114.

———. "Letting Reality Become Real: On Mystery and Reality in Bonhoeffer's Ethic" (under review).
Novak, David. *Talking with Christians: Musings of a Jewish Theologian*. Grand Rapids: Eerdmans, 2005.
O'Donovan, Oliver. *The Desire of the Nations: Rediscovering the Roots of Political Theology*. Cambridge: Cambridge University Press, 1996.
Onnasch, Martin. "Zeitgemässe Theologie? Beobachtungen zu zeitgeschichtlichen Bedingungen der theologischen Sprache Bonhoeffers." In Green et al., eds., *Dietrich Bonhoeffer Yearbook* 3, 210–18.
Pangritz, Andreas. "Who is Jesus Christ, for Us, Today?" In de Gruchy, ed., *Cambridge Companion*, 134–53.
Park, Andrew Sung, and Susan L. Nelson, editors. *The Other Side of Sin: Woundedness from the Perspective of the Sinned-Against*. Albany: SUNY Press, 2001.
Pfeifer, Hans. "Learning Faith and Ethical Commitment in the Context of Spiritual Training Groups: Consequences of Dietrich Bonhoeffer's Post Doctoral Year in New York City, 1930/31." In Green et al., eds., *Dietrich Bonhoeffer Yearbook* 3, 251–79.
Phillips, John A. *Christ for Us in the Theology of Dietrich Bonhoeffer*. New York: Harper & Row, 1967.
Polak, Paul. *Out of Poverty: What Works When Traditional Approaches Fail*. San Francisco: Berret-Koehler, 2008.
Prokes, Mary Timothy. *Toward a Theology of the Body*. Grand Rapids: Eerdmans, 1996.
Prosser MacDonald, Diane L. *Transgressive Corporeality: The Body, Post-Structuralism, and the Theological Imagination*. Albany: SUNY Press, 1995.
Prüller-Jagenteufel, Gunter M. *Befreit zur Verantwortung: Sünde und Versöhnung in der Ethik Dietrich Bonhoeffers*. Münster: LIT Verlag, 2004.
Ramsey, Paul. *Speak Up for Just War or Pacifism: A Critique of the United Methodist Bishops' Pastoral Letter "In Defense of Creation."* University Park: Pennsylvania State University Press, 1989.
Rasmussen, Larry L. "The Ethics of Responsible Action." In de Gruchy, eds., *Cambridge Companion*, 206–25.
———. "Song of Songs." In *Earth Community, Earth Ethics*, 295–316. Maryknoll, NY: Orbis, 1996.
Rich, Arthur. *Die Anfänge der Theologie Zwinglis*. Zurich: Zwingli, 1949.
Ricoeur, Paul. "Philosophical and Theological Hermeneutics." In *From Text to Action: Essays in Hermeneutics II*, translated by Kathleen Blamey and John B. Thompson, 14–33. London: Athlone, 1991.
Roberts, Alexander, and James Donaldson, editors. *The Ante-Nicene Fathers. Vol. 2: Hermas, Tatian, Athenagoras, Theophilus, Clement of Alexandria. The Ante-Nicene Fathers: The Writings of the Fathers down to A.D. 325*. 1885. Revised by A. Cleveland Coxe. 10 vols. Grand Rapids: Eerdmans, 2004.
Root, Andrew. "Practical Theology as Social Ethical Action in Christian Ministry: Implications from Emmanuel Levinas and Dietrich Bonhoeffer." *International Journal of Practical Theology* 10.1 (2006) 53–75.
Schliesser, Christine. "Verantwortung nach Bonhoeffer: Armut als Fallbeispiel." In de Gruchy, Plant, and Tietz, eds., *Dietrich Bonhoeffer's Theology*, 292–304.

Schulz, Anselm. *Nachfolgen und Nachahmen*. Munich: Kösel, 1962.
Sherman, Franklin. "Vital Center: Toward a Chalcedonian Social Ethic." In *The Scope of Grace: Essays on Nature and Grace in Honor of Joseph Sittler*, edited by Philip J. Hefner, 231–56. Philadelphia: Fortress, 1964.
Skinner, Quentin. *The Foundations of Modern Political Thought: The Renaissance*. Cambridge: Cambridge University Press, 1992.
Skydsgaard, K. E., Barnabas Ahern, Walter J. Burghhardt, Bernard Cooke, and Franklin H. Littell, editors. *The Church as the Body of Christ*. Cardinal O'Hara Series. Studies and Research in Christian Theology at Notre Dame 1. Notre Dame, IN: Notre Dame Press, 1963.
Smith, Ronald Gregor. *Secular Christianity*. New York: Harper & Row, 1967.
Sobrino, Jon. *Christology at the Crossroads*. Translated by John Drury. Maryknoll, NY: Orbis, 1976.
———. *Jesus the Liberator*. Translated by Paul Burns and Francis McDonagh. Maryknoll, NY: Orbis, 1993.
———. *Where is God? Earthquakes, Terrorism, Barbarity, and Hope*. Translated by Margaret Wilde. Maryknoll, NY: Orbis, 2004.
Soosten, Joachim von. *Die Sozialität der Kirche: Theologie und Theorie der Kirche in Dietrich Bonhoeffers Sanctorum Communio*. Öffentliche Theologie 2. Munich: Kaiser, 1992.
Steckelberg, Mathilde. Review of *Die Judenfrage* by Gerhard Kittel. *Books Abroad* 8 (January 1934) 84.
Steenberg, M. C. *God and Man: Theology as Anthropology from Irenaeus to Athanasius*. New York: T. & T. Clark, 2009.
Stoellger, Philipp. *Metapher und Lebenswelt: Hans Blumenbergs metaphorologischer, religionsphänomenologischer Horizont*. Tübingen: Mohr/Siebeck, 2000.
Stringfellow, William. *Dissenter in a Great Society*. 1966. Reprinted, Eugene, OR: Wipf & Stock, 2006.
Taylor, Charles. *A Secular Age*. Cambridge, MA: Belknap, 2007.
Thielicke, Helmut. *Being Human—Becoming Human: An Essay in Christian Anthropology*. Translated by Geoffrey W. Bromiley. 1st ed. Garden City, NY: Doubleday, 1984.
Tietz-Steiding, Christiane. *Bonhoeffers Kritik der verkrümmten Vernunft: Eine erkenntnistheoretische Untersuchung*. Beiträge zur historischen Theologie 112. Tübingen: Mohr/Siebeck, 1999.
Tillard, J. M. R. *Flesh of the Church, Flesh of Christ: At the Source of the Ecclesiology of Communion*. Translated by Madeleine Beaumont. Collegeville, MN: Liturgical, 2001.
Trinkaus, Charles Edward. *In Our Image and Likeness: Humanity and Divinity in Italian Humanist Thought*. 2 vols. Notre Dame, IN: University of Notre Dame Press, 1995.
Underhill, Evelyn. "The Future of Mysticism." In *Evelyn Underhill: Modern Guide to the Ancient Quest for the Holy*, edited by Dana Greene. New York: SUNY Press, 1988.
Vosloo, Robert. "Body and Health in the Light of the Theology of Dietrich Bonhoeffer." *Religion and Theology* 13 (2006) 23–37.

Weinrich, Michael. *Der Wirklichkeit begegnen . . . Studien zu Buber, Grisebach, Gogarten, Bonhoeffer und Hirsch*. Neukirchen-Vluyn: Neukirchener Verlag, 1980.

Wenger, John C. *Conrad Grebel's Programmatic Letters of 1524*. Scottdale, PA: Herald, 1970.

Williams, Raymond. *Keywords: A Vocabulary of Culture and Society*. Rev. ed. New York: Oxford University Press, 1983.

Witt, Ronald G. "The Humanist Movement." In *Handbook of European History, 1400–1600*, edited by Heiko Oberman, Thomas A. Brady, Jr., and James D. Tracy, vol. 2, 93–127. Grand Rapids: Eerdmans, 1995.

Woelfel, James. *Bonhoeffer's Theology: Classical and Revolutionary*. New York: Abingdon, 1970.

Wright, N. T. *Justification: God's Plan and Paul's Vision*. Downers Grove, IL: IVP Academic, 2009.

———. *Paul: In Fresh Perspective*. Minneapolis: Fortress, 2005.

———. *What Saint Paul Really Said: Was Paul of Tarsus the Real Founder of Christianity?* Grand Rapids: Eerdmans, 1997.

Wüstenberg, Ralf K. *Glauben als Leben: Dietrich Bonhoeffer und die nichtreligiöse Interpretation biblischer Begriffe*. Kontexte 18. Frankfurt: Lang, 1995.

———. "Philosophical Influences on Bonhoeffer's 'Religionless Christianity.'" In Gregor and Zimmermann, eds., *Bonhoeffer and Continental Thought*, 137–55.

———. *A Theology of Life: Dietrich Bonhoeffer's Religionless Christianity*. Translated by Doug Stott. Grand Rapids: Eerdmans, 1998.

Wyller, Trygve. *Glaube und autonome Welt: Diskussion eines Grundproblems der neueren systematischen Theologie mit Blick auf Dietrich Bonhoeffer, Oswald Bayer und K. E. Løgstrup*. Berlin: de Gruyter, 1998.

Wyschogrod, Michael. *The Body of Faith: God in the People Israel*. San Francisco: Harper & Row, 1983.

Yoder, John Howard. *Discipleship as Political Responsibility*. Scottdale, PA: Herald, 2003.

———. *The Politics of Jesus: Vicit Agnus Noster*. 2nd ed. Grand Rapids: Eerdmans, 1994.

———. *Täufertum und Reformation im Gespräch*. Zurich: EVZ, 1968.

Young, Josiah Ulysses III. *Dogged Strength within the Veil: Africana Spirituality and the Mysterious Love of God*. African American Religious Thought and Life. Harrisburg, PA: Trinity, 2003.

Zimmerling, Peter. "Gottesliebe und irdische Liebe: Religiosität und Erotik bei Dietrich Bonhoeffer." In *Dietrich Bonhoeffer: Beten und Tun des Gerechten. Glaube und Verantwortung im Widerstand*, edited by Rainer Mayer and Peter Zimmerling, 35–47. ABC-team Bücher. Giessen: Brunnen, 1997.

Index*

Act and Being, 61, 76, 78, 90, 96, 154, 167, 169, 171
Adam, xix, 61, 75, 76, 98, 99, 101, 105, 106, 167, 168, 170 *see also* humanity-in-Adam; his encounter with Eve, 180, 183
Anabaptists, 40, 41, 144; *see also* discipleship
anthropology, xi–xii, xiv, 76, 77, 80, 86n50, 148, 169, 172, 175, 176; of the church fathers, 27, 33; relation of, to ecclesiology, **91–101**
Anti-Climacus, 154, 156, 173, 174
Aquinas, Thomas, 28
Aristotle, 119
Athanasius, 27
atonement, 132n29, 148, 152, 158
Augustine, 28n9, 28, 33, 34, 42, 105n11, 106, 107, 108
autonomy: of economics, 55; ego, 80; human, 38; of the subject, 168; of the world, xvi, 108, 211

Babylonian Exile, 103, 118, 119
Balthasar, Hans Urs von, xiii–xiv, 107, 123
Barmen Declaration, 12, 13
Barth, Karl, 5, 7, 12, 15, 26, 42, 51, 71, 83n41, 142, 157; Bonhoeffer's critique of, 8, 13; Bonhoeffer's defense of, 9; criticism of religion by, 113
Beatitudes, the, 138–39, 206n68
being-for (others), xv, xvii, 34, 36, 39, 77, 80 *see also* other, the
Bender, Harold S., 128n4, 133
Bethge, Eberhard, 5, 6, 13, 18, 25n3, 81, 111, 116, 117, 166
body, the: African-American female, 177, 184; Bonhoeffer's theology of, 20, **176–90**; centrality of, in Christian community, 178, 180–81; essential goodness of, 178–79; female, as limit, 183–84; indwelling of, by God, 178, 181–82; as locus of Christian reflection, 178n2; its rights to life, 178–79; role of, as "limit" to the other, 178, 180, 183
Bonhoeffer, Dietrich: his appreciation for ancient Greece, 19, 20; in Barcelona, 7, 51; his Christology lectures, 41, 43, 44, 46, 77, 144, 146, 188, 192; his critique of philosophy, 154; economic downward spiral in the life of, 49–50, 51, 65; on education, 8–9; his family's relation to Christianity, 13; humanistic turn in theology of, 51;

---

* Page numbers in **bold** print indicate main references to the subject.

Bonhoeffer, Dietrich (cont.)
influence of his travels on the theology of, 8, 9, 51; his interpreters, **143–47**; in New York, 52; his prison theology, 72, 80, 86–89, 103, 108, 110, 147; his social conscience, 51–53; his theology as a whole, **71–90**; his theology of sociality, **72–78**
boundary-experiences, 20, 21
Buber, Martin, xiii, 21, 26n5, 73n6, 194

call of Christ, the: as a grace, 167–68, 174; to responsibility, 212–13; role of, in making faith possible, 163–64
cheap grace, 137, 142, 153, **157–61**, 164, 165, 174
Christianity: as a humanism, 25–26; "religionless," 86, 89, 112, 115, 118
Christology: Bonhoeffer's, in *Nachfolge*, **137–41**; Chalcedonian, xiv, 40, 43, 111, 144, 145, 151, 192, 193, 200, 208, 212, 213; Jewish vs. Hellenistic, 42n53; problem of, 40n50, 77, 144, 145, 151n77; relation to anthropology and ecclesiology, 91, 99
Christ-reality (*Christuswirklichkeit*), the one, xvi, xvii, 36, 45, 55, 199, 201, 207, 208; unity of reality in, 58, 122, 195
Chrysostom, John, 34
church fathers, the: Bonhoeffer's humanism rooted in, 30, 47; Christology of, 33, 34, 47; human sociality in, 32, 106; humanism of, 26, 27

church, the: as alien community, 108, 115; as the body of Christ, xv, 93, 99, 130–31, 134, 141; Bonhoeffer's concept of, *see* ecclesiology; bourgeois, vs. the proletariat, **55–57**; connection between Christ and, 103, 112, 113, 115; connection between world and, 33, 35; critique of economics by, *see* economics; as God's revelation, *see* revelation; as the new humanity, 46, 80, 99; as *peccatorum communio*, 100, 101; response of, to social issues, 55; as *sanctorum communio*, 72, 75, 94, 100, 101, 107; unity of, 136; visible vs. invisible, 93–94, 100; in a "world come of age," *see* "world come of age"
Clement of Alexandria, 27n8, 37, 37n40
Climacus, Johannes, 153, 154, 155, 156
communal existence, 121, 122
community: broken by sin, 97, 98; Christ existing as, 136; Christians as, 33n29; church as, 94, 101; as collective person (*Kollektivperson*), 74, 98–99; ethical status of the, 74–75; with God, 32, 95, 105, 106; humans as part of, 61, 73; link between Christ and, 117; *peccatorum communio* as turned-inside-out-, 100–101; responsibility for the, 196; vs. society, 107
Confessing Church (in Germany), 11, 12, 13, 102

conformation with Christ, 36, 141, 170, 174, **176–90**; as the Risen One, 188–89
conformity to Christ, 129, 130, 132, 138, 148
Constantianism, 115, 147, 151
cor curvum in se, 155, 168
creation, xvi, 21, 36, 58, 77, 80, 89, 95, 96, 100, 110, 143, 179, 208; affirmation of, 40; Christ's lordship over, 211–12
Creation and Fall, 76, 105, 178–79, 180
cross, the: the call to bear, 207; of Christ, 16, 137–38, 145; as the foundation for worldliness, 210–11; as part of authentic Christian existence, 162, 206; as part of the life of the church, 128, 134; pietistic conception of, 148
crucifixion, the, 16, 21, 89, 109, 110, 207

Dahill, Lisa: *Reading from the Underside of Selfhood*, 185
Dasein, 155
David, relationship of Christ to, 111
de Gruchy, John, 25, 26, 30
de Lange, Frits, 17, 23, 39
death of God theology, 30n14
deification (*theosis*), 27, 28, 38
Denck, Hans, 128, 131, 132, 133, 137, 139n46, 141
Dilschneider, Otto, 53–54
Dilthey, Wilhelm, 21, 108–9
discernment, xiv, xvii, 35, 36, 189n33, 196, 197
Discipleship (*Cost of Discipleship*; *Nachfolge*), 13, 41, 72, 80, 81, 82, 83, 85, 108, 137–41, 144, 148, 149, 157, 161, 163, 166–67, 172, 180, 204, 207
discipleship, **127–51**, **152–75**; Anabaptist concept of, 127–33, 147; Bonhoeffer's concept of, 82–83, 134–51, 207; in *Ethics*, 141–43; ethics of, *see* ethics; as extraordinary, 159; in Hans Denck, 132–33; Kierkegaard's concept of, **152–75**; of obedience vs. of conformity, 148, 149, 150; as participation in Christ, 206–7; as political responsibility, 206; and responsibility, 204–5; as a term, 134, 141
divinization, *see* deification

ecclesiology: central to Bonhoeffer's social thought, **102–23**; relation to anthropology, **91–101**; shift in, 113
economics: Bonhoeffer's theology in relation to, **49–68**; the church's critique of, **64–68**; influence on faith, *see* faith; as social, 62
Efterfølgelse, 153, 158, 159, 161
ego, the, 79, 80, 95
election, 121
embodiment, *see* body, the
Enlightenment, the, 11, 19, 114
epistemology: postmodern shift in, xii
Erasmus, Desiderius, 9, 10–11, 13, 128
ethical demand, 191–92, 197
Ethics, 15, 61, 63, 108, 109, 110, 141–43, 170, 179, 185, 187, 192, 191–213
ethics: application of, in specific realms, 53–54; concrete vs. abstract, xvi, 46;

ethics (cont.)
of discipleship, 152–53;
of nature, 142–43; universal
vs. specific, 192, 193, **208–13**
Bonhoeffer's, **191–213**;
Christological foundation of,
193, 198, 199–207
Christian: as Christ-formation,
34, 141–42; notion of, 192;
as participation in the will of
God, 36; universality of, 194
Eucharist, the, 30, 33–34, 146, 181

faith: and the call of Christ, *see* call
of Christ, the; correlation
of, with reason, 42–43; and
economics, **61–64**; in Hans
Denck, 131; and obedience,
82–83, 153, 157–58, **161–65**;
priority of, or following,
162–63; problem of, 146
Ferry, Luc, 37–39
Feuerbach, Ludwig, 57n21, 90, 172
finitude, 153, 155
following-after, *see* discipleship
Frankfurt School of Critical
Theory, 67
freedom: balance with call to
discipleship, 207; God's,
76; human, 22, 77; and
obedience, 198; relation with
authority, 38; relation with
love, 202; and responsibility,
see responsibility
fulfillment, concept of, 114
fundamentalism: religious, 4, 23,
25; secular, xiii; scientific, 25

Gelassenheit (yieldedness), 131,
132, 139, 140
God-relation, 156
Godsey, John, 143, 144

government: Christian participation in, 140; Christ's relation
to, 142–43
Green, Clifford, 81, 103–4; his
Theology of Sociality, 72
guilt: Christian as bearer of,
137–38, 150; willingness to
bear, 194, 201, 203–5, 213;
see also individual guilt
Gutiérrez, Gustavo, 59, 66, 67

Hegel, Georg Wilhelm Friedrich,
114n47, 154
Heidegger, Martin, 155
Hildebrandt, Franz, 13, 14
Hitler, Adolf, 121n67; assassination
attempt on, 81, 149, 150
Horkheimer, Max, 67, 68
human being, the value of, **58–60**;
influence of economic structures on, 60, 65
humanism: Barth on, 15;
Bonhoeffer's Christian,
3–24, 50–53; Bonhoeffer's
Christological, **25–48**, 170;
Christian faith as basis for, 8;
classical, 6; as derived from
the church fathers; economic, *see* economics; Russian,
6; Spanish and German
resistance to, 7; values of,
having their justification in
Christ, 16–17
Christian, 4; in Africa, 3; holistic
nature of, 22, 52, 68; as
"mature worldliness," *see*
worldliness; secular objections to, **37–39**; theological
roots of, **26–37**
secular, 4, 8, 23, 28; cooperation
with, by Christians, **10–19**;
roots in Judeo-Christianity,
26; of the twentieth century,
11

humanity: affirmation of, 14, 17, 31, 145; of Christ, 145; of God, 90; ideal, 187; recapitulation of, in Christ, xv, 30–31
humanity-in-Adam, 98–99
Hunsinger, George, 81

idealism, 153, 168
identity: human, xi–xii, 29; individual vs. collective, 32
image (*Bild*), 169–71; of Christ, 171–74, 185
imagination: dangers of, 173n86; role of, in discipleship, 153, **168–74**
imago Dei (image of God), xv, 28, 39, 76, 95, 106, 168, 170
imitation, 158, 164–65
Incarnation, the: as affirmation of the world, 110, 144–45; as basis for ethics, 142; as basis for humanism, 16, 18, 170–71; and the body, 181–82, 187; church fathers on, 27, 31; as concept vs. event, 148, 151; concreteness in interpretation of, 41–42, 45; its correlation of particularity and universality, 41; as holding together transcendence and immanence, 38; "Jesulogical" vs. "logological" interpretation of, 40–41, 144–151; as pattern for the ultimate-penultimate relation, xvii, 111; as theological basis for making common cause with secular humanists, 15
individual, the: isolation of, 195; isolation of, by sin, 98, 99, 101; in relation to the community, 196

individual guilt, connection between universal sin and, 96–98
individuality: balance with the collective, 32; interdependence of, with community, 95; relation between sociality and, xii, 100, 101; *see also* self, the
infant baptism, 131
interpretation, 119–20; Bonhoeffer's accent on, xvi, 36–37, 45; in the church fathers, 37n40; secular, 147
Irenaeus, 27n8, 31
Isaiah, book of, 116, 117, 118
Israel, post-exilic, 120
I-you relationship, 73, 75, 95, 97

Janicaud, Dominique, xi
Jeremiah, book of, 116, 117, 118
Jesus: historicity of, 146, 148, 151; particularity of, 145; relationship between the Christ and, 43–44, 134, 141, 143–44
Jewish people, the, 113, 118–19, 121

Kant, Immanuel, 114n47, 154, 168n66, 169, 171, 203
Kaunda, Kenneth, 3, 23
Kierkegaard, Søren, 22; Bonhoeffer's use of the journals of, 157; *see also* discipleship
kingdom of God, 85, 88

Lasserre, Jean, 9, 82, 166
Law of God, 131
legalism 127, 129, 147
Leibholz, Gerhard, 4, 17, 18
Letters and Papers from Prison, 20, 78, 86–89, 108, 112, 115–19, 149
Levinas, Emmanuel, xiii, 23, 155n13, 194

Liberation Theology, 59, 66
Life Together, 82, 147, 180, 181, 187
life: affirmation of, 17, 18, 109, 110; autonomy of the value of, 58–59; faith as the act of, 117
Lindbeck, George, 113, 114
Løgstrup, K. E., 191, 192, 193
lordship of Christ, 205, 211–12
love of God vs. earthly love, 111
Lubac, Henri de, 27, 106
Luther, Martin, 15, 28, 43, 78, 79, 94, 96, 162, 164, 167, 209n79, 210; his controversy with Erasmus, 10–11; his doctrine of the two kingdoms, 54; Kierkegaard's criticism of, 159–60, 165
Lutheranism, 20, 41, 45, 53, 54, 131, 143, 153, 161, 165, 174

mandates, the, 142, 144, 194, 203; as concrete response to reality, **208–13**, 213
Maritain, Jacques, 5, 25
Maximus the Confessor, 106
meaning, concept of, 119
metanoia, 172
Middle Ages, the, 19, 28, 78; concept of imitation in, 152, 158–59, 161
Moltmann, Jürgen, 67, 152
Müller, Hanfried, 148, 151
mysticism, 128, 131, 139, 140, 147, 148

Nachfolge (the book), *see Discipleship*
Nachfolge (as a term), 132, 133, 153; *see also* discipleship
nationalism combined with humanism, 5–6, 7
Nazism, xi, 9, 14, 15, 44, 65, 85, 187, 205n64

New Testament, the, 21, 42n53, 54, 88, 108, 116, 141, 158, 160, 206
Nietzsche, Friedrich Wilhelm, 20, 84
nonreligious interpretation, 78, 86, 87, 147, 149, 151
Novak, David, 118–19

obedience, 204–5; *see also* faith
O'Donovan, Oliver, 44–45
Old Testament, the, 39, 112, 113, 115–18; as basis for Bonhoeffer's humanism, 21; worldliness in, 88
order of salvation, 157
other, the xiii; as bearing the image of Christ, 184; Christ as, 76, 180; Christian humanism as humanism for, 23; concrete encounter with, **194–98**, 213; God as, 73–74; as limit, 73, 180; the self and, 73; transformational power of, 184–85
otherworldliness, 83, 84, 85, 88, 89

pacifism: of the Anabaptists, 130n13; of Bonhoeffer, 13, 81, **135–37**, 139
Pangritz, Andreas, 111, 113, 114, 117n55
participation: in Christ, 32, 35, 39, 46, 109, 129, 166, 167, 170; following Jesus as, *see* discipleship; in God, 106; in the messianic event, 117; in the new humanity, 33; social, 141
passivity vs. activity, 153, **165–68**, 171; in the response to the call of Christ, 164
patristic theology, *see* church fathers

personhood, 73, 95, 106, 107; *see also* self, the
Pfeifer, Hans, 81
philosophy: its resistance to subjectivity, 155
pietism, 148
political theology, 44–45
polyphony of life, 19, 114, 115, 120, 123
postmodernism: its aversion to substantive universal concepts, xiii
poverty, 65
power, problem of, 76, 78–81
Precious Jones (film character), 182, 186, 189; compared with Bonhoeffer, 177; as an image of Christ, 185; relation to Bonhoeffer's theology of the body, 183, 184
private person, distinction between the Christian as office bearer and, 139
Protestantism, 5, 7, 10, 40, 97, 113, 127n2, 144, 156, 212; discipleship in, 152, 156, 158; liberal, 8, 12, 14, 44, 138
prototype (*Forbillede*), Christ as, 156, 158, 159, 164, 165
Psalms, book of, 116, 136

Ramsey, Paul, 115
Rasmussen, Larry, 179, 200
rationality, human, 168–69
reality, affirmation vs. negation of, 199–200
reason, correlation of faith with, *see* faith
recapitulation, *see* humanity
reciprocity, xiii
reconciliation, 91, 100, 132
redemption myths, 88
Reformation, the, 10–11, 12, 139, 152

Renaissance, the, 5, 19; humanism of, 3, 10, 11, 29; humanism of, rooted in patristic theology, 28, 29
representation, 97–98 *see also* vicarious representative action
responsibility, **191–213**; as answering to reality, 200; for Christ, 201; Christological qualification of, 201, 213; and freedom, 196–98; as rising from the encounter with the other, 194–98; the self in ethical position of, 73; social, 34, 46, 62–63; universal dimension of, 194–98, 213
resurrection, the, 18, 85, 88, 110; and conformation with Christ, 188–89
revelation, 104, 105, 146–47, 171, 210; the church as God's, 94; imagination as locus of, 172; renewed humanity as the goal of, 30; as social reality, 76
Robertson, Edwin, 135, 146

Sanctorum Communio (dissertation), xiv, 55, 91–101, 103, 180, 185, 194
sanctorum communio, the church as, *see* church, the
Sattler, Michael, 129, 139n46, 148
Schleiermacher, Friedrich, 15, 94
Schleitheim Articles, 130
secularism 4; Christian, 85, 86, 90; its critique of Christianity, 26; "subtraction narrative" of, xii, 29, 30
Seeberg, Reinhold, 55
self, the, 73; individualistic view of, 38; in relation to solidarity, *see* solidarity;

self, the (cont.)
    renunciation of, 137, 139;
    turning to the other from,
    186
Sermon on the Mount, 72, 81–83,
    84, 127, 149
sin: Bonhoeffer's understanding
    of, 92, 95–98; doctrine of
    original, 97, 98; as exercise
    of power, 78 *see also* power,
    problem of; as unbelief, 96,
    101
Sobrino, Jon, 59, 60
socialism, Bonhoeffer's critique
    of, 57
sociality: as abstract concept, 105;
    Bonhoeffer's theology of, xiv,
    xv, xvi, **71–90, 102–23**; relation between individuality
    and, *see* individuality
sociology, the church viewed from
    the perspective of, 104
solidarity: of the church with
    humanity as a whole, *see*
    church, the; in relation to
    selfhood, xii, 33
soteriology 78, 79; point of departure for Christology, 91
Stellvertretung, see vicarious representative action
subjectivity, 156, 168, 175; as necessary to become human,
    153–55; truth as, 153–54
suffering 131; of the church,
    128–29; and the cross, 162;
    of God in the world, 147,
    148, 150; participation in
    Christ's, 137; as token of
    God's love, 121; in a "world
    come of age," 109, 110; *see
    also* willingness to suffer for
    the other
supersessionism, 103, 113–14

Taylor, Charles, xii
Thielicke, Helmut, xi
"Thy Kingdom Come" (address),
    78, **83–85**, 86, 89
time, orientation in, 120
tolerance in Renaissance humanism, 11, 12
transcendence, 47, 73, 147; Luc
    Ferry's view of, 37–38;
    relation with immanence
    in Christian humanism, 39;
    sociality as, 76
Trinity, the, 32, 43
truth as subjectivity, *see* subjectivity
"turning away from the phraseological to the real," 78, 79, 80

ultimate-penultimate relation, xvi–
    xvii, 63, 103, 109, 110, 111
Union Theological Seminary,
    Bonhoeffer's year at, 9, 50
universal vs. particular in Christ,
    123

vicarious representation, 194, 201,
    202–3, 210, 213, *see also* vicarious representative action
vicarious representative action,
    74–75, 94, 203; of Adam,
    75; of Christ, 75, 99, 202; of
    the members of the church,
    99–100
violence 186; renunciation of,
    139–40, *see also* pacifism;
    use of, 149n74
vita christiana, 110, 114

wealth, dehumanizing influence
    of, 60
weltlich vs. *säkular*, 86, 89
willingness to suffer for the other,
    194, 201, 205–7, 213

word of God, the: as theological criterion, 56; the church created by, 94

"world come of age," 21, 89n63, 103, 108, 109, 110, 111, 112; the church in a, **115–23**

worldliness: affirmation of, 210–12, 213; as living unreservedly in the world, 115, 118, 166; mature, **19–23**; of the Middle Ages, 19, 41n52; in the prison letters, 72, 78, **86–90**, 143; as rooted in Christology, 90

worship as political event, 120
Wüstenberg, Ralf, 108–9, 110
Wyschogrod, Michael, 121

yieldedness, *see Gelassenheit*
Yoder, John Howard, 31n16, 206; his critique of Bonhoeffer's Christology, 26, **39–48**

Zwingli, Huldrych, 128–29, 130n12, 148